THE
REIGNING
WOMAN

THE REIGNING WOMAN

10 *Essential W's that will Totally Transform*

Your Life and Make You an Impactful Wonder

DR. DONNA M. SHERWOOD

ROYAL REIGN PUBLISHING

London

Dedication

To all the women who live with the intense consciousness that there is much more to become in God and in life.

Welcome to the exciting, stretching and life-transforming journey of the lifetime adventure of becoming…

THE REIGNING WOMAN

"Don't settle for average. You were made for greatness."

Victoria Osteen

A Woman's Mandate

RISE UP

REIGN

DO EXPLOITS

For the glory of God

The advancement of His kingdom

The service of humanity

And the awakening of your soul!

Table of Contents

Acknowledgements

The manifestation of this landmark book for The Reigning Woman brand is an absolute joy and a dream come through! I salute the King of heaven who showered me with astonishing resources (human and non-human) for the conception and completion of this project. Lord to You, I will forever be grateful andowe You everything!

I am especially grateful to my mother, Valerie Sherwood, brother Richard Sherwood who generously shared their hearts, ears and minds on their perspectives on what it means to reign for the King and to my sister, Lois Barnes, for her 'eagle eye' assistance in proofreading. Thanks to my brothers Andrew, Ted-Mark, Terry and Terrence Jr. for all your love and prayers. I am deeply grateful. Terrence Neverline Sherwood, dad, you are gone but not forgotten. You called me "Black Star"! I commit to honour and share my light to make the world a brighter and more beautiful place. I am forever grateful.

What would life be without amazing prayerful friends? Dorcia Gregory, Maxine Crawford, Janet Newel, Arleen Campbell and all the others through the years who made your hearts and ears my home. Thank you for being you.

Christine Oscar, my friend and ministry partner, the journey wouldn't be the same without you.

I am particularly grateful for my loving, supportive and prayerful church family.

I would like to also extend appreciation to Tunji Olujimi and the Mikkelsen Twin for their invaluable guidance throughout the writing and publication of this book.

Special thanks to ex-soldier Rohan Gayle for his insightful interview about his experience in the British Army. You provided deeper awareness of what it means to be a soldier in the army of the Lord. Truly grateful.

Priscilla Muyunda, my current accountability partner from The Christian Millionaire Book Club, you have been amazing! The questions, suggestions, encouragement, prayers and laughter were just what I needed. Forever grateful.

I am hugely grateful to Jessica Dinsey for skillfully managing My book launch project. The gift of strategic accountability kept me on my toes; where I needed to be. Thanks ever so much.

To other members of the Christian Millionaire Book Club for the special ways that you've helped. I am grateful.

I am thankful to all those who offered their support in all its many forms...prayers, encouragement and care. I am very appreciative.

INTRODUCTION

*T*here was an extremely rich king in the heart of India. He was so rich that all his plates, cups, cutlery, pens, etc. were made of gold, diamonds and silver. One day, he decided to go out of his palace into the suburbs to visit and see his subjects. Not wanting them to know he was the king, he disguised himself. He was immediately struck with the abject poverty of his people. He felt so bad. "How can I be so wealthy and my people be so poor?" He thought on what to do about the whole matter and came up with a plan. He fixed one day for his subjects to come to the palace and be permitted to pick anything from the palace and take it back as their own. You can imagine how subjects rushed to the palace on the said day. Everyone scrambled for a gold plate or a gold cup or a gold spoon. Finally, when others had all come and gone, there came an old lady. As she entered, she asked the King, Sir, "Do you mean I can take with me anything from your palace?" He answered that it was true. Then she walked around the palace, as if examining everything that was available. Finally, she asked the king again, "My Lord, do you really mean I can take anything with me from this palace?" He assured her it was so. Then the old woman stepped towards the king and grabbed him. "I choose to take you, my King", she said. In taking the king, she had taken everything...

This brilliant story in Theodore Effiong's book, *Why Certain Men are Poor, Remain Poor and Die Poor*, depicts a woman who refused to settle, no matter how attractive it may appear! She realised if she settled for things, however lovely they are, she would still be going back to a life that was far below the opportunity which was given to her. But she made an ace move when she chose the king. With spectacular insight, she knew that in choosing the king she gets everything; the greatest of which is the opportunity to reign with him!

Like the king in India, Jesus Christ the King, has seen the pain and suffering of humanity. As such, He is on a mission to transform mankind's brokenness. He came to earth in the disguise of flesh as the humble son of a carpenter. And in a similar way, He is also saying, "Come unto Me and you can have anything. In fact, everything!" But not every choice is equal. As such, we are advised that as we make our priority the King and His kingdom; then everything will be given to us (Mathew 6:33)! What an offer. What will our choice be?

Why struggle and barely live, when we can reign? And why reign once, when we can reign forever? It's our choices that will determine the quality of our lives. Not many women live in the highest dimension of the reality of the kingdom of God that is possible for them! Your duty is to be one of them. And my duty is to be the transformation catalyst to help to get you there.

We may be dissatisfied with the quality of our lives. We ask ourselves, "Why is my life not at the level that I know is possible for me?" Why am I not experiencing the promises which are made to me in the Holy Scriptures?" We have cried many silent tears in the night after the preachers' words have ended and we've said a confident amen, so shall it be in Jesus' name. Alas, we go home with an ache in our hearts searching for solutions in the essential areas of life. We speak words of hope but they feel like they're bouncing off the ceiling because even as we seek to worship God, we are distracted by the struggles in our relationships, finance, wellbeing, workplace and the wisdom to live a full and satisfying life elude us! We are caught in the quagmire of pain and hopelessness. Every day is a struggle. How can you face the world with all its demands with joy, fearlessness and warmth when you work hard and long and have very little to show for it; you feel like you're standing on shifting sand. As a daughter of Jesus Christ, the King, you know deep in your heart that there is and must be a better way to live in and for Him, who is Lord over everything!

God has given us the dominion mandate to rule and reign. He wants us to live well-balanced lives. God, through Jesus Christ, His Son, who by "His divine power hath given unto us all things that pertain unto life and godliness" (1Peter 1:3). Therefore, He has graciously and lovingly made provision for both "life and godliness" and we've also been given "all things". What a blessing! To ignore or to esteem of lesser value either one or to dismiss both, is to do so to our own peril. Growing up in the church, very little tools were given to deal with life. Mainly the godliness side of the coin was highlighted and taught. I will hasten to say a lot has changed and many improvements have been made since my days of growing up.

The Word of God is a composite of teachings to address all facets of life. God has given us *all things* (1 Peter 1:3) and He earnestly desires that we grow up in *all things* in Christ (Ephesians 4: 15)! We can and must become *all* that is possible in God using *all things* He has given us to grow in *all things.* And *all* that we do must be for the glory of God! All God's children (men and women) are given the mandate to reign. However, in this book, we will examine what it means to reign for God's glory through the lens of a woman; the female gender.

God has heard your heart's cry. He has sent help; the type that is void of the fluff, but that will get you the results that you need and that which will totally transform your life into the trophy of His boundless grace. As you continue to turn the pagesor listen to the audio of this book, you will get practical solutionsthat, if acted on, will usher you in a new season of hope, joy and help.

The contents of this book, by God's grace, will introduce you to the new you a wonder that makes an impact wherever you go. You will be getting the tools to partner with the King in designing a life of dominion, authority and triumph; no more living below your rights and responsibility of a citizen of the kingdom of God.

First, you will be able to discover what dimension you are living in the ten essential areas that will totally transform your life. You will know for certain if you have settled for winning, if you are waning - deteriorating from your former high standards or living in the wandering zone going around themountain too many times than you care to remember? Don't panic, help is here, the opportunity is in your hand; strategies, tools and mindset shift that will equip you to be the wonder that you were born and designed to be. The Father is saying, "Come unto Me you who are weary, worn and wandering, and I will indeed give you deep rest and abundant life." He is calling us to discover or rediscover the transforming power and wonder of living for Christ and what it means to truly reign.

Reigning. Can you imagine what our lives would be like if we developed the intense consciousness that we are royalty and we were born to reign? We were created to have dominion and to exercise the authority and rulership which are entrusted to us by God. Specifically, *what does it mean to be a reigning woman?* First of all, she isn't a feminist! *The Reigning Woman*, the one that has become a wonder, is a woman who has said a complete yes to the King of kings and the Lord of lords. In fact, she hasn't just said yes, she has said, "Yesssssssssssssssssssssssss"! It is a commitment to live wholly, solely and boldly by kingdom principles as is outlined in the Scriptures and to honour Jesus Christ, the King.

This in turn creates a wonderful Christ-centred life experience, with all its ups and downs and joys and sorrows, in becoming like Jesus Christ. She is hungry for God and is therefore a God-chaser. The reigning woman of wonder is totally surrendered and as such, she is unstoppable and immovable. She is a threat to the kingdom of darkness. Satan needs his Paracetamol when she opens her eyes in the mornings, "Here comes the King's surrendered daughter!"

This command to reign is not only for the sweet by and by. Martin Luther King, Jr. spoke of "the fierce urgency of now", and it is with this intense sense of 'nowness' that the call is going forth to women everywhere to arise and reign. Now. It is heeding the call to reign in "the fierce urgency of now" that will make us partakers of the eternal reign! This reign is now for eternity! The 'now' phase of the reign is the preparation for the eternal phase. Will you be The Reigning Woman that the world needs?

Failure to reign has always been a major concern of

God's heart! Solomon, the wisest man who ever lived states, "There is an *evil* which I have seen under the sun...I have seen servants upon horses, and princes walking as servants upon the earth" (Ecclesiastes 10: 5, 7). What a picture! Living a boring off-centred life without impact and influence is not the Father's will for us. It doesn't please God, serve humanity nor honour one's self. Little wonder that this run-of-the-mill life is called "*evil*". This is a strong word used to describe *royalty* that is not in its rightful place. We are daughters of the King; which make us princesses. As royalty, are we in our rightful place? Are we reigning?

Reigning is the central mandate in the kingdom of God. Reigning is kingdom living. This is to such a degree that the curtailment of reigning and extreme servitude has been used as punishment from God and whichever other powers He sovereignly chooses to use! In Isaiah 3: 4 God said to Israel, "And I will give children to be their princes, and babes shall rule over them." Now is the time to be transformed into the extraordinary. Now is the time to reign. So, let's position ourselves in the starting block. Get ready. Set. Go forward! Let's learn how to reign; now and for *eternity!*

WHY SHOULD WE REIGN NOW?

One can never overestimate the need for and the value of reigning; especially at such a time as this! The world is ravaged by the atrocities of the works of darkness from the kingdom of Satan in tragic proportions. This dismal outlook is further complicated by the challenging realities for many living in an almost unrecognisable Covid-19 traumatised world. Women everywhere must Rise Up...Reign...Do Exploits for Christ!

THE REIGNING TIMELINE

JESUS

CREATION

Dominion Given   ADAM
           & EVE   BORN AGAIN   BAPTISM   JESUS'
RETURN

MILLENNIUM &

ETERNITY

FALL OF MAN   DOMINION REGAINED

Dominion Lost   Reconciliation for Reigning

Let's examine 7 major reasons for the importance of reigning:

1. Reigning is the first explicit instruction given to mankind by God at creation. We bear the image of God and as such it has been encoded in our spiritual DNA to have dominion and to exercise our God-given authority. Genesis 1:26-28 clearly outlines our dominion mandate:

   And God said, "Let us make man in our image, after our likeness: and let them have dominion over the fish of the sea, and over the fowl of the air, and over the cattle, and over all the earth, and over every creeping thing that creepeth upon the earth. So God created man in his own image, in the image of God created he him; male and female created he them. And God blessed them, and God said unto them, be fruitful, and multiply, and replenish the earth, and subdue it.

To not be reigning, is to be living a life of the ordinary, a life of mediocrity and a life of drudgery! We were born for more.

2. To decide to reign gives us a seat around the table of kingdom influencers as global change-agents. It plays an active role in bringing the will of God to the earth. In Matthew 6:9-10 the model prayer that Jesus made states, "Our Father which art in heaven, Hallowed be thy name. Thy kingdom come, Thy will be done on earth, as it is in heaven." It has been frequently said, "If we aren't prepared to be a part of the answer to our prayers, then don't make them!"

3. It gives people, whose highest core value is spirituality, the opportunity to live out their reverence for the Lord God of heaven. Reigning affords us the privilege to honour the King, for it is in God that we live and move and have our beings. Reigning at the highest level makes God the Chief Executive officer (CEO) of our lives which puts Him on the throne of our hearts.

4. The opportunity to reign is a royal invitation from God to mankind, and women in particular, to leave their place in 'Lodebar'; a place of nothingness (2 Samuel 9). So even though we may be lame and limping by the adverse circumstances in life, the King has summoned our presence and is graciously awaiting our arrival. "Come and dine", the Master is calling. In the presence of the Lord is where He puts us on His

potter's wheel where He patiently and lovingly transforms us into His image.

5. Reigning with the King is a place for presence, power, protection and provision. It is taking the noble stance of responsibility in honouring the brotherhood of the saints. It is using your life to demonstrate that you are glad to belong to the greatest family on earth, the family of God.

6. Belonging to Jesus connects us to the only brand of royalty that is both *now* and *eternal*. Jesus dismantled the middle wall of partition (Ephesians 2:14) and became the Connector that spanned the chasm and reconnected us to the King (John 3:16)!

7. Reigning *now* provides the bridge for us to transition from this transient world with its struggles to eternal bliss where all sorrow will be wiped away (Revelation 21: 3-4). "For God did not appoint us to suffer wrath but to receive salvation through our Lord Jesus Christ" (1 Thessalonians 5:9).

You may be asking why am I so passionate that every woman becomes a transformed wonder that knows her God? Why do I desire that she is endued with divine strength and is making a huge impact in the world? I have been serving in women's ministries for over fifteen years in different capacities and I know first-hand the difference it makes when a woman's soul is awakened by the Spirit of the Living God! I have ministered to many women whose primary struggle is that there is limited realisation that they are daughters of the King with rights and responsibilities. I desire with my whole heart to give women a queue jump and shorten the path to becoming the God-ordained version of themselves. Thus, preventing them from living with the ache and brokenness for the rest of their lives.

My greatest delight is being able to share the principles from the Scriptures for the transformation of the lives of God's children. I am an educator with a Doctor of Philosophy (PhD) and a Master's degree in education. In addition, as a John Maxwell Certified Speaker, Coach and trainer, I'm able to provide keynote speaking, seminars, workshops, coaching and administering The Maxwell DISC Personality Indicator Report that will advance your personal and professional growth by means of the study and practical application of John Maxwell's proven leadership methods (See Resources at the back). I eagerly anticipate being your transformation catalyst and coach to responsibly and sensitively take your hand and together we can go forward for God.

Wherever you are on the journey of becoming *The Reigning Woman*, welcome to heaven's finishing school. This is where the Master's touch, with your cooperation and partnership, will transform your life into the God-intended version of wonder that you were meant to be.

Let's set the stage before we delve into the ten essential W's (Transformation Agents); a chapter at a time.

SETTING THE STAGE

Yes, we were born to reign. But not all *reigning* is equal! The Hebrew word, 'pilai' is the same for face and the presence of God. This one word captures the essence of this book and its royal invitation from the heavenly King for women everywhere to press our faces into His glorious, life-transforming presence!

THE REIGNING DIMENSIONS

TRANSFORMATION AGENTS (TA) & CHARACTERISTICS				
	1D	2D	3D	4D
DIMENSIONS	WANDERING	WANING	WINNING	WONDER
TA #1 WORDS	Ignorant of the Truth Idle chatter Misaligned words	Complacently knowledge-able	Application-Focused Results-Focused Mastery of Vocabulary	Practises radical obedience Truth-Aligned Living Epistle Correctly-Timed Words Confidential

TA #2 **WORSHIP**	No Worship Lip only worship Vain Worship	Inconsistent Worship Eclectic Worship	Heart Worship Fellowship with others Dedicates time to worship	Authentic Lifestyle Practice Easily prompted to Worship
TA #3 **WISDOM**	Unwise Inconsistent Belief Systems	Earthly Wisdom Idolises other's Words Unsure of Convictions	Heavenly Wisdom Creative Thinking	Filled with all the Fullness of God Highly Sought-after Advisor Commoditized their wisdom Creative Thinker Intentionally asks strategic questions
TA #4 **WORTHINESS**	Low Self-esteem & Identity Crisis	Unstable Self-esteem & Identity	Stable Identity & Self-Esteem Forgive self & others	Secure Christ-focused Identity & Self-Esteem Strong awareness of history & destiny
TA #5 **WELLBEING**	Minimal Health-Consciousness Ill-health	Diminishing Health-Care	Health-Conscious living Knowing the link between body, mind and soul	Intentional Personal Care Multifaceted Healthy Living
TA #6 **WARM-HEARTEDNESS**	Closed & Resistant Withdrawn	Moody	Polite & Friendly Happy	Loving & Irresistibly Magnetic Joyful

TA #7 **WORK**	Inactive Unwilling to work Economic & Social Exclusion	Settling for mediocrity Off-course Incomplete Tasks	Purpose-Driven Hard-working Committed	Servant-hearted God-Exalting Service Completes with Excellence Operates with Best Practices Build quality Networking
TA #8 **WEALTH**	Indebted (without an elimination plan) Struggling to cope Dependent on benevolence	Surviving Financial decline Hesitant to give	Thriving Financial Freedom	Wellspring of abundance Covenant wealth Benevolent
TA #9 **WARRIOR-STANCE**	Fearful MIA (Missing in Action) Warrior Victimhood mindset	Wounded Warrior Wounds refusing to heal Sensitive Scars	Confident Healed Warrior	Defended – knows when to stand still & let God Triumphant Warrior Scars become testimony Courageous Victorious
TA #10 **WARDROBE**	Unkempt Fashion not in alignment with Godly values	Minimal effort Overtly attention seeking	Effective Signature Style	Attire of modesty & elegance Not a slave to fashion The body is God's temple not her trophy

The nature of the process of reigning is not static, it can go backwards and forwards. There is a plethora of Scriptures that speak of and warn us against drifting from the faith (Hebrews 2:1, 1 John 2:15, 1 Timothy 6:10, Hebrews 12:1). Equally so, there are many Scriptures that encourage us to get closer to Christ and come up higher in Him (Revelation 4:1, Isaiah 56:6-7, James 4:8). As royal women of God, we must intentionally exert effort to stay in the position of 4D reigning. This requires divine commitment and tenacity. John reminded us in Revelation 3:11 that Christ is soon to return for the church and that we are to hold fast to that which we have been given so we don't lose our crowns.

Anything that is not maintained falls into disrepair. As such, our relationship with Jesus Christ, the King can deteriorate even to the degree of no longer being called His child. This is reflected in several scriptures, such as the prodigal son (Luke 15:11-32), Lot's wife becoming a pillar of salt (Genesis 19:26) and Esau selling his birthright (Genesis 25: 29-34). On the other hand, the reigning status can be repaired and regained. This is done through repentance and heeding the instruction to go and sin no more.

Upon actively saying yes to the Lord, we get to decide on the depth of the relationship that we foster with Him. Do you want to become a wonder, a winner, a 'waner' or a wanderer? By our own free will we get to choose. In 4D living, being a *wonder* is the ultimate reigning dimension and which is the Father's heart towards His dear children. Becoming a wonder is to look expressly like Jesus. This is where we will be enraptured by God's love. This is when we covenant to love God with all our heart, and with all our soul, and with all our mind, and with all our strength (which is the first commandment). We have also decided to love our neighbour as we love ourselves; which is the second commandment (Mark 12:30-31, emphasis mine)! So, we have accepted the challenge to honour the mandate to reign and to be filled with all the fullness of God (Ephesians 3:19).

For most, if not all things, and even people there are very close look-alike. So, *winning* closely resembles being a *wonder*. But there are crucial distinctions between the two. Becoming a *wonder* includes *winning*. However, *winning* doesn't necessarily include being a *wonder*. In a general sense, winning is primarily the apex of the personal development industry. And oftentimes this is the overt message and mantra we are told to go win in life. There is nothing wrong with this encouragement. In fact, it is necessary, but there is so much more. In general, winning focuses on being successful in this present world. It addresses the time era of reigning and not the eternal phase. Again, the pertinent questions are, "Why merely live when you can reign and why reign once when you can reign forever?

The 1D Wandering Dimension life lacks a sense of purpose. It's an aimless living. It is characterised with a deep sense of pointlessness and helplessness. There is much movement but little to no progress is being made!

The 2D *Waning* Dimension indicates an erosion of royal living and reigning standards. The eroding of the standards may be gradual or drastically sudden.

In general, 3D is usually used to capture the perception of the highest dimension of mankind's reality. The third dimension (3D) is the peak of man's realm and 4D reality is Spirit-saturated living! Third Dimension is where *winning* happens. However, there is a fourth dimension (4D) which includes winning but goes beyond and captures the 'next level thriving' of becoming a wonder. This is reality at its ultimate. We were born to live in the Fourth Dimension. Our destiny is 4D. This is where your life has been turned into a *wonder*! Winning isn't enough. If this is all we attain, we will fall into the personal development trap where it's an end in itself. When we tick the boxes for success and achievement, what is the point and to what end? Living in the fourth dimension encompasses and takes 3D living to the next level and ultimate level. What 4D does is to choose the Almighty God as the purpose of winning and ascribe the honour of winning to Him. He is the reason for the win!

This book seeks to address this deficit and encourages the reader to reach for deep transformation and reach beyond winning to become a wonder! It also seeks to give practical tools and solutions on how to upgrade from the 2D life of *Waning* and 1D life of *Wandering* to cross-over to use their potential to enter into the possibilities of becoming a *Wonder*! Reigning in a life of wonder is the zenith of abundant life possibilities. My prayer and deepest desire for you is that as you read or listen to this book, it will lead you to the King (even if already saved, go deeper) and that you will become further transformed into the image of Jesus Christ, His Son. Let God introduce you to the God-ordained version of yourself that should have been, could have been and can still be!

Forgive us Oh God for settling when we should be reigning. However, today marks the beginning of yielding to You because of who You are and because we love You. Lord, our highest desire is that the nail-pierced hands of Your son transform us into *wonders*. Let's have a look at the 10 essential W's.

TRANSFORMATION AGENTS

My colleague, Alima*, is an excellent cook that specializes in Asian cuisine. I salivate even now simply writing about her delicious cooking; especially her hot spicy pakoras! I loved them so much that I decided to make them at home. She gave me her recipe of what I needed: chickpeas flour, spinach, chili, salt, turmeric, potatoes, onion, garlic and so on. I was brimming with anticipation of making my very own pakoras. I prepared the mixture, fried them, and drumroll for the taste. Oops. They weren't quite like Alima's, but they will have to pass.

The next day I told Alima about my pakoras adventure. I told her of the ingredients I used and effortlessly she diagnosed the missing ingredient baking powder! It wasn't a surprise that my version of pakora was let's just say a bit on the hard side. Armed with the knowledge of what was missing, I decided to make them again; and what a difference a little tweak can make!

In a very similar manner, the making of *The Reigning Woman* requires some essential ingredients which I call Transformation Agents. To reign in the fourth dimension of being a wonder necessitates that none of the 'ingredients' is missing, each is well-developed and they are combined in such a way to create a well-balanced life. This is marked by the fragrance of heaven and a love for Christ that surpasses knowledge. Above all, she is filled to the brim and overflows with all the fullness of God (Ephesians 3:19! She showcases the reigning DNA of Purpose, Excellence, Abundance and Contribution. In this book I am going to walk you through step by step in a sequential order, the ten essential Transformation Agents starting with 'W' with which a woman of wonder is made! Depending on where you are in your royal journey, you'll be able to identify your missing ingredients and those that you already possess but need to be upgraded. Every ingredient is crucial to the outcome of you becoming a 4D reigning woman of wonder.

The 10 essential Transformation Agents are:

1. WORDS

2. WORSHIP

3. WISDOM

4. WORTHINESS

5. WELLBEING

6. WARM-HEARTEDNESS

7. WORK

8. WEALTH

9. WARRIOR-STANCE

10. WARDROBE

As you read the chapters devoted to each of the ten essential W's, you may realise that you have great strengths in some areas, require significant growth in others and some may even be totally missing. However, all the Transformation Agents are of uttermost importance! Poor performance in or absence of any will negatively impact the attainment of others. Fortunately, the reverse is also true. Improvement in or addition of a Transformation Agent creates a compounding effect which will lead to improvement in other areas of your life! There is a synergy amongst all the Transformation Agents. By the power of the Holy Spirit, they work together to give birth to the wonder in you! As we commit to making progress, every day there will be an unveiling of an emerging wonder which is the one-of-a-kind glory that is the sign that the King of glory is in residence!

It is important to note that this book is an overview that serves as an overarching introduction in The Reigning Series. Consequently, the chapter addressing each Transformation Agent, provides a foundation examination; given the weightiness of each. Other books will follow to address different aspects of the Transformation Agents in greater depths. The first two books to follow later this year will be on worship and wealth.

THE REIGNING MINDSET

The mindset plays a critical transformative role in the way people live. Therefore, it is important because it is the starting block for human change and development. The mindset is a reflection of people's beliefs, value systems and attitudes; thus, governing their way of being. Mindset drives thoughts and thoughts shape behaviour. Your mindset determines your 'life set'.

The reigning woman is extraordinary and it shows in the ways she thinks. People become what they consistently think of. "As a man thinks in his heart, so is he" (Proverbs 23:7). The reigning woman's way of thinking and living are different from others.

To reign at the highest dimension requires a shift to the kind of mindset that will act as a compass to take you to the destination of living in dominion. To experience total and lasting transformation necessitates the transformation of the mind! "And be not conformed to this world: but be ye transformed by the renewing of your mind, that ye may prove what is that good, and acceptable, and perfect, will of God" (Romans 12:2).

It is both comforting and challenging to know that mindsets can be transformed and shifted into that which we desire. The four dimensions of reigning-wonder, winning, waning and wandering have a unique mindset positioning.

In the wandering dimension, the mindset is generally wishy-washy; being unsure of who to be and what to do. This manifests in being inauthentic 'wanna-be' of whoever catches her fancy and or the latest personality trend. Being a clone of even the most admirable individual will never do your equally amazing self any justice. Ask God for the grace to be the God-ordained version of your authentic self. The best copy is still a copy.

The mindset of the 2D waning dimension is that of being wounded and worldly. This mindset is encumbered with the limiting belief that the situations which are unhealed is how life will be. Consequently, they are dealt with in ways that are worldly rather than Christlike.

In the 3D reigning category, a woman's winning mindset is well developed and she is willing to do whatever it takes to fulfil her dreams, purpose and goals. Achieving the wish-list attached to them is one of her priorities.

In the ultimate fourth dimension of being a wonder requires a mindset that is well balanced. She adapts the belief that every area of life impact on all the other areas. As such, she is teachable and aims to be world class in her field of endeavour. Above all, the mindset of a woman of wonder is that of seeing and living life for and through

Christ. Jesus is her everything. Consequently, He becomes the anchor and compass of her mindset!

How does *The Reigning Woman* live in dominion?

HOW TO REIGN

Every woman is a manifestation of the creative genius of Almighty God. You're a rare gift from the treasure chest of God's infinite intelligence. To reign, we must be transformed. The gold standard for transformation is Jesus Christ. The objective is that we become the God-intended version of ourselves which is to accept, love and reign with Christ *now* and for *eternity*. "For God so loved the world, that he gave his only begotten Son, that whosoever believes in him should not perish, but have everlasting life" (John 3:16). The reason for our birth, deliverance and transformation is to reign. And yes, you can reign!

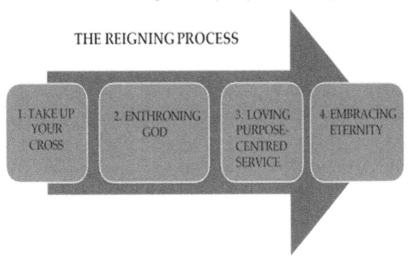

THE REIGNING PROCESS

1. TAKE UP YOUR CROSS   2. ENTHRONING GOD   3. LOVING PURPOSE-CENTRED SERVICE   4. EMBRACING ETERNITY

From beginning to end, God's primary desire is to have a loving relationship with humanity! *Enthroning God* is the starting point of the relationship whereby we exercise our free will to choose the god to whom we will devote our lives to. To *Take up Your Cross* is to choose Jesus which represents a desire and commitment to deepen the relationship with Him. Manifesting *Loving Purpose-Centred Service* is an indication of our response toGod and the depth of our relationship with Him and others. And *Embracing Eternity* represents both a stretch (connecting the possibilities of *now* to the future reign) and a reward for the decisions and commitment we have made along the path of our transformation journey. Let's explore a bit further…

Step 1: TAKE UP YOUR CROSS

Taking up our cross is never easy! It's not a stroll on the Christian lullaby highway. It will simply require all of us for all of Christ. It will reduce the *self* in us to nothing and exalt the Christ in us to the overflow. But be encouraged, it is possible and can be implemented. It has systems and strategies which make transformation repeatable and scalable! The King, Jesus Christ, for whom we reign, has revealed the secrets to an extraordinary life in and for Him. Who better to tell you how to please and impress an individual than the person himself? So here is Jesus Himself sharing with those wise enough to choose Him and learn at His feet. He said in Luke 9:23, "If any man will come after me, let him deny himself, and take up his cross daily, and follow me."Let's unpack this life-transforming verse.

• Deny Yourself

We truly have to deny ourselves in order to reign both now and for eternity! Self-denial is being willing to say no to our desires and demands to satisfy our greedy out-of-control flesh. This is done to become mature in Christ and to live a lifestyle of holiness and total surrender to God.

Allegiance to God will cost. It is the willingness to pay the cost for the choice to honour God whom we've put on the throne of our hearts! Unless an innermost death to self is fully exercised in our lives, we will not be transformed in this life nor be ready for eternity. Transformation is the prerequisite for reigning.

• Take up Your Cross

There is never a crown without a cross. Taking up our cross is never easy, but it is essential! In the Christian faith, we operate our lives with the Joshua declaration. And resoundingly we echo his words, "As for me and my house, we will serve the Lord" (Joshua 24:15)! Today we make crystal clear that our God, Jesus Christ, is the only wise God. And we choose Him. Alone! The King of glory is worthy of and requires our total unconditional commitment. A. W. Tozer states, "The value of the stripping experience lies in its power to detach us from life's passing interests and to throw us back upon eternity." Let's decide to obey God despite the possible pain and temporary lack in our lives. Our greatness is often disguised in suffering and sacrifice.

• Daily

It is obvious that consistency, intimacy and freshness matter to God! Yesterday's surrender and self-denial won't suffice. On pondering, I realise that God is fair. He doesn't give His children yesterday's manna, yesterday's blessings, yesterday's...mercies yesterday's anything! He is the Divine, so He is the endless supply of everything and all that we need. Every day we receive new grace, new mercies, new feedback...new everything. Lamentations 3:22-23 states, "It is of the Lord's mercies that we are not consumed, because his compassions fail not. They are new *every morning*: great is thy faithfulness." God is the God of the new. We should reciprocate and show up with kingdom commitment, radiance and authority *daily*!

- ## Follow the King

Follow suggests an active choice and participation in surrendering our will to make Jesus the King of our lives. It is pursuing Him; going after and letting Him lead the way and our lives. It is by Him, for Him and through Him that we reign. We are the sheep of God's fold and sheep follow and obey the Shepherd's voice. In the personal development circles, the mantra is, "Becoming the best version of ourselves." This may sound good, but it is flawed. To begin with, 'the self' (which is fallen and broken) becomes the template. How can 'the self' be the 'disease' and the cure? Deciding to follow Jesus is a stance of humility (accepting that we are broken) and that we need a Saviour. This is a wise and empowering choice.

Step 2: ENTHRONING GOD

Now that we are followers of Jesus Christ, who gets the most exalted place in our lives? Who is on the throne of your heart? Make no mistake, Jehovah is holy, majestic and faithful. But He is also jealous. He will never be content to be one of our collectibles. As it is often stated, "He must be Lord of all or not at all." As women in the kingdom of God, we intentionally put on our CROWN! What is our CROWN? It is the Christ-like Reign Over Worldly Norms. What are 'Worldly Norms'? They are anything and everything that seeks to exalt themselves above the knowledge of God's truth! This means living a totally surrendered life for Jesus Christ and simultaneously taking your rightful God-ordained place on the earth! This lifestyle is most strongly evidenced by obedience and actively fleeing from Satan by the enabling power of the Holy Spirit and with the Word of God as its foundation. A reigning woman of wonder can't hide! She humbly yet boldly wears her CROWN and exudes God's image and influence.

Step 3: LOVING PURPOSE-CENTRED SERVICE

We were saved by Love for love! As we serve humanity and bring solutions for their many needs, we must first be love ambassadors! A purpose-centred life is powerful and there is no adequate substitute for it! Let's embrace our God-given identity and ask Him to reveal our purpose or to make us advance in it. Find out what you were born to do and do it! Everything Jesus did aligned with His divine purpose and assignment...to preach good tidings to the poor, heal the broken-hearted, proclaim liberty to the captives, open prison doors of the bound, and console those who mourn in Zion (Isaiah 61:1-3; Luke 4:17, 18). Such purpose-driven living is one of the characteristics of reigning.

Step 4: EMBRACING ETERNITY

Reigning spans time and eternity. The reign in the nowness of time ought not to eclipse our desire, focus and preparation for the eternal phase of the reign with Jesus Christ. He has placed eternity in our hearts (Ecclesiastes 3:11). The power has been given to whosoever will to become the sons and daughters of God through the sacrificial death of Jesus Christ. If we surrender, the Holy Spirit (the wonder creator) will come within and upon us in such unmistakable manner that we will be led by the Spirit.

Embracing eternity now is possible, necessary and captivating! It ushers in the transformation of the mind and reality that is unrivalled. It bends reality, through Jesus Christ, outward and upward and connects now to forever. Reigning…what an amazing way to fully thrive!

When we live God's way, it goes deep within and engrafts us with the Reigning DNA!

DNA of The Reigning Woman

God, with great intentionality, made you a woman! What a gift and responsibility. As the feminine image-bearers of God, we carry deep within our soul a desire to express our uniqueness. The DNA of *The Reigning Woman* is the fundamental and distinctive characteristics that act as an anchor and a compass as she encounters the opportunities and challenges of her life, as she surrenders to and navigates the process of becoming a wonder with great impact. These fundamental characteristics facilitate her development, functioning, growth and 'reproduction'. The reigning revolution begins deep within. The four parts of The Reigning Woman's DNA are:

1. PURPOSE

There is a certain darkness that the soul can't out-run, satisfy nor silence until it enters the light, effort and joy of purpose! When the voice of purpose calls, answer "yes" even if you're trembling.

Beloved daughters of the King, before we were even born, God had an amazing plan for our lives. We were born for a purpose. Firstly, we were born to be positioned in Christ the King and to become and to execute what we were hardwired to be and do for the glory of God. Purpose is the global positioning system (GPS) for reigning. It identifies where you are in relation to God's predetermined destination for your life. Therefore, when your purpose, goals, and priorities are aligned, your productivity and progress are certain. Your YOU-nique identity and wiring come with YOU-nique responsibilities. Purpose then becomes a reference point for decision-making. Your purpose must be the primary point of reference for selecting the focus for your growth and development. Mark Twain aptly said, "The two most important days in your life are the day you were born and the day you find out why." Have we discovered why we were born? It has been frequently said, "Our potential is God's gift to us, and what we do with it is our gift to Him."

2. EXCELLENCE

Can it be said of us that we have an excellent spirit like it was said of Daniel (Daniel 6:3)? Every reigning woman hates mediocrity! Why bother to do something half-heartedly and misrepresent the King whom you serve; who is a God of excellence! To be excellent is to aim to operate at the highest standard possible. It is the quality of being first-class that makes you exceptional. Excellence demands that we use the resources available (including The Word and The Holy Spirit) to us with maximum efficiency and possess a keen attention to detail. Excellence births dependability. People know who will show up and be and do their best! Are we excellent to the extent that we can be trusted? And best of all, God greatly delights in His saints who are excellent (Psalm 16:3). However, excellence should not be mistaken for perfectionism which births analysis paralysis. Staying unnecessarily stuck is not required for excellence. Do you best and let it go; but be committed to growth.

3. ABUNDANCE

Our heavenly Father isn't only a King, but He is also El Shaddai! In Hebrew 'Shaddai' means breasts or teat. As the breasts of a breastfeeding woman contain the milk to give her child nourishment for life, so it is that 'the breasted God', the El Shaddai, provides all that His children need for spiritual and temporal sustenance. Jesus' transaction at Calvary gives us total access to the fullness of God's unlimited resources for the execution of our vision and mission. We don't have to chase abundance. We already possess it! God gave His Son to give us all that we need for life and godliness. Adopt an abundance mindset and reject the scarcity one. There is always more than enough to meet your needs and that of others. Hence, abundance is our birthright! Jesus came, died and rose again, so we may not only live; but have it with amazing abundance (John 3:16).

Reigning is shalom living! People use 'shalom' as a greeting and readily identify its often used meaning of 'peace'. However, there is a much deeper meaning to 'shalom' than is customarily used. According to Strong's Concordance (7965) 'shalom' means welfare, health, prosperity and peace. It also means wellness, happiness, favour, wholeness and rest; to complete and restore. 'Shalom' comes with a strong perfume whose fragrance permeates every area of life! 'Shalom' will change you. Indeed, Christ came that we may not just have life, but an abundant and impactful life! Importantly, abundance must be responsibly managed for it to remain a blessing.

4. CONTRIBUTION

Contribution presupposes that we have something to give. It's hard, if not impossible, to give what we don't have and also to give what we think you don't have! Do believe that everyone has something to give. You do have something to give. Becoming a contributor committed to serving others is not just a good idea, it's an instruction. Jesus said to Peter, "When you are converted [transformed] feed my sheep." Making a valuable contribution requires that we have grown and been transformed. It is pointless to possess your YOU-niqueness and keep it hidden under the cover of fear, mediocrity and insecurity. Give the gift called YOU to those in need, which is everyone you meet! We carry heaven's treasure, so let's be a blessing. We are alive for such a time as this!

Jesus modelled the mindset to be an active contributor. We must do the same. However, it requires being lifelong learners; which means just that. Learning for a lifetime. Not only should we intentionally embark on the process of transformation to become world-changers, but more importantly we do so to become 'reproducers'! Let's not only think of motherhood when you hear the word 'reproducers'. It includes it but is not limited to it. Every woman is potentially a reproducer! It is said, "success is not a success until there is a successor."

A vital aspect of becoming a contributor is to actively equip others to become the plan God has for them. To whom much is given, much is required (Luke 12:48). In what area of influence are you reigning? Which of the seven mountains of society are you exercising your influence and dominion in? Is it media, government, education, economy, family, religion or celebration (arts and entertainment)? Which one or ones? Go forth and make disciples of others.

By the way, being an equipper is a huge responsibility. We must ensure that what we replicate is of the highest standard. If we are broken and half-baked, those that we impact will be of the same calibre. If we are transformed and operate with the spirit of excellence, we too will 'reproduce' after our own kind. It is a law, the law of sowing and reaping. Live in such a way that death cannot kill you, because you have emptied and replicated yourself! For example, I believe my mother, Valerie Sherwood, can never really die. When her appointment with death arrives, she will take her final bow and go to rest until the next phase of reigning comes. She will live on in the hearts and minds of her children, grandchildren, in-laws, nieces, nephews, other relatives, brethren, community members and even her critics all over the world. She modelled and taught what it means to reign with Jesus Christ and live with strong convictions for which she was prepared to be counted! Do you possess the DNA of the reigning woman?

As it relates to God's Holy Words and our words, where are we operating? Are we wonders, have we settled for winning, are we waning or simply wandering? Let's find out in Chapter One which focuses on words.

Chapter One
Transformation Agent #1
WORDS

"Handle them carefully, for words have more power than atom bombs."

Pearl Strachan Hurd

One afternoon, my brother Richard and I were about to go to the hardware store. As he was about to drive off, he said, "Donna we should have gone a bit earlier. It's about to be the rush hour for school pick-ups and we are going to lose the parking spot." I immediately asked him if he wanted to lose the parking spot and suggested that he should say what he wanted. He good-naturedly chuckled, agreed and we both said that we wanted to get parking on our return. You must have guessed it by now. On our return from shopping, we got a parking spot! We even got the same one we had left! What do we want? Are we consistently speaking what we want? And even more importantly, are we speaking in alignment with what God says?

The individuals with the most impact and who will inevitably be world-changers are those that understand, appreciate and employ words for the desired outcome. Our words will never be in alignment with our mandate to thrive in dominion until we are soaked with the Words of God. Your life is the creation of your words.

Recently I was with a young lady and she began to tell me the specifics of the negative things which were said of her in the past. I listened with much empathy. After some time, I picked up an item and asked her to identify it. She said it was wet wipes. I opened the container and took out the few wipes which were left in it. I then asked her if I could change the content of the container. She said, "Yes". I asked her what would eventually happen to the label if she puts whatever she desired to fill the empty container and speak about it. She silently pondered for a while. I began peeling off the label and her eyes lit up! There is little to no profit to dwell on and repeatedly speak of what we don't like about our life. Let's make the transformation we desire and speak often about them. It's possible. And we can!

Our words help to design our wonder or they are our detonators! When we take command of our words, our world will come into alignment with the promises of God for us. Take authority over your words and you'll take authority over your world. Our words are reflections of your thoughts. Let's focus on filling our minds and mouths with life-transforming words. God's Word is the cornerstone of our reign.

Let the Words of God dwell in us richly (Colossians 3:16). This will help to make the impossible possible. Your miracle is your mouth! Cindy Trimm says "An idle word, is a word spoken which does not have a kingdom assignment."

The Ultimate Expert of Words

"In the beginning God...and God said" (Genesis 1). The Word is the foundation of a kingdom woman's reign! The spoken and the embodied Word were from the beginning. If you want to build a skyscraper life, build it on the Word of God. It's the only foundation that can bear the weight of your destiny! If you want to build a life of significance and impact to display the worth of the King of Glory, let the Ancient Word be the Cornerstone of your palace, your life.

At the beginning of creation there was chaos all around and pitch darkness permeated the space. Imagine chaos plus darkness. For many, this would be intimidating; choosing to either ignore it or simply run away. But not the Omnipotent One. He faced it with much gusto and intentionality. He knew what He wanted and as such He used the power-packed thing He had, His word; because He is The Word. He partnered with the Spirit and His Son. And then and only then did He begin to issue commands. He wasn't lamely making suggestions about what He desired. No. He was commanding. "Let there be." And it was so. *Everything* He commanded was established.

The Bible is the best manual to empower women of wonder with strategies that will catapult us into our destinies; the purpose for which we were born. God's Words teach us how to make evidence-based decisions in this life and for the life which is to come! "Thy word have I hid in mine heart, that I might not sin against thee" (Psalm 119:11). Without the compass of God's Words, we are lost at best; numbed by sin. Alas, what a catastrophe when the weight of sin acts as gravity at the first resurrection roll call. So, it doesn't matter how off-course and how far we have wandered from the standard of kingdom living. We are given this moment called *now* as an opportunity for transformation to say "Yes" to the call from the Father's tender heart.

The first and foundational principle that a woman needs to ever reign as joint-heir with Jesus Christ, is a deep revelation of the Word of God. If this foundation concept isn't in place, nothing will last, no matter how high she is elevated. Until a woman comes into a surrendered alignment with all of God's Word, she cannot reign. The most powerful force on the earth is the Word of God. This world with all its grandeur was created by His spoken word. In Psalm 33:4 it states that "By the word of the Lord were the heavens made; and all the host of them by the breathof his mouth."

Think of how amazing the galaxies, planets, stars, moon, sun, mountains, lakes, seas, rivers, trees, flowers...caves are! I am almost dizzy trying to comprehend the sheer power that must have impregnated every word, that such astonishing order and complex arrangement of life and beauty could have emerged from chaos and darkness. The Spirit of the Lord moved and then God said, "Let there be." And without exception when God said, "Let there be", there was a manifestation of His declarations. Not only was this the case, but He lingered and evaluated His progressive acts of creation and He deemed that they were good. God Himself was impressed by His Own Words. This is to the extreme extent that He honours His Words above His name (Psalm 138:2), He watches over them to perform them (Jeremiah 1:12) and not one of them will return to Him without accomplishing what it was sent to do (Isaiah 55: 11). These calibre words can certainly take us to a different realm and cause the miraculous to become the norm in our lives!

New Address

Let's do a rebranding and put our lives under new management. First, let's be washed and cleansed by God's infallible Words (John 15:3). If not, we'll take our old lifestyle of the grime of sin to the new season of life where the Spirit of the Lord is guiding us to. Before there is a hello, there needs to be a goodbye. Goodbye to old mindset, old strategies, old prayers, old believing and certainly old speaking! Even before the Word of God was canonised and presented to us in Bibles, mankind was always expected to live by God's instructions.

One of the necessities we must do to reign for the King of glory is to ask Him to detox us from every misconception we have concerning His Word and leave nothing except His undiluted truth. Reigning necessitates a transformation of our desires and reconstruction of our determination to please and honour God according to the principles of His Words. We live in an era (in most parts of the world) where the Word of God is readily available in multiple versions, on CDs, DVDs, Bible apps, book format, braille, to name a few. In spite of the accessibility of the Scriptures, sadly many of us are experiencing famine in our souls because we prioritise the non-essentials over spending time in the Word. It is like working in a restaurant and being diagnosed with malnutrition! Isn't it interesting that while some have little regard for the Scriptures, there are others who are risking their freedom and their very lives to have access to the precious Word of God!

It is illegal in some countries to have a Bible. Let's make good use of it while we can. Know assuredly that we can't reign and become an impactful wonder and bear much fruit unless we abide in Christ, the Living Word (John 15:4-5)! It is the Word that informs us of how to reign and possess the kind of influence that will leave a permanent mark in our generation and generations to come.

Words Dimensions of Reigning

Jesus Christ heralded His entrance on the stage of His reign as the Word. "In the beginning was the Word, and the Word was with God, and the Word was God" (John 1: 1).

• 1D Reigning: Waning

In the 1D realm, a woman is wandering. She isn't careful with her spoken words and the words she allows to influence her in songs, books, movies, art, conversations, thoughts and self-talk.

The popular adage "Garbage in, garbage out" holds true. Everything we see is an expression of someone else's words as the building block of ideas. Words were the prime medium of exchange all along the creation process. Remember that the trees, moon, stars, everything were manifestations of God's spoken words. The same holds true for us too. Could it be that whatever is missing from our lives is the need for sufficiently potent words? Let's ponder on this possibility and implication. In the 1D realm, a woman simply doesn't know the power of the tongue!

Misaligned words are out of sync with the absolute truth as is reflected in the Scriptures. Some of the reasons for wandering in words is being unwilling to gain more knowledge, satisfied with our own thinking, believing that we are right and idly using words.

• 2D Reigning: Waning

In the 2D realm, this woman is waning in her words. She is complacently knowledgeable. Although expanding your vocabulary is important, it isn't the only objective. Understanding and applying a deep awareness of the power of word as a tool to be transformed and to reign is what are required. This important depth is absent in the waning dimension. What you know is an expression of words; whether it's words listened to, read in a book or spoken by God. Right words are priceless. Therefore, to be knowledgeable and simply sit around and do nothing or very little with it is to be on the path of a steady decline; diminishing your potential. When our words are transformed, they will always need and seek useful expression. To not do so, is to sabotage the transformation process of words! To be complacent with words and not aspiring in this area, we have devalued the power of our own words and their ability to transform our own destiny! Words are universal.

• 3D Words Reigning: Winning

In the 3D winning realm, a woman knows how to win with her words. She is applications and results-focused. She has an extensive vocabulary and has gained mastery with words. This winning woman is careful to use the right words and is careful in her mannerisms along with the expression of her words. "The Lord God hath given me the tongue of the learned, that I should know how to speak a word in season to him that is weary: he wakeneth morning by morning, he wakeneth mine ear to hear as the learned" (Isaiah 50:4).

• 4D Words Reigning: Wonder

A woman living in the 4D realm understands that God's Word and the impact of her words are literally shaping her destiny. Our experiences, good or bad, are the result of the shaping of someone's words; the most powerful ones being ours. She is led by the Holy Spirit and so she copies her King. In that before she begins to speak, she ensures that the Spirit moves; first.

Although a woman expanding her vocabulary is important and needful, it isn't the primary objective in the 4D space. The potency of words as a tool to reign is. Our words, when uttered, simply don't disappear. They impact ourselves, others and even the environment forever.

No matter how potentially powerful a tool is, if misused and done outside of its correct season, it is rendered null and void. This is why the Scriptures and our words are always connected to wisdom, which we will explore in Chapter 3. The Word is the foundation for wisdom. I specifically pray and ask God to grant me, what I deem as the 'Issachar anointing'. This tribe in Israel was the smallest; only two hundred men and their claim to fame wasn't being mighty men of war like the other tribes of Israel. Their distinction was simply but powerfully that they "Understood the times and knew what Israel should do" (1Chronicles 12:32). There is great power in knowing what and when to speak and to whom. The timing of our words is critical. Wars have been fought, lives lost, reputations tarnished, friendships broken and families destroyed because of wrong and ill-timed words. A woman in 4D reigning is diligent in safeguarding her words and that of others. She is confidential.

In the fourth dimension of wonder, a woman deeply understands the power of words and uses it as a powerful agent for transformation. It's not simply a means of communicating, it is actually a tool to shape our experience. She has allowed the Word of God to transform her life to the extent that she has become a living epistle of Jesus Christ that is known and read by all (2 Corinthians 3:2)! As the saying goes, "Preach the gospel and use words, if necessary!" She has allowed the Holy Spirit, in conjunction with the power of the Word, to bring her into alignment with God's truth. She refuses to settle for and substitute truth for personal opinions, denominational persuasions, the situation-imposed less-than-ideal options, nor societal norms. "Sanctify them through thy truth: thy word is truth." (John 17:17). She is sanctified by *the truth,* not just *a truth*!

In a world that is largely governed by situational ethics and the subjectivity of whatever ideology is trending, to be a reigning woman governed by the truth of Scriptures will not be popular nor easy. God's Word is the absolute truth. It is our ultimate point of reference. God's truth becomes her truth. Do we embrace or do we actively reject God's truth?

> *Preach the word; be instant in season, out of season; reprove, rebuke, exhort with all longsuffering and doctrine. For the time will come when they will not endure sound doctrine; but after their own lusts shall they heap to themselves teachers, having itching ears; And they shall turn away their ears from the truth, and shall be turned unto fables (2 Timothy 4:2-4).*

Word Plus Holy Spirit Equals Dynamite

God's Spirit bears witness of His Word. God's Word is spirit and life (John 6:63). Flesh can't fully comprehend that which is spirit. It takes spirit to understand spirit. Thank God for the Holy Spirit, which is the Helper that will lead us into all truth and grant us revelation and illumination (John 16:13). For us to reign, we must live in alignment with the revealed truth of God's Word. It is the power of the Holy Spirit that empowers us to live an authentic life to the glory of God. God's dear children who believe in Him have been given the power to do so (John 1:12). The Holy Spirit is the power we need to reign. And the reign that will be established is built on righteousness as revealed by Scriptures; not denominational and cultural persuasions. Warren W. Wiersbe in his book, The Best of A.W. Tozer quoted A. W. Tozer having profoundly said the following of the Holy Spirit in relation to its magnetic force of casting the vision of and securing an almost tangible experience of eternity *now*:

> *Reality is its subject matter, reality in heaven and upon earth. It does not create objects which are not there but reveals objects which are already present and hidden from the soul. In actual human experience, this is likely to be the first felt in a heightened sense of the Presence of Christ. He is felt to be real...and to be intimately and ravishingly near. Then all other spiritual objects begin to stand out clearly before the mind. Grace, forgiveness, cleansing take on a form of almost bodily clearness. Prayer loses its unmeaning quality and becomes a sweet conversation with Someone actually there. Love for God and for the children of God takes possession of the soul. We feel ourselves near to heaven and it is now the earth*

and the world that begin to seem unreal...and soon to pass away. The world to come takes on a hard outline before our minds and begins to invite our interest and devotion. Then the whole life changes to suit the new reality and the change is permanent.

Benefits of God's Word

To reign in the dimension of wonder, we must put a very high value on the Word of God. Love God's Word more than our very food. Food nourishes, provides enjoyment, expresses ethical and health values, creates cultural symbols, heals and restores! The Bread of Heaven provides a far more lasting and excellent 'food' for the soul. It is light unto our feet and safeguards us from sin. God's Word is the 'manna' that we need for our often famished souls. It's time to increase our portion sizes, variety, and the frequency of intake of God's Word. There are numerous versions and media to support us in accessing God's truth. There is no excuse to be malnourished. The Bread of Life has a table spread and He invites us to come and dine. The Word provides a feast for hungry and thirsty souls to be fed! Royalty-conscious women know how to dine richly in the Word of God to embed them in our hearts and encode them in the DNA of our souls!

1. The Word of God is the manual for life. It shows us how to live in the best way possible. We all can relate to when we purchase something and run ahead to use it, only to realise we are wasting our time and efforts because we don't really know how to operate it. In the end, we had to refer to the manual. Shall we be wise to refer to the Words

of our manual, the Bible, from the beginning? This is the ideal. However, let's be encouraged if we haven't done this. It doesn't matter how much we have blundered in our futile attempt to live without the Manual, we can make a u-turn and change our lives by the power of God's all-purpose Words. We reign by implementing the Word of God. The Word of God (and our Scripture-aligned words too) is the foundation for our 4D reign. It's not a surprise that we are instructed in Colossians 3:16 to "Let the word of Christ dwell in you richly in all wisdom."

2. Our mindset determines the altitude of our lives. What is the best mindset transformer known to mankind? Categorically, it is the Word of God. "Be not conformed to this world: but be ye transformed by the renewing of your mind, that ye may prove what is that good, and acceptable, and perfect, will of God" (Romans 12:2). The written Word reveals the Living Word; Jesus Christ, the King!

3. The Words of God provide sustenance for our journey of transformation. The Word God, the Bread of Heaven, supplies knowledge, wisdom, joy, strength, hope, faith, change, prosperity and good success. "All scripture is given by inspiration of God, and is profitable for doctrine, for reproof, for correction, for instruction in righteousness: That the man of God may be perfect, thoroughly furnished unto all good works" (2 Timothy 3:16-17). In fact, the Word is "able to save your souls" (James

1:21). Therefore, it is critical to remember that it is not the hearers of the Word that will be transformed in order to reign, it is the doers.

4. It expels darkness with light. Individuals, families, churches, communities and nations are direct representatives of their adherence (or the lack thereof) to the Word of God. It is a lamp unto our feet and a light unto our path (Psalm 119:105).

5. God's Word is the petrol in our 'tank'. It is the fuel that we need in order to accelerate on the highway of life. Without this satisfactory petrol we will be prone to fill our 'tanks' with inadequate substitutes.

6. The Word increases our faith. "But without faith it is impossible to please him: for he that cometh to God must believe that he is, and that he is a rewarder of them that diligently seek him." (Hebrews 11:6). We cannot please God without faith. It is vital that we infuse our lives with God's Words. "So then faith cometh by hearing, and hearing by the word of God" (Romans 10:17).

7. The Word of God is the generator of our words; providing the power that we need to use our mouths with authority and accuracy. Our words represent our thoughts. Let's not damage our future and put ourselves in bondage by the words we speak. Do not speak against the things we are believing God for. It is important to hold fast to our confessions.

We need it All!

We need all of God's Word in order to thrive. For too many people, the only parts of the Words of God that are readily embraced are the bless-me-Jesus-bless-me parts. We live in a time where God's Word is treated like a buffet line. We take a little bit of this and a little bit of that and a whole dollop of our favourite Scripture sauce; while other portions are completely ignored! This results in undernourished or malnourished spirituality.

There is also no private understanding of Scriptures, but the Holy Spirit will lead us into all truth. The Word of God must be interpreted, applied and understood holistically. The Word of God is like a cake. It's delicious when every ingredient comes together in the correct order and correct proportion and 'baked' at the correct temperature and time duration. So too, the Words of God must be administered in the right environment under the care of competent Word administrators (teachers, preachers, pastors and prophets and apostles).

The Master Chef is so particular about His Words that He calls Himself the Word. Not only that, He said that until heaven and earth pass away, not one jot or tittle of His Word will (Mathew 5:18). It also will never fail but will accomplish its intended outcome (Isaiah 55:11). God even honours His Word above His own name (Psalm 138:2) and He watches over His Words to perform them (Jeremiah 1:12). I hope we are impressed by how God views His own words. High and holy. They are must-haves and mandatory. To view them otherwise is to lack the wisdom that is God-enthroning and self-advancing; without which we cannot reign. The Word of God is both a sword and a balm. It cuts and it heals. The Word is the all-purpose antidote for that which ails women and humanity in general.

Have you ever wondered how the Word of God is so powerful, and why is it that all of God's children aren't living amazingly impactful lives? May I propose that three factors determine the results and rewards concerning the Word of God. The quality of the seed (the Word), soil and surrender matter very much!

1. Seed:

God's Words are powerful and they are sharper than any two-edged sword (Hebrews 4:12). However, the dissemination of God's Word has a direct impact on its quality; in terms of its effect. Not every Bible study is equal. Therefore, some people teach and preach God's Word from a biased and possibly compromised standpoint. This aborts the effectiveness embedded in God's Word. It is therefore critical for believers to ensure they are indeed attending a Bible-believing and practicing church. The transformation and blessings promised in God's Word are dependent on them being 'rightly divided' (2 Timothy 2:15). If they are 'wrongly divided', they're castrated. God is under no obligation to bless that which is twisted and out of alignment with the already defined intention of His Word.

We must be grateful that we have the help of the Holy Spirit and those assigned to our lives to help keep us learning, but also safe and abiding in the truth. The revelation and illumination we receive in God's Word are usually progressive; receiving new and deeper insights from God. Life is a journey and we go from glory to glory. Therefore, when studying the Scriptures, we ought not to be afraid to throw overboard that which is old, dead and bears no fruit. Be prepared that we may need to unlearn some of the 'truth' we hold dearly. Refuse to stay stuck in the shallows of our understanding because we would rather be faithful to yesterday's revelation rather than today's fresh rhema word. What is God saying is usually a better question to ask rather than what did God say? This requires a willingness to swim beyond the boundaries of our comfort zone, possibly our denominational persuasions, experiential learnings (or lack thereof) and into God's endless oceans of truth.

2. Soil:

The seed can be compromised and so too can the soil. Often you hear people recount experiences in a service in which you were present and your perception and response to the same word is like East to West and North to South. Matthew 13: 3-8 outlines a very useful proverb that gives great insight about the different types of soil that the Word of God can be sown in:

- Some seeds fell by the way side which were devoured by fowls.

- Some fell upon stony places, where they did not have much earth. As such, they were withered by the sun because they lacked depth of earth nor they had no root.

- Some fell among thorns. Then the thorns sprung up and choked them.

- But others fell into good ground! And they brought forth fruit. They increased by 100%, 60% and 30%.

Indeed, soils are different which have huge consequences forthe outcome of the seed!

3. Surrender

We can never be 4D women of wonder if our lives aren't marked by the sweet aroma of surrender. Total surrender to the whole counsel of God's Word; which is His will! Do we still tremble at the Word of God or do we shred to pieces the parts we deem to be archaic, irrelevant and unreasonable? Isaiah 66:2 states candidly that God has a divine date with a special set of people. Will He find us in this special endangered species? He says, "But to this one I will look, to him who is humble and contrite of spirit and who trembles at my word." David in Psalm 119:120 trembles and expresses reverence for the laws of God.

King Darius, the heathen king of Babylon, in Daniel 6:26-27 must have gotten a deep revelation when he uttered these striking words throughout all the nations after the plot to have Daniel become lions' meal failed.

I make a decree, that in every dominion of my kingdom men tremble and fear before the God of Daniel: for He is the living God, and steadfast forever, and his kingdom that which shall not be destroyed, and his dominion shall be even unto the end. He delivers and rescues, and he worketh signs and wonders in heaven and on earth, who hath delivered Daniel from the power of the lions.

Wow, what words of exaltation of God and what deliverance of Daniel. When you are living in the dimension of Wonder in your words, those that accuse you falsely will be defeated. "And every tongue that shall rise against thee in judgment thou shalt condemn. This is the heritage of the servants of the Lord, and their righteousness is of me, saith the Lord" (Isaiah 54:17).

Let's be reminded of the instruction that Mary, the mother of Jesus, told the disciples, whatever He tells us to do, let's do it (John 2:5). If not, we will begin to follow strange deceptive voices and will fall prey to vain teachings. Oftentimes we sing hymns and refrains of surrender, but when the Word informs us how to surrender; we quickly walk through the door of excuses and enter the room of disobedience with its own annex of deception. The devil will attempt to discredit God by enticing and deceiving people into rejecting God's total truth. Instead, we settle in believing half-truths and outright lies. The deceiver will try to make us question and disbelieve the character and integrity of God as is revealed in the Scriptures.

He gets us to doubt God's goodness, faithfulness, promises, timings and even His capacity to do what He said He will do. Consequently, we make decisions without the deep belief and confidence that God is who He says He is. God's Words are spirit and life (John 6:63). You may be asking, "What is the believer's source of strength against the devil's intention and attempts to deceive and devour us?" The strength of believers is based on the Word of God infused by the Holy Spirit into our lives and our willingness to be radically obedient. The former works in conjunction with the latter. Anything that is deemed to be revealed by the Holy Spirit that contradicts the Word is not the truth, hence not of God.

Aligning our words with God's Words

The power of God's Words is real. God's Words ought to saturate our words. Words matter. Words are the building block of our thoughts and our thoughts are in the driving seat of our actions. What we think eventually becomes who we are. "For as he thinks in his heart, so is he" (Proverbs 23:7). And without fail, our words come from the treasure house of our hearts. "A good man out of the good treasure of his heart bringeth forth that which is good; and an evil man out of the evil treasure of his heart brings forth that which is evil: for of the abundance of the heart his mouth speaks" (Luke 6:45). Wow. There is a direct relationship between what we think and what we speak. Our words both reflect and determine our attitudes. Our attitudes affect us the most and those in our environment to a far lesser degree! Often, we choose an attitude as a weapon for others, not realising that the other edge of the attitude sword is also destroying us.

The opposite is also true. When we use our words as blessings, the other edge of the 'attitude sword' is carving out a life of empowerment and elevation. We get to choose our attitudes. In any environment, we are exposed to the same stimuli, but oh what vast differences in our attitudes towards them! Our self-talk is either useful or unhelpful. One of the hallmarks of a woman who reigns is that her words are saturated with the principles of God's Word and absolute faith in Him. Therefore, her words are established.

We can't reign if we don't know how to use our mouths as legislative devices. Women become unstoppable when we know the authority we carry in our mouths. The words we speak are the catalyst of our realities; for better or for worse. The mouth isn't simply for eating. It is a creative instrument. More importantly, our mouths were made to partner with God in sculpturing our destiny!

Self-Talk

As women, we are sometimes very mean and disparaging to our own selves! Our self-talk can either make or break us! Just like the spoken word by the Father created this world, so it is that our words will create our world. Be careful of the names you call yourself. It is one thing when someone else calls you another name that is not in line with who you are and what you carry. However, if you are the one calling yourself names which are not in agreement with what God says of you; the damage is even greater. For example, Mephibosheth called himself a "dead dog", Naomi called herself "bitterness", Moses called himself "a stammering mouth" and Sarah called herself "barren". As of this moment, we will call ourselves only what is in alignment with what God says of us. We cancel negative words spoken over our lives; even by our own mouths.

The niggling negative voices will always come to our minds, but we don't have to invite them in and have tea and biscuits with them. Tell them they've got the wrong address. Let them know that you are *The Reigning Woman* and your Father forbids you to speak to strangers! Do a 'stranger danger' and close the door to the negative thoughts bombarding your mind.

Let our words confirm our wonderful worth and give the same gift to others. We must daily speak words of affirmation over our lives and our loved ones. Words are everything! Words can either poison or empower. It is an instrument of creation or carnage. How do you speak about yourself? What we believe and speak about ourselves tend to be what others believe and think of us. Have you ever wondered how two people can have the very same experience and their words about it are completely different? Are we reacting or are we responding? Words matter. They are irreplaceable agents for the transformation we need and long for.

Invest the time to become a keen observer of your own words. Consciously study them, correct them, improve them and watch the astonishing speed with which things will begin to change for the better. When the words we speak to ourselves change, the words we speak to others will inevitably change. Ruth's words transformed generations.

"Entreat Me Not to Leave You!"

Let me reiterate, the power of words can't be overestimated! "A closed mouth is a closed destiny!" Are your words commanding or cancelling your destiny? Ruth, a widowed Moabite, made the decision to leave the land of her birth and its many gods and clung to her mother-in-law as she prepared to return to Bethlehem. In the book of the Bible that is named after her, Ruth uttered words that catapulted her into an amazing destiny and shifted ensuing generations; including being featured in the genealogy of Jesus Christ. Ruth is a prime example of a woman whose life was totally transformed and who became a wonder with great impact. She said in Ruth 1:16-17:

> *Entreat me not to leave you,*
>
> *Or to turn back from following after you;*
>
> *For wherever you go, I will go;*
>
> *And wherever you lodge, I will lodge; Your people shall be my people,*

And your God, my God. Where you die, I will die, And there will I be buried.

The Lord do so to me, and more also,

If anything but death parts you and me.

When Ruth made this rather bold declaration to Naomi, an exception to the rule of excluding all Moabites and their descendants from entering God's congregation forever, even to their tenth generation! Ruth's words catapulted her beyond the limitations and curse of her generation because she spoke the right words. What destiny altering words do we need to speak to the right person today? Ruth did. Will you?

❖ **People:** When Ruth opened her mouth and declared, "Your people will be my people" (Ruth 1: 16), her words literally gave her people. As she said it, she got it! First, there was Naomi, her mother-in-law and mentor. Then this divine connection led her to Boaz and the ensuing generations, which included Jesus Christ, our Lord and Saviour. Precious lady, your words can and should help to bring people into your life, as it did for Ruth.

❖ **Place:** In God's kingdom-logistics, He has a designated place for everyone; with no exception. During harvest time, people weren't allowed to reap all their produce. The corners of the fields were reserved for those less fortunate, such as the poor, widows and orphans (Leviticus 23:22). In alignment with God's plan, Ruth's words led her to the corners of Boaz' field at the right time of the year. Your words have the power to help to take you there wherever your *there* is!

❖ **Permission:** Ruth was permitted by Boaz to reap only in his field. He later permitted her to move closer; from the field to the house. She later upgraded from gleaning to reigning and from a destitute stranger to a beloved wife.

❖ **Provision:** Ruth tapped into the destiny that is possible when you change your bearings and fix your gaze on the True and Living God. Ruth's greatest blessing was finding refuge in a loving, sovereign, merciful and truly tender God; who is no respecter of persons. Boaz was a bonus thrown in for good measure. But what a good measure he was! Indeed, whosoever puts their trust in the Almighty God will never be ashamed (Psalm 37: 18-19). Look around you right now. With observant eyes you will be sure to find lots of handfuls intentionally made available to you like Ruth from El Shaddai. This is a classic example of a woman's life being totally transformed and suddenly she was transported from gleaning to reigning. And transported from abject poverty to great wealth.

❖ **Purpose:** Ruth did not arrive in a strange land and culture twiddling her fingers and with a spirit of pity and complaint! No. She made the decision to leave Moab and was willing to do and become whatever it takes to have great success for herself and her mother-in-law! To think that the offspring of this Moabite young woman gets featured in the genealogy of Jesus is truly amazing. The Moabites were not allowed in the congregation of Israel up the tenth generation (Deuteronomy 23:3)! What a woman you are when God chooses to break His own rules in order to make a way for you and to use you mightily. Thank God for His sovereignty, He gets to make whatever decisions that suit His divine will.

WORDS TRANSFORMATION STRATEGIES

1. Embrace the Scriptures as the truth and manual for your life. Just like when we are using our GPS to get us to a specific destination, if we miss our turn, we don't abort the trip. It recalibrates to get us there. But be prepared we sometimes have to make complete U-turns, but it will be worth it.

2. Our attitude towards the Scriptures is important. Approach God's Word with childlike faith and trust; with a heart that is open and ready to obey; no matter the cost. Precious sisters we shouldn't allow our circumstances (whether they are dire or opulent) to dictate to us how to live or whether or not we will obey God.

3. The Word of God is the ultimate terms and conditions of our lives. Notice I didn't say the Word of God dictates the terms and conditions of our lives. Repeatedly throughout the Scriptures, our free will is honoured. God will never override nor take away our self- governance of choice. Never. The word "if", highlights our freedom to make our own choices. *"If* ye be willing and obedient, ye shall eat the good of the

land: But *if* ye refuse and rebel, ye shall be devoured with the sword" (Isaiah 1:19-20). See also Deuteronomy 28:1.

4. The Words of God is a perennial staple for every kingdom- focused woman of God. The way the written Word is read, memorised, meditated on, studied, taught and pursued should be with a view to develop intimacy with Jesus, the Living Word. The best way to position oneself as we engage with God's word is in relationship; not as an end in itself. Loving God's Words should lead to loving God more deeply. Aim to not only know the Word of God but also to know the God of the Word.

5. Extra-Biblical aids (such as commentaries, different versions, character studies) can be very useful. However, great diligence must be exercised when selecting and using them. Some are steeped in personal and denominational opinions which are not in keeping with the intended truth of God's Word.

6. Totally and actively rely on the Holy Spirit to guide you into all truth. It's a promise, so make the best use of it.

7. We must be prepared to say goodbye to every denominational persuasion, mindsets, cultural norms, family traditions, clubs and societies...everything that contravenes God's truth. Unlearning is a vital prerequisite of new learning. This will take courage, humility and integrity. This will take God.

8. Timothy knew the scriptures from his youth (2 Timothy 3:15). Similarly, let's ensure that we life-changing, conscience-sorting, yoke-breaking, mountain-moving...decision-making treasure of the infallible Word of God. Seize every opportunity to teach them. "You shall teach them diligently... and shall talk of them when you sit in your house, when you walk by the way, when you lie down, and when you rise up" (Deuteronomy 6:7). Our entire household needs the sanctifying truth of God's Word.

9. Make a covenant with God about your mouth. Here is an example found in Proverbs 8: 6-8, "Hear; for I will speak of excellent things; and the opening of my lips shall be right things. For my mouth shall speak truth; and wickedness is an abomination to my lips. All the words of my mouth are in righteousness; there is nothing froward or perverse in them." Be very mindful of the destructive practices of anger, malice, gossip, sarcasm, belittling, swearing, flattery, boasting, lying, and other such practices which are destructive to our reign and do not promote the righteousness of God. If we are having significant struggles in these areas, we may decide to become accountable to someone to help us break the stronghold of these vices.

10. Practise listening rather than being quick to speak; let your words be few. When we are focusing on becoming all that we can be in Christ, we cannot afford to be dissipating energy through unnecessary words. Proverbs 10:19 states, "In the multitude of words there wanteth

not sin: but he that refraineth his lips [are] wise."
In essence, when we speak too much, we'll
inevitably sin. "The tongue can no man tame; it is
an unruly evil, full of deadly poison. Out of the
same mouth proceedeth blessing and cursing. My
brethren, these things ought not so to be." (James
3: 8, 10).

11. Commit to practise the law of kindness with
your tongue. Let it be said of us, "She opens her
mouth with wisdom; and in her tongue is the law
of kindness" Proverbs 31:26.

- Pause before speaking. The mental 'counting to
ten' before speaking can be useful. In some
situations, we may have to count to twenty
to remind ourselves that we are under the
Kingship of Christ; new government and
management.

- Before speaking, we must think; since our
thoughts are reflected in our words. We
could ask ourselves the following sobering
questions implied in Philippians 4:8 to help
us speak with integrity. Is what I am about
to say: True? Honest? Just? Pure? Lovely? Of
a good report? Virtuous? Praise-worthy? If
the answer to any of these questions is no,
then perish the thought. We are told
forthrightly in Ephesians 4: 29 how to speak,
"Let no corrupt communication proceed out
of your mouth, but that which is good to the
use of edifying, that it may minister grace
unto the hearers. Let's remember who we are
in Christ and to each other! Therefore, we

solemnly pray, "Let the words of my mouth, and the meditation of my heart, be acceptable in thy sight, O LORD, my strength, and my redeemer" (Psalms 19:14).

- The world, especially since the global lockdown, has become a large online village. It is vital that we reread before pressing the send icon in the online spaces. Remember "you are the master of the unspoken word and slave to the spoken ones." It is true that our silence can only be misinterpreted but never misquoted.

12. Prayerfully identify a topic of focus from the Scriptures to become an expert of. A focus ignites a passion and passion ignites focus. There is much merit in being an "inch wide and a mile deep rather than being a mile wide and an inch deep." For example, wisdom is Dr. Mike Murdock's and leadership is Dr. John Maxwell's foci. I have started my focus on transformation.

13. Consider implementing (or continuing to do so) a yearly word focus. A few years ago, I began asking God for a word to focus on for the upcoming year. This has been life-changing! God will literally use the words to transform you deeply. The last two years my word was 'transformation' and this year my word is 'wonder'. Recently in a prayer encounter with my beloved kingdom sister Barbara, I got my general anchor word for my life, which is "Yes"! For the rest of my life, in a deeper and fresher awareness, my answer is "yes" to Christ, my King and

Master! In response to the gift of these words, I read, attended trainings, use them as prayer points, shared the insight with others and developed content.

14. Practise doing Word-based prayers, singing and declarations as an integral part of your lifestyle of worship and transformational growth. For example, I consistently pray concerning Ephesians 3: 19 and Isaiah 11:2-5. My favourite Bible verse declaration is Proverbs 21:1. And a few word-based songs that I sing are Psalms 23, 46:10, 61: 1-3, 121, Isaiah 22:22 & 50:4. Make a list for yourself.

15. Integrate topical word studies on various subjects. Find and study Bible verses in areas of your focus such as trust, healing, marriage, holiness, children...forgiveness. I have been finding Scriptures on 'trust' and have been having a great time studying them.

16. Practise using your 'faith muscles' and confessing God's truth over every situation. If not, we will lose confidence in the Word and eventually succumb to the 'fiery darts' of the enemy, especially that of disbelief, disappointment and disobedience. Can you imagine the pointlessness and damage we do when we constantly whine and say thingslike, "I am broke", "I want to run away", "I am shy" and "I can't"? Our words are a vivid reflection of the condition of our hearts.

17. Intentionally ask questions to have your grey areas addressed by those competent in the areas

you need answers in. For example, if you want to learn about leadership, you could include John Maxwell's work. If you desire to learn about wisdom, you could include Mike Murdock's and so on. Decide how you will capture the answers you are given so you can follow up.

18. The Word of God must be shared with a view to glorify God and meet the needs of the people. Hence, it is critical that we are sitting under a church leadership which is in alignment with God's Word and your plan for growth. The Word of God tends to be transmitted across generations, so a wise choice is needed to facilitate the transmission of a legacy of truth.

19. Decide to exert consistent effort to improve the quality and quantity of your words. In ways such as delighting in and studying God's Word, join your local Toastmaster, learn at least one new word or way to use an existing word every day, practise purposeful speaking, read books, listen to audio, use a dictionary and thesaurus and get feedback on your communication skills.

God's Word is the cornerstone of the existence of the world. It is the foundation of everything that is! Jesus is the Written and the Living Word. He is the Template from which we pattern our lives in order to please Him. He is the Lord that reigns supremely. If we are to reign in Him and for Him, we must bring our lives in alignment with the gold standard of His Word; starting with our words.

Our world changes at the speed and quality of our words! Words are the building block of our lives and the world. When we pray, sing, if we want a degree, change jobs, enter a new relationship, negotiate a deal...whatever; we do so via the pathway of words. Our lives are the evidences of the manifestation of words. Therefore, to lack word (in quality and quantity) is to be at a disadvantage. It would do us much good to heed the advice in 2 Timothy 2:15 "Study to show thyself approved unto God, a workman that needs not to be ashamed, rightly dividing the word of truth."

In addition, the timing and seasons of words are critical. "A word fitly spoken is like apples of gold in pictures of silver" (Proverbs 25:11). The right word said at the wrong time becomes the wrong word. Wrong words are very damaging. They break relationships, forfeit negotiations and can even cancel our destinies. Words are powerful; and power is always accompanied by great responsibility.

The depth and extensive possibilities and responsibilities of a woman becoming a wonder even in the dimension of words, requires the immovable foundation of God's Word and the alignment of her words with His!

God is relational. He is always saying, as He said to John, "Come up here, and I will show you things" (Revelation 4:1). There is absolutely nothing that can transform our lives, both inside and outside, quite like God's penetrable Words. Absolutely nothing! The Word is calling us. Can you hear Him?

The Written Word leads us to the Living Word and He calls us to worship, which is the focus of the next chapter.

WORDS TRANSFORMATION TASK

1. In terms of the Reigning Dimensions regarding *Words*, where are you? (Tick one)

Wonder ☐   Winning ☐   Waning ☐   Wandering ☐

2. Develop a Words Declaration: Eg. My words are in alignment with God's Word; I am secure in my identity!

_____

_____

3. Which of the Words Transformation Strategies would give you the maximum impact now?

_____

_____

4. Set a SMART (Specific, Measurable, Attainable, Realistic and Time-bound) words goal.

_____

_____

_____

5. Motivation: Why is this goal important to you?

_____

_____

_____

6. Accountability: Which person or system will hold you accountable?

_____

7. Review Date:

_____

8. Reward: How will you celebrate achieving this goal?

_____

_____

Chapter Two
Transformation Agent #2
WORSHIP

*"Worship is a response to the revelation
of just how great God is."*

Darlene Zschech

Worship is the purpose, priority and privilege of *The Reigning Woman*. All other interests and occupations are side dishes. Worship is the main course! Worship is derived from the word which means 'worth-ship'. Forever our Lord reigns and ,oj worthy of all our worship. Worship is about ascribing reverence, adoration and admiration to God. 'Proskuneo', the Greek word for worship, means to bow down to God or kings. The home of worship is the heart and it's a lifestyle!

Father, we Your daughters, bow our hearts lower than our knees can ever bow to declare You as the King of our lives. You are our everything! Who can be compared to You oh God? None! In honour of Your worth and majesty-mountains salute, starry hosts dance, trees clap their hands, lightning and thunder praise, fountains exclaim, innocent children scream in delight, men pay homage and oceans twirl with gladness! As redeemed women of Your kingdom, we too join in the symphony of worship. Our souls simply stand in total awe of You! As You reign, we reign in You and for You.

There's nothing as beautiful, sweet and glorious like the fragrance and sound of worship. Jesus died the death of a common criminal so that we could become royalty. He wore a crown of thorns so that we can wear a crown of radiance and glory. He died so that we can have an extraordinarily abundant life. There is no greater beauty to behold than to see a sanctified woman worshipping God with her whole heart. She worships as a lifestyle; not just a one-day of the week affair. A. W. Tozer reminds us that:

> God wants worshipers before workers; indeed, the only acceptable workers are those who have learned the lost art of worship. It is inconceivable that a sovereign and holy God should be so hard up for workers that He would press into service anyone who had been empowered regardless of his moral qualifications. The very stones would praise Him if the need arose and a thousand legions of angels would leap to His will.

Mankind was created out of nothing as is recounted in the creation story in Genesis 1-2. And God by His divine spoken Word and breath converted our nothingness into the apex of His creation as a tripartite being- body, soul and spirit. We bear the express image of God. We were made to worship our Creator with our whole heart bestowing unto Him our everything! "Thou art worthy, O Lord, to receive glory and honour and power: for thou hast created all things, and for thy pleasure they are and were created" (Revelation 4:11).

The only worship that touches God's heart is the one done after His design. There is a special brand of worshippers that God seeks; it is those who worship Him in spirit and truth (John 4: 23-24). The only accurate scale for what constitutes true worship and will include us in the category of true worshipers, is God's Holy Words. Jesus in His passionate prayer to His Father asked Him to, "Sanctify them through thy truth: thy word is truth" (John 17:17). What does it mean to sanctify? What was Jesus really asking His Father to do? Sanctification is the process of being separated from everything that defiles and makes us unclean before God. Worship necessitates a leaving from and a laying down; a transformation indeed.

It is needful for us to be very conscious that we serve a Holy God that requires that we too, as His dear children must be clean, holy and set apart! "For I am the Lord your God: you shall therefore sanctify yourselves, and you shall be holy; for I am holy" (Leviticus 11: 44.) Many Christians believe and behave as if holiness was for the Old Testament era and hence is no longer applicable to this grace dispensation. Well, if under the Mosaic Law with the blood of bulls, rams, pigeons and other animals required holiness, how can the dispensation purchased by the blood of Jesus Christ require less than holiness? The standard must be the same or more, not less!

We are not talking about self-assigned holiness. Rather, the holiness through the finished work of Christ. All our own righteousness is like repulsive filthy rags (Isaiah 64:6). But by the power of the Holy Spirit, we exercise the effort, by God's grace, to honour Him. Genuine worship is allowing the Elohim to take over our lives through living the kingdom principles revealed in His Words and energised by His Holy Spirit. He becomes Lord of all and has become the pinnacle of your value system. This is why idolatry is an insult to God because someone and or something else has taken His place; a place that should be unrivalled.

Worship Dimensions of Reigning

• 1D Worship Reigning: Wandering

At the first dimension of wandering, this woman actively chooses not to worship. Albeit, possibly unknown to her, she is still worshipping! On the other hand, when she chooses to worship, it is from the lips only. On the surface, everything may appear alright, but the worship activities are done for the purpose of ticking the boxes. Her heart is not in it. The heart of reigning is about our hearts! Here is a classic example in 2 Chronicles 25:1-3:

> *Amaziah was twenty and five years old when he began to reign, and he reigned twenty and nine years in Jerusalem. And he did that which was right in the sight of the Lord, but not with a perfect heart.*

In the end, not worshipping God with a totally surrendered heart amounts to vanity; having no point and substance which will not lead to the desired outcome of being a genuine worshipper in a covenant relationship with God. "But in vain they do worship me, teaching for doctrines the commandments of men" (Matthew 15:9). Vain worship also includes doing whatever worship activities that we do, but it's with a wrong motive; possible for a show and ego strokes.

In essence, we are worshipping and saying it is done to God, but alas, it is not what God required of us and or it wasn't done from a heart where God alone is enthroned. At the end of our worship, let it not be said of us as it stated in Matthew 7: 21-23:

> Not everyone that saith unto me, Lord, Lord, shall enter into the kingdom of heaven; but he that doeth the will of my Father which is in heaven.

> Many will say to me in that day, Lord, Lord, have we not prophesied in thy name? and in thy name have cast out devils? and in thy name done many wonderful works?

• 2D Reigning: Waning

In the 2D realm, worship begins to wane and is inconsistent. It is deteriorating from the standard of what God expects and what used to be practised by the worshipper. For example, this worshiper waits for a special day, choir leader and praise and worship team to actively engage in worship. She is dependent on worship props to light the worship fire in her soul; which is often cold and thirsty. Not so with the 4D worshipper, she comes with her own fire and comes with the mindset to start a worship revolution. When worship is waning, the worshiper is usually skilled at making excuses and complain about the worship service- the praise and worship session is 'dry', the preacher is cold, the prayers and the service are too long and the offering plate is passed around too often (that was before Covid-19 struck). Any and everything gets on these worshipper's nerves. The 2D worshipper, by virtue of all the fault-finding and complaining, is a distracted and lukewarm worshipper. Distracted worshippers become a danger to themselves and are a threat to the health of the church fellowship.

With eclectic worship, there are other gods competing for the throne of the heart that ought to be reserved for Jesus Christ, alone. Yes, we recognise Jesus as Saviour, but we give God the leftovers because He isn't given the first place. This manifests in picking and choosing when to obey the instructions of the Lord. It's a case of if God requires lamb, we give turkey, if he desires honour, we give dishonour. If He requires clean, we give unclean, if He says fast, we eat, if He requires justice, but we give Him oppression, if He says worship, we whine and complain. The question in Luke 6:46 is pertinent, "And why call ye me, Lord, Lord, and do not the things which I say?" One of the hallmarks of transformation in the context of reigning for Christ is the mindset and heart-set of obedience. "Why then are the people of Jerusalem slidden back by a perpetual backsliding? they hold fast deceit, they refuse to return" (Jeremiah 8:5). This was the tragic state of God's people, Israel. May it not be said of us and if it is so, we must return to (or go to) God and He will abundantly pardon us.

• 3D Reigning: Winning

In the third dimension of *winning*, your heart is focused on your worship and is happy to engage in the disciplines of worship such as singing, praying, and fasting. This winning woman knows that worship is a matter of the heart. She belongs to a local church and consistently engages in fellowship with a community of believers. Importantly, she dedicates time to worship both privately or corporately.

• 4D Reigning: Wonder

In the fourth dimension of wonder, worship is a lifestyle. It's not viewed nor treated as a slot in the service nor pseudo reverence on a specific day. To reiterate, we were made in the image of God. We are joint-heirs with Christ who were born to reign. In this next level of thriving, we engage in authentic worship. This matter is so deep that it goes beyond the scope of this chapter. This is why my next book will be totally dedicated to Authentic Worship. Worship is a full-time occupation for the woman who has become a wonder as she yields to the Lord!

This calibre of worshipper is easily prompted to worship. As she thrives in God's benevolent glory, she sees His majesty and handiwork in nearly everything and responds with worship. She sees God's glory in the heavens (Psalm 19:1), a new-born babe, a squirrel, the sea, mountains, trees, food, flowers, animals, tests, trials, neighbours...herself. No matter what has happened or isn't happening, she can find much to worship God for. She knows that God is always worthy and deserving of her praise!

Which Worship?

Genuine worship is the only path to escape life's nothingness. We were born to worship. It's just going to be a matter of whom or what we worship; because we are all worshipping beings. As we have said, our Heavenly Father is holy. And as such He doesn't accept every worship! It doesn't matter if we label whatever we do as worship. If it doesn't measure up to God's standards of truth as prescribed by His Word, He isn't pleased. "But the hour cometh and now is, when the true worshippers shall worship the Father in spirit and in truth; for the Father seeketh such to worship Him. (John 4:23).

This is what God explicitly said, "This people draweth nigh unto me with their mouth, and honoureth me with their lips; but their heart is far from me. But in vain they do worship me, teaching for doctrines the commandments of men" (Matthew 15: 8-9). Worship that isn't heart-centred and Word-aligned is deemed as vain! God is never impressed by that which has no substance and is fake! Acceptable worship must saturate our entire life; it must become a lifestyle devotion. The following texts establish the fact that our lips and heart can be *feigned* in worship.

1. *Hear the right, O LORD, attend unto my cry, give ear unto my prayer, that goeth not out of feigned lips. Psalm 17:1*

2. *And yet for all this her treacherous sister Judah hath not turned unto me with her whole heart, but feignedly, saith the LORD. Jeremiah 3:10*

What are feigned lips and heart? In this context, this is when worship is insincere and pretentious! Jesus' question in Luke 6:46 is worth deep pondering: "And why call ye me, Lord, Lord, and do not the things which I say?" In addition, idolatry angers God greatly and we are advised to avoid it at any cost (Jeremiah 17: 5; Exodus 20: 3-5). Here are a few erroneous ways to worship which must be avoided:

1. Self-Worship

This worship makes the self the centre and object of worship. The centre-stage and adoration are given to things that are passing, such as intellectual prowess, the beauty of the body and the allure of numerous other accomplishments. In this brand of false worship, the sense of self is exalted and the holy God is relegated to the side-line; if at all in the picture.

Thus says the Lord: "Let not the wise man glory in his wisdom, let not the mighty man glory in his might, nor let the rich man glory in his riches; But let him who glories glory in this, that he understands and knows Me, That I am the Lord, exercising lovingkindness, judgment, and righteousness in the earth. For in these I delight," says the Lord (Jeremiah 9: 23-24).

2. People Worship

There are some persons that have larger-than-life personalities and possible achievements. As a result, based on this faulty and shaky premise, they have become the object of worship. Some are happy to be worshipped and others may be oblivious that they are being worshipped. However, when they are happy to receive worship, they are usually proud, self-absorbed, very demanding and they themselves have put the true God on a lower self and the people must stretch beyond their assigned place for God' to get to them! What an insult to the King of glory.

3. Creation Worship

The creative works of God's hands are amazing, but ought not to be the object of worship. Instead, they should inspire us to worship the Creator; not the created! The sun, moon, stars, trees, oceans, sky, rain, children, spouses and others. Creation worship can also be the worship of the created things of men's imagination. Any and everything can become the object of worship; a car, house, business...whatever. I have heard of people loving and adoring inanimate objects to the degree that they fall in love with them to the extent that they make wedding vows and marry them! Imagine someone marrying a car, the Eiffel Tower in France and countless other inanimate objects. "There shall no strange god be in thee; neither shalt thou worship any strange god. But my people would not hearken to my voice...So I gave them up unto their own hearts' lust: and they walked in their own counsels" (Psalm 81:9-12). Yes, creation worship is real but not accepted by God. God our Creator is the only Being worthy of our worship.

4. Worshiping outside the 'Door'

Jesus said of Himself in John 10:9, "I am the door: by me if any man enters in, he shall be saved and shall go in and out, and find pasture." Many people desire to be saved but are, for many reasons, stopping outside the door rather than entering through the access point of Jesus Christ! This amounts to nothing; simply vanity and disappointment. Acceptable worship can only ever happen by entering through The Door of Jesus Christ. He is the only one that can lead to salvation. It gives status, refuge, safety, provision, a new identity, hope, a brighter future and eternal life!

5. Sin-stained Worship

God will not coexist nor tolerate our sins. He is a jealous God. Idolatry will always be an abomination to Jehovah. Joshua, Moses' successor, told the people as they faced the battle, "Sanctify yourselves: for tomorrow the Lord will do wonders among you" (Joshua 3:5). For God to do wonders in, for and through us, we must be set apart from that which defile. God is holy and He views sin with utter disgust. However, He loves sinners to the extent that He is always calling us unto Himself. Rejection of this royal invitation to relationship breaks the Father's heart.

As women, our Egyptian bondage can leave us battered, bruised and broken. It sometimes leaves us with the proclivity to worship strange gods. The gods of self, illicit sex, drug abuse, eclectic worship practices and stories of miseries and regret. Today, right now, we are being reminded that we should have no other god before the Lord (Deuteronomy 5:6-10). There are always serious consequences for choosing to worship other gods. Pause and read 1 Samuel 5:1-7 and take note of God's response to the ancient Philistine god of Dagon. Idolatry kindles the wrath of God to the extent that He may destroy us! Do you want to be a reigning woman of wonder with Jesus Christ? If yes, let's put away all strange gods and sanctify ourselves. Jehovah M'Kaddesh, is The Lord our Sanctifier, let's all go to Him for our needed sanctification.

It is not easy to worship God acceptably. We are fallen and broken; bent out of shape by sin. However, through Jesus Christ, we can! In addition, let's praise God for the help of the Holy Spirit. So, whatever we do to worship Yahweh, it must be engineered and fuelled by the divine unction of His Spirit. Worship awakens us to know and value who our Source is. He is Elohim, the Lord God Almighty. The magnetism of this mutual relationship serves as a place of refuge, comfort, birthing place and wisdom downloads. Let's take a look in the mirror of truth and see where we are in our worship. When we know this, we can make the needed changes for greater transformation.

Dealing with Sin

Repentance is needed for reigning. It is godly sorrow for violating the standards of God and more importantly, forsaking them. Sin causes reproach (Proverbs 14:34). We can't deal with our sins by our own efforts. We will fail even with our best determinations. The righteousness that avails, is bestowed upon us through the transforming gift of Jesus at Calvary. Our self-constructed, denomination-constructed and world-constructed versions of righteousness are altogether vanity. We need to put on the sanctifying robe of righteousness in Christ alone. So based on the finished work of Calvary, we in turn, must respond by becoming sanctified by the Word, Blood of Jesus and the power of the Holy Spirit, which will make us abhor all works of darkness and of the flesh.

Our lives will then be marked by submission, obedience and gratitude. We should not be content with missing the standards of God; which is what sin is. The daughters of Zion are like a comely and delicate woman. Sin destroys our friendship with God and invites worldliness into our lives; which causes us to wane and wander and cancel the likelihood of becoming a wonder! James 4:4 speaks expressly, "Know ye not that the friendship of the world is enmity with God? whosoever therefore will be a friend of the world is the enemy of God".

John Wesley said, "Give me 100 men who hate nothing but sin and love God with all their hearts and I will shake the world for Christ!" Here is my remix, "Give me one woman who hates nothing but sin and loves God with all her heart and she will shake the world for Christ!" Will that one woman be you as you read (or listen) this book by divine appointment? Do you want to impact the world for Christ? Well, here is the formula: hate only sin and love the Lord your God with all your heart and your neighbour as yourself! Consistently do this and you will, without fail, greatly impact the world for Christ. May God grant us grace as we go forward from glory to glory and from conquering to conquer for His dear name's sake! Have we been allowing God to use His Word, prayer, Holy Spirit and fasting to help us deal with the things that defile our life?

Love Inspired Worship

Genuine love is built on the foundation of a deep and committed affection for the heavenly Father. In Mark 12:30-31 we are instructed to, "And thou shalt love the Lord thy God with all thy heart, and with all thy soul, and with all thy mind, and with all thy strength: this is the first commandment. And the second is like, namely this, thou shalt love thy neighbour as thyself. There is none other commandment greater than these." God elevates only those who love Him unreservedly and have bowed their hearts to Him. Him alone! No trinkets can be there.

What is Your "One Thing"?

"One thing have I desired of the Lord, that will I seek after; that I may dwell in the house of the Lord all the days of my life, to behold the beauty of the Lord, and to enquire in his temple. (Psalm 27:4).

David's "one thing" was to live in the presence of the Lord and to behold His beauty! Amongst the multitudes of all our desires, what is our "one thing"? To whom do we give our worship? Let's be real and honest. Some women's "one thing" is to get a husband, see their names with an illustrious title on an office door, get a lovely house, travel the world, become a billionaire, migrate, become a president or prime minister, raise children, meet a specific celebrity, to be healed, to conceive, to be slimmer or gain some weight and others "one thing" is absolutely nothing! With the exception of wanting absolutely nothing, there is nothing wrong with any of the forgoing desires. However, if they are our "one thing"; our highest desire, we have truly missed the boat! We have missed having a noble reason for reigning and understanding what it really means to worship God, no matter what!

Do you see why we have to choose the King like the woman in the story at the beginning of the introduction? If Jesus isn't enthroned in our hearts and we are truly dead to ourselves...our "one thing" will be temporary, laughable, and pointless in the end; even though it might be impressive, win the applause of men and even though it is a very good thing! Paul puts it this way in Philippians 3: 8-10:

> *Yea doubtless, and I count all things but loss for the excellency of the knowledge of Christ Jesus my Lord: for whom I have suffered the loss of all things, and do count them but dung, that I may win Christ. And be found in him, not having mine own righteousness, which is of the law, but that which is through the faith of Christ, the righteousness which is of God by faith: That I may know him, and the power of his resurrection, and the fellowship of his sufferings, being made conformable unto his death.*

Genuine Worship

God-approved worship is only possible when we, with the help of the Holy Spirit, commit to a lifestyle of holiness! God has bequeathed His righteousness to us as a gift through Jesus. The only reasonable response to this amazing gift is total consecration. The lifestyle of holiness means we'll treasure the righteousness given to us through Jesus Christ our Lord. This means that we will hate sin and endeavour to please God by walking in obedience according to His Words. Even though perfection in Christ is the aim, I'm very glad and grateful that God chooses to still use imperfect vessels.

The righteousness of Jesus Christ is bestowed on His children at the finished work at Calvary. However, we have a responsibility to allow Him to transform us into His image. The Fruit of the Spirit (addressed in greater detail in Chapter 6) is evident in the lives of women who are drawing near to God. It is vital that with the help of the Holy Spirit and in alignment with God's Words, we mortify the sinful nature of our flesh. The death of our 'fleshy' disposition is usually not a pleasant experience; everything within us will resist it. However, discomfort is a necessary part of practising a lifestyle of progressive sanctification; so that we'll bear a closer resemblance to our Heavenly Father. This will indicate that we are in His family. Our divine nature and prominent likeness of Christ will be a witness to convince and attract others that we are daughters of the King; and indeed, we've been with the Lord.

However, we can never have a strong resemblance to God until we yield to the Holy Spirit for assistance to mortify the works of the flesh. These are, "Adultery, fornication,uncleanness, lasciviousness, Idolatry, witchcraft, hatred, variance, emulations, wrath, strife, seditions, heresies, envyings, murders, drunkenness, revellings, and such like. Those who practise these things will not be able to inherit the kingdom of God" (Galatians 5: 19-21).

Intentional transformation involves the engagement of the will to consistently pursue God even when setbacks are experienced and mistakes are made. Holiness is not only about doing the right deeds, but is more importantly having the right positioning of the heart before God. We can't earn the Father's love; it's a free gift. However, we can certainly live in such a way that brings delight to Him. We are His daughters and as such He loves us no matter what! This is the reason God pleads with His children to come out of sin and He has given us the power to do so. In the end, sin will destroy us and it is never God's desire that we are separated from Him. God has given us the ultimate gift of salvation which costs Him the life of His only child, Jesus. Therefore, our response should be choosing the genuine worship that is possible through Him.

Total Surrender for Total Transformation

It is time to pause to commit or recommit and reconnect to the God who made and called us. It's not enough to choose Him thirty years ago when we met Him, or on our baptism day, or on that hospital bed when we stared death in the face, or even yesterday as we knelt in prayer. Every day and every moment we must choose the King.

Joseph didn't only choose God the first time Mrs. Potiphar made her illicit sexual pass at him or even the second time. She was relentless and Joseph was surrendered and committed. Hence, he refused to sin against God (Genesis 39:9)!

In the anguish of Gethsemane, Jesus had to surrender His will. It was His *nevertheless* that change his life and later the world to this very day (Luke 22:42)! In a similar way, it is your *nevertheless* that will change your life; your world and the world! If you handle your *nevertheless* well, God will make your life astonishing! You will become a sign and wonder in your family, job, business, ministry, local community, county and indeed the world.

Let us take another worship pause and sing the song of commitment and surrender below that God gave me in December 2019 during devotion one morning. You may find this worship song, 'For a Lifetime' on *The Reigning Woman* YouTube channel.

> *For a lifetime, Lord I say yes to Your call.*
>
> *For a lifetime, Lord I will give my all.*
>
> *For a lifetime, Lord I am Yours.*
>
> *For a lifetime!*
>
> *For a lifetime, Lord I say yes to Your call.*
>
> *For a lifetime, Lord I will give my all.*
>
> *For a lifetime, Lord I am Yours, for a lifetime!*
>
> *Totally Yours, totally Yours, for a lifetime.*
>
> *Totally Yours, totally Yours, for a lifetime.*
>
> *Totally Yours, totally Yours, for a lifetime.*
>
> *Totally Yours, totally Yours, for a lifetime.*

Let's join in with John Wesley's poignant and timely prayer of surrender...

> *Lord, I am no longer my own, but Yours. Put me to what You will, rank me with whom You will. Let me be employed by You or laid aside for You, exalted for You, or brought low by You. Let me have all things, let me have nothing, I freely and heartily yield all things to Your pleasure and disposal. And now, O glorious and blessed God... You are mine and I am Yours. So be it. Amen.*

Worship... It's a Family Gift

Family is God's idea and we all belong to one in some way. The most authentic and effective way to introduce children to the Almighty God is to model a lifestyle of genuine worship in a God-honouring family. Thank God we belong to the body of Christ, so we don't have to do the difficult task of raising children alone! A well-known African proverb states, "It takes a village to raise a child". Whatever way we impact the lives of children; whether as a mother, grandmother, great- grandmother, auntie, sister, grand-aunt, by fostering…adopted aunt of your friends' and church brethren's children. Our greatest investment in children is to diligently nurture their tender hearts to honour the true God.

Remember we have the noble responsibility of inspiring and equipping children to be able to make God-centred decisions in the home, at school, university and in adult life. We want them to personally and deeply know God and will turn to Him in all their ways and throughout their lives.

One of the vital ingredients of a healthy family is shared worship which can take a myriad of formats and done at different times suitable for your family. Thank God it doesn't need to be a super-early call to worship used by my parents! However, our children should see us practising our faith as a way of life. They should be witnesses to our praying, singing, fasting, giving, studying the Scriptures and being joyful and grateful. Psalm 145: 4 declares that, "One generation shall praise Your works to another, and shall declare Your mighty acts". Let's not wait for a special day of the week to dust off our Bibles (for those who still carry a physical Bible), put on church apparel and then try to appear as worshippers. This is fake and it doesn't work. In fact, this façade damages children's desire and appreciation for a God that, as adults, we don't consistently honour.

Let's seize every opportunity to tell our children of the greatness and goodness of God who is faithful and mighty to save! Let's be faithful in praying for them and put the blood of Jesus over their lives. Pray that generational curses be broken from our children's lives (and our entire bloodline). Do everything to position them to become a worshipper of Jesus Christ. Deuteronomy 6: 6-7 admonishes that:

> These words which I command you today shall be in your heart. You shall teach them diligently to your children and shall talk of them when you sit in your house, when you walk by the way, when you lie down, and when you rise up.

Don't be put off by children's protests as you introduce them to spiritual disciplines. Expect them to! I can vividly recall when my parents would wake my siblings and I between 5-6am for family worship, I wasn't amused at all. It felt like death by design. I pulled every trick in a child's 'antics toolkit' to get out of joining in; but to no avail. I would pretend to be fast asleep when they were waking us for worship, I would pout and sometimes fall asleep in worship. My parents thought that morning worship was important for their family. Therefore, no bargaining and antics were accepted. In the end, I simply joined in and after some time began to engage enough to benefit from the experience. Today, I'm grateful for those times of worship that helped to bend my heart towards God! Thanks mum and dad for not giving in, nor giving up.

And oh, how much my life has been transformed. Thank You Jesus! Now, I am deeply disappointed when I miss worship sessions for whatever reason. Let's not give up on our children and young people due to their resistance. If God could change my heart, He will do the same for those who have not yet surrendered their hearts to the Lord. Consistently model genuine worship and God's life-transforming love, trusting that God will one day save our children and other loved ones. And keep on praying...

Prayer

Prayer is having a dialogue with God through Jesus Christ which is done by the empowerment of the Spirit. For prayers to be effective they must be done in alignment with the Words of God; which is the will of God. If not, we would be praying amiss. When praying, aim to remember the elements of adoration, repentance, petition and thanksgiving. Listening is also crucial in effective praying. Oftentimes, this is the most neglected part of our prayers. Don't be too hasty to rush out of prayer without quieting your spirit to deeply listen to God. Imagine having a very special friend who calls you every day, outlines a long 'shopping list' of requests and hardly ever pauses to hear what you have to say! How would this make you feel?

Many women remain at the place of frustration because we are too busy to pray in the first place, and even busier to spend time listening to the answers God is desperately trying to communicate to us. How many times have we rushed away from prayer before God can sing over us and give us corrections, witty inventions, kingdom expanding ideas and answers to our myriad of questions? Let us do ourselves a favour and resist the habit of constantly rushing out of prayer. Linger in God's presence. He truly wants to fellowship with, guide, transform and bless us!

Importantly, when we pray, we shouldn't waver; being double-minded and unstable. If we do, we will receive nothing from God (James 1:6-8). Rather, we should be filled with faith knowing the fervent prayers of the righteous avails much (James5:16)!

Functions and Blessings of Prayer

- Prayer provides the platform for an authentic lifestyle of praise and worship.

- Prayer is a posture of surrender and hope.

- Prayer helps to engineer our total transformation from within to without.

- Prayer aligns our will with the Father's.

- Prayer provides a vehicle through which God corrects and comforts His children.

- Prayer releases divine power and favour.

- Prayer stills the anxieties and trembling of the soul.

- Prayer reveals your divine identity and purpose.

- Prayer seats you in heavenly places and fosters intimacy with God.

- Prayer is the vehicle of kingdom breakthroughs and unites anticipation with the manifestation of our expectations.

- Prayer undergirds us with kingdom authority and power.

- Prayer gives courage, commitment and confidence.

- Prayer paralyses the artillery of the enemy.

- Prayer is the key to heaven's treasures.

- Prayer is the dynamite that blasts through that which appears impossible!

- Prayer is a medicine for the soul.

- Prayer is the oil and fuel that keeps our spiritual engine in tip-top condition.

- Prayer helps to propel us into our destiny.

- Prayer gives us access to consistent abundant joy.

Prayer does all these and more…

When God says "No"!

God loves His children very much. Like all loving fathers do, He sometimes tells us, "No." And none of our bargaining and theatrics will move Him to do otherwise! What we often don't realise is that God's "no" is equally a gift to us as His "yes" because they are both born out of love and complete knowledge.

Paul in 2 Corinthians 12: 7-10, pleaded with God to be delivered from the thorn in his flesh. His request wasn't granted. Paul didn't pray just once or twice. He prayed three times. He pleaded to God, but to no avail. He was told: "My grace is sufficient for you, for My strength is made perfect in weakness". Paul accepted that God knew what He was doing and he made the greatest decision in his life. He decided to trust God no matter what! Paul chose to boast in his infirmities, that he might experience a greater measure of the power of Christ. For the sake of Christ, he also took pleasure in his weaknesses, criticisms, necessities, oppressions and sufferings. Paul learned that it was in his weakness that Christ's strength was most profoundly revealed.

Sometimes being told "no" is actually an instruction to wait; because we aren't ready. So rather than engaging in wrestling matches with our Father, let's yield and focus on following His will.

Feasting on Fasting

Surface cleaning can't address certain issues in a woman's life. We need to get to the very root of the problems; if not, they'll spring back again. Prayer alone can't handle certain things. It requires the dynamite of fasting! "Howbeit *this kind* goeth not out but by prayer and fasting" (Matthew 17: 21). As women in general and women of God in particular, we have several *"thiskind"* in our lives that need fasting.

There are many blessings in turning down our plates with a focus to seek God's face for that which we need. And without any contest, our greatest need is for God Himself and to be transformed into His likeness. Beloved, let's not be preoccupied with the hand of God and treat Him like a tap to turn on and off to get the *stuff* that we need. Rather, our will, our mind and our total being must fall in love with Christ Himself. We must be so enraptured by God that if He never lifts a finger to do anything else for us for the rest of our lives, we would still totally devote our lives to Him. Fasting shouldn't be reserved for when there are difficult situations in our lives that we do a knee-jerk reactionary fast. Instead, fasting must be a worship lifestyle practise.

By the way, not every fasting is acceptable to God. In Isaiah 58, God's people lamented that they were fasting but weren't getting the results they required. If we are in a similar dilemma, let's see what Israel did wrong and accept God's remedies.

Fasting Offences

1. They were having fun and pleasure when they were fasting.

2. While they were seeking God in fasting, their hired labourers had to work and couldn't seek Him too.

3. They had the wrong motive for fasting. They did it for strife and debate, and to smite with the fist of wickedness and to be seen and heard by others!

4. They also deliberately went about their fast with a sorrowful attitude and face and made it rather obvious that they were fasting.

5. They were violating the principles of acceptable Sabbath observance.

   • Having fun and pleasure on God's holy day.

   • Didn't treat the sabbath as a delight and that which is holy and honourable.

   • Their conversations were not befitting.

Remedies to get Answers

1. Stop practising wickedness and be merciful to the less fortunate, afflicted and oppressed.

2. Treat their employees with care.

3. To practise radical generosity by feeding the hungry, provide shelter for the homeless and give clothes to those who had none.

4. They were also to remember to look after their families.

5. Observe the Sabbath according to God's Word.

6. Live a lifestyle of delighting in the Lord!

God's Faithful Promises

1. Then shall your light break forth as the morning, and thine health shall spring forth speedily: and thy righteousness shall go before thee; the glory of the Lord shall be thy reward.

2. When we call on God, He will gladly answer and reveal Himself to us.

3. God will remove the burden, accusations and vain speaking.

4. We will be elevated and have great impact; being removed from obscurity into much relevance and influence. God will celebrate you and cause your name to be known and to be great.

5. God will consistently guide us.

6. He will satisfy our souls even in times of crisis and scarcity; such as these unprecedented times!

7. We will experience uncommon prosperity. Our souls shall be satisfied and be like a well-watered garden; forever flourishing.

8. We will become renowned in our spheres of influence and will become trend-setters.

9. God will empower us to establish His standards which were trodden on for generations. We will raise up the broken standards and call our generation to worship the King of heaven! God will give us a name for righteousness!

10. Finally, God promises that the Abrahamic heritage will be clearly manifested in your life (See Genesis 12: 2-3). This is spoken by the unfailing mouth of the Lord!

Indeed, fasting shouldn't be a ritualistic event. If it is reduced to a tick-box event that ignores God's set standards, it will bear little to no fruit. It ought to be a heart-centred devotion built on the strong foundation of total surrender and a deep desire to know and please God. How can we worship God with songs?

Singing

There is a beauty and a stirring of the soul that comes with singing songs unto the Lord. It's like a spoon that stirs our souls to unprecedented adoration for the King who owns us and loves us dearly.

When God's children sing from that deep place of wild abandon and with no other agenda but to adore Him; it ushers us into a state and space like no other. Singing is often the catalyst for spontaneous songs to erupt from deep inside our souls. It ignites the prophetic and drops wisdom nuggets too awesome to be uttered.

A reigning woman of wonder joins with the angels in heaven singing, "Holy, holy, holy. You are worthy to receive majesty, glory, honour, dominion and power!" Kingdom wonders aren't content to know and bask only in the acts (blessings and miracles) of God. Like Moses, they want to know His ways. The heart is the heart of worship. In 4D reigning, not only do we sing, compose, play musical instruments and dance, but more importantly, we allow God to make music with our lives. Let's pray: O Lord, let my life become the music-a song of grace, a song of triumph, a song of celebration and song that makes demons tremble at the sound; the special sound that You gave me on the earth.

Can We Worship God in the Turbulence?

If ever there is a time that we need to genuinely worship God, it's when we are facing challenging times! Yet sometimes it's the hardest thing to do. Since Covid-19 the saying, "We are living in unprecedented times," has become very popular. Challenging times may be compared to being caught up in extreme turbulence on the flight to our holiday destination. From a meteorological standpoint, turbulence is simply an irregular motion of the atmosphere denoted by gusts and lulls in the wind. This irregularity of wind pressure is what tests the capabilities of the plane and flight team and can induce stress on the passengers. My sister, Lois, shared with me a profound thought she received from the Lord while flying to North Carolina from Dallas, Texas, during extreme turbulence. The inspiration of the Holy Spirit was, "The more your life seems out of control is when more power exudes from the throne".

Turbulence can be likened to the pressures of life we face as women. Sickness, divorce, death of loved ones, joblessness, homelessness, persecution, and financial ruin are a few of life's turbulences. One of the challenges with experiencing turbulence is that you can't request for the flight team to allow us to get off the plane in mid-flight! We're too far gone on our journey.

Do the jolts of the 'turbulence' often send us into panic mode? We want to cry, scream or grab the hands of the stranger seated next to us. But that individual seems so in control of their emotions and you begin to wonder, "Why am I so terrified? You begin to muster up some composure and fake your calmness throughout this turbulent time. Little do you know that the seemingly in control individual seated next to you is screaming like a baby inwardly.

Have you ever noticed that when turbulence is reaching its highest peak, the pilot is often calm as he announces his scripted lines, "Ladies and gentlemen we are currently experiencing turbulence… Stay seated, fasten your seat belts and we'll land in just a minute." Your trembling lips want to say, "Sir I already know we are experiencing turbulence. I can feel the violent shaking of the plane." And by the way, how long is your minute? Before you can even respond to his one hundredth repetition of pilot school calming speech, he goes silent. Are you kidding me? The pilot, of course, has gone back to doing his job, that is, navigating the plane.

Similarly, why is God seemingly not saying anything to us and we've just been diagnosed with stage four breast cancer or have lost our jobs and our mortgages are overdue? "Hello God, are you there?" Silence in the midst of turbulence! At this point, as worshippers we're sometimes battling not to throw a temper tantrum or are too numb to speak. Am I not supposed to be trusting God? We often fall off the 'spiritual wagon' during times of silence. We crave the crumbs of a word... any word...somebody...anybody... please say something. Are these the times when you question God and His credibility to get you out of your turbulence?

Here is my proposal- let's turn to God in His Words and prayers for our answers. Consider this, no matter how severe the turbulence, have you ever seen a passenger demand to see the pilot's qualification during turbulence? No. Never. So why is it that we often confront God with our demands for proofs and signs when we hit challenging circumstances? Hanmer Parsons Grant states, "We must free ourselves of the hope that the sea will ever rest. We must learn to sail in high winds." Don't forget, God is God- even in turbulence! Are we so addicted to operating in the physical realm and living as a 1D and 2D worshipper, that the seeming silence of God will result in us giving up on our God-given pursuits and possibly on Him too? God's silence does not mean His unawareness of our situations. On the contrary, His silence would suggest a great measure of trust and confidence that He has equipped you to deal with life's turbulence. Make a commitment that when you are afraid that you will trust in God(Psalms 56:3-4) knowing that your gut-wrenching turbulence is temporary!

Trusting God in the Unknown

We can only worship Yahweh in the turbulence if we have a rock-solid trust in God and the many promises that He has made to us. More importantly, we must believe that He is who He says He is- faithful, true, loving and holy! More than ever, it is when life is smashed to pieces that we must believe that He keeps His covenant to a thousand generations. And like David, our heart must be fixed, trusting in the tender love and mercies of the Lord (Psalm 112:7). Here are some Scriptures that highlight the benefits of trusting in the Lord. Commit them to memory; it's both fun and very empowering!

1. Trust in the LORD with all thine heart; and lean not unto thine own understanding. In all thy ways acknowledge him, and he shall direct thy paths. Proverbs 3:5-6

2. So do not fear, for I am with you; do not be dismayed, for I am your God. I will strengthen you and help you; I will uphold you with my righteous right hand. Isaiah 41:10

3. Blessed is the man that trusts in the LORD, and whose hope the LORD is. Jeremiah 17:7

4. They that trust in the Lord shall be as mount Zion, which cannot be removed but abides forever. Psalm 125:1

5. He that trusts in the LORD, mercy shall compass him about. Psalms 32:10

6. The Lord redeemeth the soul of his servants: and none of them that trust in him shall be desolate. Psalm 34:22

7. My God, I trust in thee: let me not be ashamed, let not mine enemies triumph over me. Psalm 25:2

8. The fear of man bringeth a snare: but whoso putteth his trust in the Lord shall be safe. Proverbs 29:25

9. The LORD [is] my strength and my shield; my heart trusted in him, and I am helped: therefore,

my heart greatly rejoiceth; and with my song will I praise him. Psalms 28:7

10. And they that know thy name will put their trust in thee: for thou, LORD, hast not forsaken them that seek thee. Psalms 9:10

11. God is a shield unto them that put their trust in Him. Proverbs 30: 5

What amazing rock-solid promises to those whose trust is in the Lord who made heaven and earth! It pays to worship Jesus. I speak from the deep confidence in my heart. What do you say?

Relationship and Fellowship

We need a church fellowship for corporate worship, service and accountability. Let's not spend a lifetime looking for a perfect one. We imperfect beings are the church. With much due diligence and prayer, let's commit to one and roll up our sleeves and work for Jesus, lovingly serve His children and expand His kingdom. Charles Spurgeon insightfully said, "If I had never joined a church till I had found one that was perfect, I should never have joined one at all; and the moment I did join it, if I had found one, I should have spoiled it, for it would not have been a perfect church after I had become a member of it. Still, imperfect as it is, it is the dearest place on earth to us." Let's arise and passionately be the church and serve people through a local assembly.

Unfortunately, to the other extreme, some Christians treat their denominations like when gangs are having postcodes wars (conflicts over specific territories); not as brothers and sisters who are also part of the kingdom of

God. The shed blood of Jesus at Calvary invited us into the body of Christ, not into denominations. Too many times, the denominational affiliations are more exalted than Christ Himself. Hence, the fertile soil for cross-pollination of Biblical teachings is aborted in self-isolation chambers called "my church".

An authentic church mindset is a warm and safe space where Jesus Christ is at the centre; not a larger-than-life personality. There is 'gold' in the church family across the road from ours. Let's radically love the body of Christ and be willing to learn from each other and engage in the corporate expansion of God's kingdom. Don't be unnecessarily put off because the name on a church building is different from ours. Connect to hearts, value God's people everywhere. It is in the melting pot of church corporations that deeper transformation can also take place.

The King Deserves Our Best

A little sprinkling of the flavour of worship will never be accepted by the King of glory! In Mark 14:3-9, a woman demonstrated very well what sanctified unrestrained worship looks like. There in the midst of it all, with Jesus being with Simon the leper, a woman was audacious enough to come to worship Him with an extravagance that could not go unnoticed. Firstly, she disrupted the moment. Sometimes worship will disrupt the status quo.

Secondly, she came with her best. She worshipped Jesus with the reigning DNA of abundance, excellence and contribution and she certainly was a woman of purpose! "A woman came with an alabaster jar of very expensive perfume, made of pure nard" (Mark 14:3, NIV). This wasn't a cheap perfume; it was very costly. Does our worship cost us a lot these days?

Thirdly, she gave everything. It wasn't two little squirts on Jesus' head and then she popped it back in her bag. No! She broke it and poured it all on the King! Glory to God.

Fourthly, she ignored the critics. "Some of those present were saying indignantly to one another, "Why this waste of perfume? It could have been sold for more than a year's wages and the money given to the poor. "And they rebuked her harshly" (Mark 14:4-5). Can we handle the stares, ridicule and those who will state the opinion that it doesn't take all that to worship (whatever the 'all that' is)?

Finally, Jesus acknowledged and honoured her worship! This ought to greatly encourage us.

Our worship is for God. He alone is the qualified judge of our worship. Jesus defended the woman's worship. He said, "Leave her alone... Why are you bothering her? She has done a beautiful thing to me." (Mark 14:6). Wow. Does Jesus think our worship is a "beautiful thing"? Will He say we have done what we could? Here is an example of a woman who became an impactful wonder, "Truly I tell you, wherever the gospel is preached throughout the world, what she has done will also be told, in memory of her." What will be said of us in honour of our worship? Our worship now should prepare us for the worship that will never end. Are we ready?

Worship's Ultimate Reward

In an article entitled, *Are We Ready* which appeared in the *Bible Advocate* (March-April, 2020), I wrote the essence of the following which warrants reiterating the question, especially as we examine worship, Are we ready for worship's ultimate reward?

Every bride will tell you that she didn't just saunter down the aisle in her regular clothes; and certainly not her nightwear! Her long-awaited wedding day and subsequent marriage required much preparation: deciding who to marry, premarital counselling, planning the wedding day, deciding where to live and others.

An earthly wedding and marriage are usually not microwave experiences but require detailed preparation. What about preparing to reign for eternity as the bride of Christ? The magnitude of eternity requires that we pause, reflect, and most of all, get and stay ready.

It is often said, "There is no such thing as an ugly bride." But is that true of the bride of Christ? Are we being diligent in our preparation to make ourselves beautiful for His return? Are blemishes of sin making us unsightly? Our marriage to Jesus suggests we are a new creation; old habits, lifestyles and status have changed. In Christ Jesus, all things have become new. Revelation 19:7-9 gives us an advice and a promise:

"Let us be glad and rejoice and give Him glory, for the marriage of the Lamb has come, and His wife has made herself ready." And to her it was granted to be arrayed in fine linen, clean and bright, for the fine linen is the righteous acts of the saints. Then he said to me, "Write:

'Blessed are those who are called to the marriage supperof the Lamb!'" And he said to me, "These are the true sayings of God."

Beautiful City

As the bride of Christ, we have so much to prepare for, so much that awaits us! The Alpha and Omega, who is true and faithful, has promised us that one day New Jerusalem will come from God out of heaven, prepared as a bride who has made diligent preparation for her husband. Imagine the newness of all things and being enraptured by the holy God that our hearts have long waited for. Imagine the sublime existence when God himself, and not another, will wipe away all our tears. Goodbye to the separation of death, to sorrow, to crying and to all versions of pain.

Most importantly, imagine the grandeur of the foursquare city of God, Holy Jerusalem, described in Revelation 21:10-26. The city will be splendid with the glory and light of God. John writes that its high wall has twelve foundations named after the twelve apostles and is adorned with all manner of precious stones. The city also has twelve gates, each a different pearl with an angel and the name of one of the twelve tribes of Israel. The streets of the city are made from gold.

To top it off, there will be no temple in the New Jerusalem because God Himself will be there, and the brightness of the Lord will render the sun and moon of no effect. This is an experience, existence, and place not to be missed. What a glorious time this will be when all worshippers who overcome will reign with the King of kings and the Lord of Lords permanently, inheriting all things!

WORSHIP TRANSFORMATION STRATEGIES

1. The starting point to become a wonder is to be captivated by Jesus Christ. It is only the touch of God that can inspire and maintain genuine worship. Jesus Christ is the greatest gift you can ever receive! Solomon wisely states in Ecclesiastes 12:1 that youth is the ideal time to remember and serve God while our health is in good condition and before our appointment with death. Indeed, we can't worship God from the grave. However, isn't it so lovely to know that even when we missed the ideal time in our youth, God is delighted to embrace us whatever time we choose Him as Lord and Saviour who is worthy to be worshipped. Accept the righteousness of Christ Jesus by faith in order to inherit eternal life. Remember you were repositioned by grace and you are loved!

2. Let our songs, fasting and prayers be based on and be compliant with the Scriptures. For example, Isaiah 58 outlines how we should fast and Mathew 6:9-12 gives us a model prayer. Make God's Word the cornerstone of your worship.

3. Schedule time and place for personal and corporate worship. Timing and space matter to God and play a big part in the richness of our worship. Over time, this secret and sacred place will represent a place of encounter, intimacy and expectation. When possible, always linger in the atmosphere that is soaked in the spirit of worship. Be observant;

listen, look and sense what God is doing. Be diligent to capture what your Father is saying and doing. Practise stillness and silence as an integral part of worship; both personally and corporately.

4. The power of a journal is inestimable. Journaling as worship and also journaling in worship is life-changing. Over time, your journal will become a masterpiece filled with precious memories. For example, do a gratitude journal. Practise recording the good things God and others have done for you. Magnify the Lord on paper or electronically- for those who prefer online journaling.

5. Practise using every experience (good, bad and the in- between) to lead you in extolling the worthiness of God.

6. Do whatever it takes to safeguard the purity of your heart. The essence of worship is a matter of the heart. Every day aim to experience intimate worship with God!

7. Begin to share your faith more intentionally. Nothing elevates your worship like displaying and sharing the God that you worship.

8. Regularly evaluate your worship and set goals in this area of your life. You may ask yourself these and other questions:

    - Is my intimacy improving with the Lord?

    - Am I enjoying God's presence or is it just a routine?

- How can I make my scheduled worship time better?

9. Prepare to minister in God's presence. Remember, He is the Excellent God that requires our excellence too. There is a place for spontaneous worship, but this is not the same as lazy and unprepared worship.

10. Let's heed Solomon's summary of life, "Let us hear the conclusion of the whole matter: Fear God, and keep his commandments: for this is the whole duty of man. For God shall bring every work into judgment, with every secret thing, whether it be good, or whether it be evil" (Ecclesiastes 12: 13-14).

Worship is when everything in us bows in reverent adoration for the King who is majestic and worthy. The wonder of a woman that genuinely worships Yahweh is breath-taking; a trophy of God's grace. Genuine worship can only come from God to be given back to Him. Worship is a lifestyle, not just an event. This is embraced through submission to Him; not outward compliance to traditions and rules. It is also activated within a framework of love and done by the power of the Holy Spirit. Worship is a reflection of the state of our hearts. Real worship can only effectively function in an individual who has said a complete and deep "yes" to God. Giving God the worship that He finds acceptable; not that which we find convenient and easy, is the worship that transforms everything!

Jesus has issued a royal invitation to worship Him in a pleasing manner according to His Word, and as such we can embrace the opportunity to reign for Christ now and eternally. What we can't afford to do is worship God on our own terms and conditions and then end up being eternally cast away with the pronouncement of, "I never knew you: depart from me" (Matthew 7:23).

It takes great sacrifice and paying a high cost to worship Jesus as a woman of wonder called to be His new creation. However, indescribable rich rewards await those who do. Are we ready to meet our Beloved, or is our worship a construction of our own making? Jesus has gone to prepare a place for us and promises to return for us so we can continue our reign with Him forever (John 14:2-3). If we diligently prepare ourselves, we'll be the spotless bride He's coming for. Let's get into our 'secret places' and pray, fast, sing... become a true worshipper in spirit and in truth. So that at the end all will be well and our reign with and in Christ will never end!

WORSHIP TRANSFORMATION TASK

1. In terms of the Reigning Dimensions regarding *Worship*, where are you? (Tick one)

Wonder ☐   Winning ☐   Waning ☐   Wandering ☐

2. Develop a Worship Declaration: Eg. My worship is a lifestyle practice and it deepens every day!

_____

_____

3. Which of the Worship Transformation Strategies would give you the maximum impact now?

_____

_____

4. Set a SMART (Specific, Measurable, Attainable, Realistic and Time-bound) worship goal.

_____

_____

_____

5. Motivation: Why is this goal important to you?

_____

_____

_____

6. Accountability: Which person or system will hold you accountable?

_____

7. Review Date:

_____

8. Reward: How will you celebrate achieving this goal?

_____
_____

Chapter Three
Transformation Agent #3
WISDOM

"Every problem is always a wisdom problem."

Dr. Mike Murdock

ave you ever considered why wisdom is often referred to as a woman? Wisdom is the beauty of God's daughters. It brings to every person and environment something that nothing else can. There is no substitute for wisdom. It is indeed the principal thing (Proverbs 4:7). Everything that we desire and seek will only be unlocked by the master key of wisdom! There is nothing as attractive as a wise woman! Nothing. Imagine a woman with the virtue of God's wisdom unapologetically bringing grace, value and delight everywhere she goes. This could be you. This could be me. In fact, let's declare it; this is you and I; women full to the brim with God's life-transforming and beautifying wisdom. Let's embark on the journey that will lead to this desired outcome. We reign by wisdom! In Proverbs 1: 1-3 (TPT) it is stated:

> *Here are kingdom revelations, words to live by, and words of wisdom given to empower you to reign in life,*

written as proverbs by Israel's King Solomon, David's son. Within these sayings will be found the revelation of wisdom and the impartation of spiritual understanding.

Use them as keys to unlock the treasures of true knowledge Those who cling to these words will receive discipline to demonstrate wisdom in every relationship and to choose what is right and just and fair.

Types of Wisdom

James in James 3:13-18 makes it very clear that all wisdom isn't of the league! A wise person is endued with knowledge! Endued means to surround, enclose, encompass; to be robed, dressed, and clothe. Earthly wisdom isn't from above. Rather, it is sensual and devilish. It is characterised by bitter envy, strife, confusion and every evil works! Women of wonder certainly need to stay far away from the brand of wisdom.

On the other hand, Godly wisdom is from above. It is meek and is lifestyle-based. In addition, heavenly wisdom is, "First pure, then peaceable (the fruit of righteousness is sown in peace), gentle, and easy to be intreated, full of mercy and good fruits, without partiality and without hypocrisy." (vv. 17-18)! What a gem! It is the duty of every woman that desires to reign in the ultimate 4D realm to seek God for the only wisdom that is indeed wise. This comes from Him who dwells in the heavenly realm. God's heavenly wisdom is revealed in His Word; hence God is wisdom.

We reign by wisdom, so let's examine where we are in the reigning dimension categories.

Wisdom Dimensions of Reigning

• 1D Reigning: Wandering

The *wandering* dimension of wisdom is 1D living. A marked characteristic of operating in the 1D dimension of wisdom is being wishy-washy regarding one's core values and ensuing convictions. After some time, it will become evident that foolishness and being driven about by "every wind of doctrine" have become the norm. "That we henceforth be no more children, tossed to and fro, and carried about with every wind of doctrine, by the sleight of men, and cunning craftiness, whereby they lie in wait to deceive" (Ephesians 4:14).

Doctrine shouldn't only be understood as church teachings. Doctrines are tenets of beliefs and core teachings concerning any area of life such as doctrines (teachings) of relationships, finances, science, investment and others. It is vital that, as believers, we ensure that what we believe and teach are indeed Biblical and not just denominational persuasions. It is the infallible Scripture that has the strong foundation to hold us up. Anything else will fail.

• 2D Reigning: Waning

A woman operating in the 2D realm is usually set in their limited way and lacks a teachable attitude. This leads only to a dead end where it doesn't manifest the blessings of God in terms of possessing value to help others. In a sense, this man-made wisdom tries to do its job, but in the end, it destroys its own self, which leads to waning. The more you become conceited in your own wisdom and become wrapped up in yourself, that arrogance kills the initial wisdom. Who wants to be in the presence of a woman that is arrogant and is unwilling to learn from anyone? No one. "Here are kingdom revelations, words to live by, and words of wisdom given to empower you to reign in life" (Proverbs 1:1 TPT).

• 3D Reigning: Winning

The more superior wisdom, heavenly wisdom, is in operation in the 3D realm! The reigning woman with 3D wisdomknows how to tap into and apply the rich heavenly wisdom which is from above. She consistently hones her thinking skills by seeking more opportunity to grow and to apply that which is learnt. As such, the more they acquire knowledge they more they become influencers in their circles of operations.

• 4D Reigning: Wonder

When we allow God to make us wonders in the fourth dimension of wisdom, we are filled with all the fullness of God (Ephesians 3:19). Consequently, people will seek your counsel because you possess the heavenly wisdom which is from above; not the earthy wisdom. In this realm of ultimate reigning, you have the ability to commoditize your wisdom as witty inventions in ways that it can be used to add value to the lives of others. This commoditization of wisdom can be demonstrated in creative products, outstanding job prospects and wealth creation strategies (seminars, motivational speaking, books and content creation).

This commoditization of wisdom ensures that the wisdom is preserved. However, be diligent that your wisdom becomes scalable so that you aren't constantly exchanging your time for money and in ways that are out of alignment with your purpose. This is part of the manifestation of the Abrahamic heritage and blessing that we carry. For example, you will begin to train others, have recordings of your persuasions so that what you believe can be accessed 24/7 in every time zone.

This packaging of one's wisdom is done for the glory of God, the advancement of His kingdom and to meet the many needs in the lives of individuals. Heavenly wisdom is from above and it is humble. Proverbs 9:10 states, "The fear of the Lord is the beginning of wisdom." In James 3:17, 4D wisdom is described in great detail. This will be unpacked in the upcoming section on wisdom. Isn't it interesting that Socrates says, "Wonder is the beginning of wisdom?" However, as we consider how majestic, faithful, merciful, awesome...holy God is, it does inspire a deep sense of wonder. It is understandable and appropriate that His name is also Wonderful!

The Impact Trio

My son, if thou wilt receive my words, and hide my commandments with thee; So that thou incline thine ear unto wisdom, and apply thine heart to understanding; Yea, if thou criest after knowledge, and liftest up thy voice for understanding; If thou seekest her as silver, and searchest for her as for hid treasures; Then shalt thou understand the fear of the Lord, and find the knowledge of God. For the Lord giveth wisdom: out of his mouth cometh knowledge and understanding. He layeth up sound wisdom for the righteous: he is a buckler to them that walk uprightly. Proverbs 2: 1-7

The trio of knowledge, understanding and wisdom are mentioned repeatedly in the Scriptures. Each has its distinction and can't be adequately substituted by the other.

1. **Knowledge**

Being knowledgeable is having accurate and relevant information about a matter. When we do, we are better able to manage our emotions and attitude. Lord teach us how and when to speak. Give us a desire for knowledge and how to use it wisely; not destructively. In whatever way we will offer value in the marketplace, there is an expected knowledge base. We must be diligent in building strong knowledge bulwarks in order to be relevant and even be ahead of the trends in our particular industry. The opposite of knowledge is ignorance, which is very destructive. God Himself made a very insightful diagnosis in Hosea 4:6, "My people are destroyed for lack of knowledge: because thou hast rejected knowledge, I will also reject thee."

Those who are wise will seek knowledge, wisdom and understanding earnestly. We are instructed to, "Buy the truth, and sell it not; also wisdom, and instruction, and understanding" (Proverbs 23:23). Lacking relevant knowledge in all areas of life is costly. Loving ignorance is to forfeit the call to reign and the beautiful possibility of becoming an amazing wonder in God's hand. Ignorance renders us impotent in fulfilling our purpose, it excludes excellence and abundance and there will not be much to offer as value to others. The reigning woman appreciates the necessity to consistently unlearn, learn and relearn. The reigning woman knows that the highest and most life-transforming knowledge to be acquired is God's truth; His holy Words.

2. Understanding

Understanding means to have insight and an explanation for acquired knowledge. This sense of enlightenment is advantageous since it gives depth to that which is learnt. There is little value in just knowing specific information. It begins to increase in value when it is understood. The Impact Trio is like a ladder. It takes you from one level to the next and none of the steps can be omitted. It is impossible to understand what you don't know! It is the combined knowledge and understanding that will usher in wisdom. I'm appreciating on a deeper level the verses that instruct us to worship God with understanding that He is King (Psalm 47:7) and that without knowledge we are destroyed (Hosea 4:6). To go from glory to glory in Christ, we must become hungry for life-transforming knowledge, intentionally seek to deepen our understanding and take it to the next level of living in and by divine wisdom!

3. Wisdom

Wisdom is the principal thing (Proverbs 3:4). It is the consistent correct application of knowledge and understanding for a desired goal. Applying the right knowledge and understanding, at the right time, at the right place, with the right systems; yields the right results. Since the fear of the Lord is the beginning of wisdom. Consistently pray for the wisdom of God; since there is a foolish and failing wisdom of men.

Earthly wisdom is when God's wisdom has been corrupted. Mankind gets caught up in their vain ideologies and tries to pass them off as wisdom. Little wonder God's wisdom is deemed as foolishness to man. And in a similar manner, God deems mankind's wisdom as utter foolishness. God is the giver of all good gifts; including witty inventions. Man's wisdom allows them to become puffed up and vain in their own conceit.

God is wisdom and wisdom created the world. Wisdom is the primary tool for creativity. In a general sense, people can be exposed to similar knowledge, but the distinction happens in how they choose to apply it. The more we allow the Word of God to dwell in us richly, the Holy Spirit to lead us and we intentionally put ourselves in enriching environments, it will be that divine wisdom will increase in our lives and we become wonders indeed.

Divine wisdom is like perfume. You don't have to say you're wise, your life will testify without you having to say a word. God accepts your surrender and He begins to showcase His wisdom through the vessel of honour you've become. This is done with only one aim and that is to lift up the name of Jesus that He is Lord. The wisdom lifestyle declares boldly that His return is near and that we ought to be prepared for the second return of the King of glory. Ultimately, wisdom is living by kingdom principles in a practical way. We were never born to be average. It is the wisdom of God in us and through us that will make us a history maker for the honour of God!

How can we consistently become ardent learners with a godly intention and a servant heart mindset?

Continuous Learning and Development

For every area of endeavour in our lives, there ought to be accompanying consistent learning to be able to improve our undertakings and ultimately become a more useful tool in God's ambidextrous hand.

• Mentorship

Mentorship is a relationship whereby one that is experienced and skilled in a given area passes on their wisdom to their mentees. Modelling and teaching are at the heart of mentorship. The mentorship model of gaining wisdom is evident through scriptures. The mentorship of mature saints can be invaluable; as they nurture and guide us. One of the benefits and responsibilities of being a part of the body of Christ is offering and receiving support. It's where we give and gain wisdom. In Titus 2:3-5 it is stated that older women have a responsibility towards the younger women.

> *The aged women likewise, that they be in behaviour as becometh holiness, not false accusers, not given to much wine, teachers of good things; That they may teach the young women to be sober, to love their husbands, to love their children. To be discreet, chaste, keepers at home, good, obedient to their own husbands, that the word of God be not blasphemed.*

Every strong and future-prepared church, business, school whatever the organisation; ought to have some form of mentorship in place.

• Coaching

A coach is an individual who comes alongside another in a supportive, goal-focused and dynamic relationship. Unlike mentoring, coaching doesn't provide answers. Rather, it'sasking questions in such a way that allows the individual to become aware of the answers they possess in relation to achieving a set task. Therefore, at the heart of effective coaching is the establishment of rapport, asking effective questions and identifying effective goals.

Importantly, the coachee must be aware of his own reality and what are the possible obstacles that may prevent them from achieving their goals and putting strategies in place to minimise the risk of them happening. John Whitmore states:

> The best way to develop and maintain the ideal state of mind for performance is to build awareness and responsibility continuously throughout the daily practice and the skill acquisition process... The coach is not a problem solver, a teacher, and advisor, an instructor or even an expert, he or she is a sounding board, a facilitator, a counsellor, and awareness raiser.

He further states that Coaching is a highly transformational process and possesses the ability to increase the capacity of coachees to achieve their set goals. Some of the qualities of an effective coach are self-awareness, good listening, integrity, confidentiality, perception, support, and genuinely caring about the goals of the coachee.

• Masterminds

Napoleon Hill first coined the term Mastermind in the early 1900's. In his classic book, *Think and Grow Rich* he described a Mastermind as a group of people coming together to work towards a definite goal in the spirit of harmony and goodwill. Of vital importance is the contribution of effort and knowledge of all members for the success of everyone. In the midst of this group is the emergence of what Napoleon Hill calls a third invisible force. The mastermind has now become a very popular method employed across many industries to foster growth, cooperation and the sharing of best practice ideas.

Not only should we sharpen our minds, but we must develop mastery in handling our emotions and responding to others well too. It is self-evident that if a woman will reign as a wonder, she must feed her mind with the best information from individuals who are the best in their fields of endeavour. And more importantly, she must be connected to the Source and embodiment of wisdom that is God Himself.

However, what about managing one's emotions?

Emotional Intelligence

The inability to be aware of and skillfully manage our emotions will cause us to self-sabotage the work we've invested in for personal and professional growth and development! Daniel Goleman in his iconic book, *Emotional Intelligence* defines Emotional Intelligence as "Being able...to rein in emotional impulse; to read another's innermost feelings [and] to handle relationships smoothly. He states that it includes self-control, zeal and persistence, and the ability to motivate oneself."

Daniel Goleman categorises Emotional Intelligence into four domains and twelve competencies that make individuals highly effective:

1. **Self-awareness**

   - *Competency: Emotional self-awareness*

2. **Self-management**

   - *Competencies: Emotional balance, Adaptability, Achieveand Positivity*

3. *Social Awareness*

- *Competencies: Empathy and Organisational Awareness*

4. *Relationship Management*

- *Competencies: Influence, Coach, Conflict Management, Team Work and Inspire*

Isn't it profound and interesting that the Emotional Intelligence domain with the most competencies is Relational Management! Wow. We can't reign effectively and by no means can become wonders without relationship mastery. Whatever it takes to grow and develop in this area will yield a significant return on investment and you and the people in your environment will be glad you did! More than anything else, lacking the competencies for relationship management makes for a kind of poverty that is more far-reaching than a financial one!

The first competence in Emotional Intelligence is self-awareness, so the more self-aware we are, the better the quality of our relationships. The better the quality of our relationships is the better the quality of our lives. A tool that is very useful and thorough in helping to bring about self-awareness, is The Maxwell DISC Personality Assessment.

As a Certified Maxwell Method DISC Behavioral Analysis Consultant, I know the massive insight this tool can provide in bringing awareness to the blind spots in people's lives and how enlightening and empowering this can be. The four DISC styles are Dominant, Influencing, Steady and Compliant. Each behavioural style has its unique strengths and general characteristics, weaknesses with scope for growth and even their greatest fears. When the behavioural analysis is done, you are given a detailed report about your unique personality dispositions.

The Law of Awareness by Dr. John C. Maxwell states, "You must know yourself to grow yourself." It is difficult, if not impossible, to be our best in any relationship if we lack self-awareness. See the Resources at the back of the book about how you can do your DISC Assessment. It's a priceless gift you get to give to yourself and those you love. The quality of all your relationships will improve, including the one with yourself!

Benefits of Emotional Intelligence

According to the Institute for Health and Human Potential, emotional quotient (EQ, also called Emotional Intelligence) is useful both at the personal and work levels.

At the individual level, EQ helps individuals to:

1. Improve relationships with the significant others in ourlives

2. Address uncomfortable issues without hurting other people's feelings.

3. Empower us to manage our own difficult emotions;especially when feeling overwhelmed and stressed.

At work, Emotional Intelligence can help us:

1. Resolve conflicts

2. Coach and motivate others

3. Create a culture of collaboration

4. Build psychological safety within teams

Fortunately, Emotional Intelligence is not a fixed ability. It can be learned and there is much we can do to improve it over time with intentional observation and practice.

We need wisdom to navigate relationships well.

Wisdom in Relationships

Every wise woman builds her house, but the foolish destroys it by her own doing (Proverbs 14: 1). It truly takes great wisdom to excel in managing the terrains of relationships in order to foster peace, collaboration, productivity and growth. However, this requires self-awareness.

All our relationships; whether platonic or intimate, are meant to be platforms of love. It is critical that we learn how to manage conflict in a healthy manner so that it doesn't become toxic and damaging. When we care, there will be times when it's necessary to address conflicts in an appropriate manner and at the right time. Daniel Goleman states that a myth that individuals believe is that having emotional intelligence means just being a nice person-whilst it may very well mean being to the point and assertive; especially when communicating unpleasant truths. In these times we need God's wisdom more than ever and can't afford to be considered foolish. How do we know when folly is at work in our lives?

Indicators of Folly

As women of God, we are instructed by our Father to live in ways that bring glory to Him. To do otherwise is to practise foolishness...

1. Not reigning with delight now and excitedly

'living forward' for the second coming of the Lord. (1 John 3:3, Matthew 6:19-21)

2. Despising wisdom and instruction and not fearing the Lord. (Proverbs 1:7, Psalm 74:18)

3. Not treating God's Word as the ultimate answer, which is spirit and life. (2 Timothy 3:16, John 1:1)

4. For those who are married, being unsubmissive to their husbands (1 Peter 3:1, Colossians 3: 18, Ephesians 5:22) and other levels of authorities such as parents (Ephesians 6:1- 3) church leaders (1 Timothy 5:17-18), management at the workplace (Ephesians 6:5-7) and each other in general. (1 Peter 5:5, Ephesians 5:21)

5. Denying God when life gets tough rather than living with integrity. (Job 2:9-10)

6. Destroying your home rather than building it. (Proverbs14:1)

7. Not consistently renewing your inner self. (2 Corinthians 4:16)

8. Being loud, simple and knowing nothing. (Proverbs 9:13)

9. Being contentious and nagging. (Proverbs 19:13)

10. Like the foolish virgins, having no reserve built into our lives; whether spiritually, emotionally, relationally nor financially. (Matthew 25:1-13)

11. Speaking too much. Let's not waste our words. Sometimes the only 'word' we need is silence.

Not pouty malicious silence. Rather, intentional constructive silence. (Proverbs17: 27)

12. Being deceived (2 Timothy 3:6). As women, we ought to exercise a lot of wisdom in what we deem worthy of the investment called 'you'; your soul, time, energy, money and affection. We sometimes overstay our time in relationships which are destructive in that they break our focus to become all that God has called us to be and do.

T.D. Jakes offers lifesaving advice concerning this matter:

Stop watering things that were never meant to grow in your life. Water what works, what's good [and] what's right. Stop playing around with those dead bones and stuff you can't fix, it's over...leave it alone! You're coming into a season of greatness. If you water what is alive and divine, you will see harvest like you've never seen before. Stop wasting water on dead issues, dead relationships, dead people, a dead past. No matter how much you water concrete, you can't grow a garden.

This isn't suggesting having a disposable mindset towards relationships. However, it is truly better to enter the kingdom of God no matter what, rather than be eternally lost.

Master the Art of Saying No and Meaning It!

An out of balance 'yes woman' can't please God! As reigning women living in a liberal and largely anti-God world, we must develop and refine our choice of refusal; the ability to say "no" with courage. We need a heightened sense of belonging and identity in Christ to be willing to go against the grain...no matter who, when and where. A reigning kingdom woman hears a different drumbeat, from a different world, played by a different Drummer! Be prepared, some people will call you weird, rebel, crazy, stupid and even words that cannot be written in Christian literature. However, don't forget that Jesus was called Beelzebub, gluttonous, blasphemer, winebibber and a friend of sinner (See Matthew 11:19).

A woman who has not mastered the ability to say " no" to honour her convictions can't be a winner, let alone a wonder! To be a reigning kingdom woman who isn't ashamed to rock her CROWN- Christlike Reign Over Worthless Norms, she must be able to say, "No." "No" to compromise. "No" to lies. "No" to sexual impurity. "No" to procrastination. "No" to waning. "No" to wandering. "No" to settling. "No" to unforgiveness. "No" to shame. "No" to resentment. "No" to guilt... "No" to *everything* that does not agree with who God says you are and can be through Jesus Christ! "No".

The power of saying "no" with authenticity, wisdom and courage cannot be overemphasised and is often undervalued. Without a suitable "no", our "yes" loses most, if not all value. God is looking for daughters who are willing to learn and master having a holy and impactful "no". There is a brand of "no" that have no room for negotiations. This is when the answer is "no"; take it or leave it!

Joseph mastered the choice of refusal. When Potiphar's unfaithful wife wanted to have sexual relations with him, he said "no"! His "no" was categorical. He wasn't going to think, pray, fast, contact a friend or consider it at a more convenient time. It was a "no", full stop.

When Joseph did the right thing, the consequence of

saying "no" led to demotion, imprisonment and being forgotten; albeit temporarily (Genesis 39 & 40). However, in the end, his holy and resolute "no", catapulted him into his destiny. This included becoming the Assistant Prime Minister in Egypt and not to mention saving his family from certain starvation (Genesis 41 & 42).

One choice can change the entire trajectory of your life, family, ensuing generations, business, country and even the world. What is the quality of our choices? Invest assigned time to examine the quality of your choices. If we want to change our lives, we must change our decisions concerning our choices!

The Wise Woman Abigail

Abigail's life that is outlined in 1 Samuel 25 is an amazing story of a woman whose wisdom catapulted her from the humdrum of being married to a fool to protecting the destiny of David; to later becoming his wife! Firstly, Abigail is identified as being a woman of good understanding and stunning beauty. Abigail, which means, my father's joy, brought joy to the king in David and prevented him from throwing away his destiny!

When a wise woman is married to an absolute fool, like Nabal, it's a very difficult situation to be in! As such, Abigail's wisdom was a welcome light against the bleak backdrop of folly in her environment. Suffice it to say that foolishness is very costly. Nabal's foolishness would have costed him and all the other men in his household their lives, had it not been for Abigail's outstanding wisdom.

- She still respected her husband's headship and leadership.

- She took action based on her convictions and she acted swiftly. She knew that time was of the essence.

- She exercised moral courage and did not succumb to the wrong choice of her husband.

- Abigail was aware of the current affairs of the times in which she lived. Hence, she knew who David was and the plans God had for him.

- She also knew the law of cause and effect when she identified to David that if he committed murder, he would forfeit his throne and his purpose.

- Abigail knew the right words to influence the angry made- up mind of King David. It is often said that there is a king and a fool in every man (I would say there is a queen and fool in every woman too). Abigail spoke to, connected with and inspired the king in David.

I pray thee, forgive the trespass of thine handmaid:

for the Lord will certainly make my lord a sure house; because my lord fighteth the battles of the Lord, and evil hath not been found in thee all thy days. Yet a man is risen to pursue thee, and to seek thy soul: but the soul of my lord shall be bound in the bundle of life with the Lord thy God; and the souls of thine enemies, them shall he sling out, as out of the middle of a sling. And it shall come to pass, when the Lord shall have done to my lord according to all the good that he hath spoken concerning thee, and shall have appointed thee ruler over Israel (1 Samuel 25: 28-30).

- She didn't adopt an I-am-right-and-so-I-am-brash stance. Rather, she was meek and as she spoke to the king, she respectfully and humbly fell on her face before David and bowed her head as she spoke.

- She was very generous.

- She knew when to speak. She didn't rush home and beganspeaking to her husband, Nabal, in his drunken state! She waited until the next day to speak with him.

- Abigail knew how to identify worthwhile opportunities. As such, she said "yes" when David requested her to be his wife.

Abigail was an extraordinarily wise woman. We can be too.

WISDOM TRANSFORMATION STRATEGIES

1. If you lack or want more wisdom, simply ask God becauseHe is wisdom and also the source of it! James 1:5 states, "If any of you lack wisdom, let him ask of God, that giveth to all men liberally, and upbraideth not; and it shall be given him". God will give you wisdom with much generosity.

2. Treat the Scriptures like the best university known to mankind, and it really is! Spend quality time every day interacting with the Scriptures- whether listening, reading, watching it in movie form, or having Word-based conversations with others (witnessing, encouraging and admonishing).

3. Intentionally place yourself in environments that will stretch you. If you are always the 'fountain of wisdom' in your associations, it's time to develop a teachable attitude. Learn from great men and women who possess tried and proven wisdom on the relevant subject matters you want to learn. Be strategic in cultivating destiny-propelling relationships.

4. Be diligent when choosing mentors, coaches, masterminds, clubs and other such connections. They can either make or break your dreams and goals. Be diligent to do the relevant research and ask specific questions of the right sources. Ensure also that you get divine wisdom for the guidance that you need. Pray about everything!

5. Be willing to pay the price in terms of energy, focus, time and finances to equip ourselves to thrive with excellence and to become the highest expression of the amazing potential treasures inside our souls.

6. Schedule daily quality thinking time with a strategic, robust and easily retrievable system to capture your ideas.

7. Don't be afraid to try new things outside of your comfort zone. Everything needed to catapult us into purpose, excellence, abundance and contribution with great impact is in our stretch zone.

8. Create a wisdom atmosphere and culture in your home and other environments where you can influence. Have a collection of books and

other learning materials that will support the area of your expertise.

9. Be adventurous with your time in using it to learn and apply knowledge. For example, converting your travel time into learning moments.

10. Be very committed to passing on your legacy of wisdom to your children, teammates… clients. Begin to share your wisdom. Everyone has something that they can teach others. It will also concretise your knowledge. It is often said, "Expression deepens impressions."

11. A wise woman knows when to speak, how much to speak and to whom to speak! It's only a foolish woman that speaks everything that is on her mind. The famous term, "keeping it real" is frequently overrated and grossly misguided. Aim not to offend in your speech.

12. Be patient with yourself. A woman of wonder is never done in a microwave. We must be patient to be in God's and life's Slow Cooker to get to our optimal state where we embody God's highest intention for our lives.

13. It is worth examining Daniel Goleman's work to get a deep understanding of the transformational concept of Emotional Intelligence.

14. Be intentional in learning how to be a competent communicator. It is one of the most transferable knowledge and skills.

We don't stand a chance of being totally transformed and to reign with wonder if we are devoid of divine wisdom! We can agree that wisdom is the main thing. And if we are truly wise, wewould decide to keep the main thing the main thing! Wherever we are on the reigning spectrum of wisdom (even if the descriptors place us in the 4D realm) we fall on our faces before the only wise God our Saviour and we beseech You to baptise us with the wisdom which is from above. Lord, we yearn to emanate the 'wisdom perfume' from heaven, in and to a world that needs the sweetness of You. Where there are traces of fleshy wisdom and folly in us, we lay at Your feet so that You can perform surgery on our hearts and minds to make us more like You.

We promise to partner with You to seek after knowledge, understanding and wisdom. Help us to choose wisely the mentors, coaches, masterminds and other agents that will assist us in growing to become all that is possible. Teach us how to apply what we have learned as we aim to be wise women of honour and virtue. Lord, introduce us to ourselves by Your sovereign power. Increase our self- awareness and Emotional Intelligence. Help us to grow in the wisdom which is heavenly so that our relationships will begin to become that which is from above.

Grant us the courage and wisdom to live by our convictions and to know when to say "no" and when to say "yes". Make us like Abigail that speaks to the royalty that is within all Your children in such a way that they will hear Your voice. May this cause them to make the choice to embrace the destinies for which they were born and not act with reckless ego-driven ideas. Lead us to the solutions to our problems since we know that they are all wisdom problems. Lord help us, to provide solutions for the problems of others. We recognise that we must be transformed to carry the grace and glory of the wisdom for which we seek. We know that You are more than able to keep us from falling and living a life of folly. Make us into jewels of wisdom fit for the Master's use.

WISDOM TRANSFORMATION TASK

1. In terms of the Reigning Dimensions regarding *Wisdom*, where are you? (Tick one)

Wonder ☐   Winning ☐   Waning ☐   Wandering ☐

2. Develop a Wisdom Declaration: Eg. I am sought after for divine wisdom!

_____

_____

3. Which of the Wisdom Transformation Strategies would give you the maximum impact now?

_____

_____

4. Set a SMART (Specific, Measurable, Attainable, Realistic and Time-bound) wisdom goal.

_____

_____

5. Motivation: Why is this goal important to you?

_____

_____

_____

6. Accountability: Which person or system will hold you accountable?

_____

7. Review Date:

_____

8. Reward: How will you celebrate achieving this goal?

_____
_____

Chapter Four
Transformation Agent #4
WORTHINESS

"You have been criticizing yourself for years,
and it hasn't worked. Try approving
yourself and see what happens."

Louise L. Hay

To believe we can reign without a healthy dose of a sense of worthiness, is to believe that a ship can float on dry land! There is an unchangeable and foundational truth that we are worthy and complete! Part of the turmoil that every woman struggles with, at least at some points in her life, is that eroding feeling of inadequacy and deep self-doubt. If this sense of not being enough isn't taken out by its root, it can act as an emotional and spiritual contraceptive that prevents women from birthing the infinite treasures of our souls! Brené Brown in her powerful book, *Daring Greatly*, refers to this as:

Wholehearted living is about engaging in our lives from a place of worthiness. It means cultivating the courage, compassion, and connection to wake up in the morning and think, no matter what gets done and how much is left undone, I am enough. It's going to bed at night thinking, Yes, I am imperfect and vulnerable and sometimes afraid, but that doesn't change the truth that I am also brave and worthy of love and belonging.

The understanding and valuing of self-worth are essential for us to believe we can advance and live with dominion! A fractured sense of worth results in the impairment of our ability to authentically love ourselves, love others and being victorious. Therefore, if you want to have good success and reign, you must believe in yourself! A reigning woman is secured and anchored in the Lord and she categorically knows that she is royalty of the highest calibre. She knows her worth. Her noble and dignified sense of worth is premised not on that which are fleeting, but that which is immovable since her "life is hid with Christ and in God" (Colossians 3:3). For many women, this knowledge of our worthiness didn't happen overnight; it was a journey and came after living beneath our royal status and royal worthiness for a long while. Let's embark on the journey...but first where are you in your sense of worthiness?

Worthiness Dimensions of Reigning

• 1D Reigning: Wandering

In the one dimension *wandering* category of reigning, this woman usually has low self-esteem and an identity crisis. Being unsure of who you are is very crippling. This may lead to individuals copying others as opposed to being true to their authentic self. As such, they become 'wannabes' contented to be copying other people. They have not reached the place of being happy and content in their own skin.

A deep sense of unworthiness prevents individuals from believing that they are valuable and have much value to offer people. Sadly, there are some goods and services that have been marketed that exploit people's already shaky sense of worth; and women in particular. For example, the dangerous and excessive darkening and lightening of the skin and extreme cosmetic surgeries may be done out of an impaired sense of worthiness. This often feeds into the negative perception of their own beauty.

• 2D Reigning: Waning

The second dimension is where you begin to wane. Identity and self-esteem are usually unstable. This woman is in need of constant validation because she lacks the assurance of her own sense of worth and values. This makes her very needy and clingy. Self-absorption and exaltation are sometimes disguising an unstable identity and a sense of unworthiness. An unstable identity and sense of worth can also manifest in misplaced motives. It may be that we are doing the right thing with the wrong mindset and intention. For example, they are those who, if they have not gotten a lot of praise for the efforts that they have made and or if they're criticised, it really bends them out of shape. This may be to the extent where some refuse to do what they were doing before or it leads to emotional outbursts.

• 3D Reigning: Winning

In the third dimension, women have a stable identity and self-esteem. An individual's identity and self-worth affect everything. Everything. It impacts from the minute to the significant. In the areas where you are strong in your identity and self-worth, some offences will be treated like water running off a duck's back. On the other hand, where there are weaknesses in our self-worth, we are more susceptible to injury. How you view yourself will largely determine how you will respond or react in life. Eleanor Roosevelt said, "No one can make you feel inferior without your consent."

In the third dimension, women are winning. However, they may forgive, but may remain stuck which cancels their ability to press forward into their destiny. Even if our backgrounds have been fraught with many traumas, we still have the ability to press forward. Based on your past, if you don't see yourself as worthy of your amazing destiny, you will inadvertently disqualify yourself for the future.

• 4D Reigning: Wonder

In the ultimate 4th Dimension of worthiness, women have a secure Christ-focused identity and self-esteem. This sense of worth requires having the confidence to live by one's value system. Knowing the Bible's value system and your specific values are absolutely transformational! In addition, they have a strong awareness of their history and destiny, which is the bedrock of one's identity and self-worth. Many people look at their history and become paralyzed by their past trauma and find it difficult to fill this aching void no matter how God's Word describe them as "wonderfully and fearfully made!" (Psalm 139:14).

On the other hand, a positive self-worth in one area also gets translated into other areas. There are endless possibilities in Jesus Christ. In this dimension, there is a sense of freedom; no longer bound by past hurts. They have somehow managed to emancipate themselves from mental slavery. This positive mental state and attitude empower them with an even greater sense of worthiness; which serves as a catalyst for their greatness within.

As God's children, we are encouraged to come before Him with boldness as we access His throne of Grace. Sin and its consequences can be very damaging. This is why asking for and receiving forgiveness from both God and man is very important for the repairment of our sense of worthiness. To reign, we must rise above our heart's condemnation by embracing the grace Christ has so freely given. Many women (and men) find it very difficult to accept the forgiveness of God and others in order to move on with a sense of worthiness. Hence, their self-worth is short-circuited by self-condemnation. But God's grace is always greater than our heart's condemnation (1 John 3:20).

Do believe you are...

Extremely Valuable

One Tuesday evening as I was doing my grocery shopping at a supermarket in Ealing, West London. I saw a young lady picked up a bunch of flowers, looked at it, then returned it to the flowers stand. I became curious, went over, picked up the same flowers and stood there in absolute shock. There in my hand, I held the loveliest bunch of carol-coloured tulips that you can ever imagine, at the jaw-dropping price of seventy-five pence! I was totally surprised at the price. It was labelled jumbo tulips and the original price was seven pounds. I noticed that the sale price was initially reduced to less than half price of three pounds. And finally, it was reduced to less than a pound; at a shocking seventy-five pence.

Think about a jumbo bunch of tulips in excellent condition and still had four days before the expiration of its 'display by date' at a measly seventy-five pence price tag. I wondered what could have caused this drastic reduction of price for such a beautiful large bunch of tulips? Who determined its value and price? And why did the young lady return the beautiful flowers to its shelf?

Needless to say, I was too pleased to purchase these delightful tulips! It was a large bunch to the extent that it was subdivided into three smaller bunches with elastic bands. I decided to keep one of the bunches, give one to my neighbour and took the other to my workplace staff room. Oh, what great beauty and blessing this jumbo bunch of tulips at knocked down price brought to three different environments. Not to mention the countless number of people in these environments that experienced an aesthetic awakening and appreciation of stunning beauty! What can we learn about our own worth from this experience?

Full Price

We are worth the full price! Jesus thought so at Calvary. Precious woman of God, He paid not only the full price for us, but also the ultimate price! He died that we may not only live but can reign now and for eternity! Know assuredly that you are worth it! Your worth and your identity are in Jesus Christ. You're a daughter of the King of kings, forever loved by God and joint- heir with Jesus.

Only God through His Words can give us an accurate, centred and purposeful sense of identity. As we get closer to God, and get to know Him for who He is (not only for what He gives), we will know who we are! Self-knowledge is gained with Christ as the foundation and using other very useful tools and strategies such as identifying our core values, figuring out our Love Language using Dr. Gary Chapman 5 Love Languages and our personality using The Maxwell DISC Personality Indicator Report (See details in Chapter 6). Always remember that you have, "Treasure in earthen vessels" (2 Corinthians 4:7).

Not for Sale!

Many will try to force you (some may even try to do it themselves) to downgrade your sense of worthiness for their own agendas. There you are with all your inner and outer rare beauty, but alas they aren't willing to pay the full price for you. But know this one thing, you're not for sale! You are who you are. Your price tag has Jesus' blood on it! "For He hath made Him to be sin for us, who knew no sin; that we might be made the righteousness of God in him" (2 Corinthians 5:21). Therefore, don't treat yourself and the treasures that you carry as a light thing. Jesus paid the full top-end price for us. So, dare anyone to suggest otherwise and double dare us to believe otherwise. It is one thing when others want to put a 'For Sale' tag on us, but it's a different matter when we do it ourselves! You're a wonder of inestimable value! And this you must believe. Pause for a moment and answer truthfully, is there any area in your life that you've placed a 'For Sale' sign on, or allowed others to do so?

Like I said, you are oh so worth it. Examine Genesis 25: 29- 34 in which Esau despised his birthright for a pot of stew. As women, we will all face extremely trying times. Sometimes the physical, emotional, mental, financial and spiritual pain and or need can be so intense that we will feel something akin to how Esau felt. In Genesis 25: 31-32, Esau said, "Feed me, I pray thee, with that same red pottage; for I am faint… Behold, I am at the point to die: and what profit shall this birthright do to me?" Let's be very careful how we perceive and hence label our temporary, albeit intensely painful situations. It is our own short-sighted descriptions that Satan, the chief enemy of our souls, uses to leverage against us at the negotiating table in our lives and for our lives. Esau used words such as "faint" and "I am at the point to die"! What words are we using which are putting our eternal destiny at risk? Selling our souls for nought is never a wise choice.

Let's always remember, "For what will it profit a man if he gains the whole world, and loses his own soul?" (Mark 8:36). Let's make this more personal so that it causes us to be far more sensitive towards and thereby put a high and holy value on who we are through Christ Jesus. For what will it profit a woman if she gains the whole world, and loses her own soul? Nothing is worth your precious soul. Absolutely nothing. And while we are on this matter, we may be hungry; for whatever, but we are not going to die. Our 'hunger' is a temporary need that will be met at the right time and in the right way. We must hold on to our birthright; our position and inheritance. In the kingdom of God, your inheritance was secured in the death of Jesus Christ, a joint-heir with Him. Your position in His kingdom ministry of reconciliation is "You are a chosen generation, a royal priesthood, a holy nation, a peculiar people; that ye should shew forth the praises of him who hath called you out of darkness into his marvellous light" (1 Peter 2:9).

Jumbo-sized Blessing

Like the bunch of tulips, you are a jumbo-sized blessing that can and will bring beauty, value and improvement to every environment you enter! What Jesus did for you at Calvary has certainly super-sized your life! You have a trailer load of blessings in your soul, heart, mind and hands. Identify them, own them and hone them. And by all means, go and share them. There are many environments that are almost complete with only one thing missing. That one thing missing is you! God is talking to you. So, don't turn around to look at others and coyly ask while pointing at yourself, "Who me?" Yes. God says, "Go forward and be a blessing!"

It's Not Personal

Not everyone can discern your worth. Don't take the feedback from their rejection personally. Sometimes people's rejection of you is significantly more about them, not you. Some people lack the capacity to recognise your worth and blessing even if it hits them between the eyes. The young lady who didn't embrace the opportunity to purchase the tulips, was the one who didn't get to experience the great joy and aesthetic gift that they brought to me and others.

Be encouraged, the right 'shopper' who knows quality will honour your quality and pay the price for you. And guess what they are not looking for a discounted version of yourself. They are totally willing to pay your full price with all your godly terms and conditions. Celebrate what God has shaped your life into. And don't let people's rejection erode your confidence and let you begin to take shortcuts and put a "For sale" over your life. You are not for sale, as was mentioned, Jesus paid the full price for you. Therefore, be assured that the people who are assigned to your life will recognise you. Remember Ruth recognised Naomi. Boaz recognised Ruth. Elizabeth recognised the unborn Saviour. Johnathan recognised David. Elijah recognised Elisha... Be encouraged, the discerning and the deserving will identify and honour your worth.

Beyond The Package

Ensure that your life is filled with amazing attributes and skills so that people are not disappointed by what they encounter beyond your packaging. At the time of purchase, the beautiful tulips package was plastered with a bright yellow and black reduction label that belittled its contents. But the discerning could look beyond the package to see the valuable contents waiting to be appreciated. Live in such a way that your contents command respect because of what you have allowed the Master Architect to build in and with your life. May I suggest that you make both our package and the experience beyond it, a memorable and delightful one! Don't let your package detract from your contents. I will go much further with this thought in Chapter 10 which addresses Wardrobe. Until then, know assuredly that packaging can make or break closing on a 'purchase'. Make your 'content' be of greater emphasis that will complement what can be seen.

Keep Blooming

When people walk away from the opportunity to choose you, please beloved sister don't wilt and refuse to bloom because of the possible pain and shock of not being selected by some people; especially when you believed you were appreciated and chosen. The truth is, only the people who are assigned to you, will choose you and stay! In fact, they will come looking for you. Just keep on blooming…never, never, never wither. And we dare not die before our death. We must fully live to be the God-ordained version of ourselves to declare the works and glory of the Lord.

Unlike the tulips, we have the capacity to pour water and fertiliser on ourselves. We can also ensure we are in the right environment that nurtures our growth. It's our time to fully utilise our throne-room radiance and gifting for the Father! Remember that, "There are diversities of gifts, but the same Spirit. But the manifestation of the Spirit is given to every man to profit withal" (1 Corinthians 12:4-12). We are endowed with specific gifts by the power of the Holy Spirit, for the betterment of the body of Jesus Christ.

Let's operate in our gifts with excellence and love within the scope of the grace we've been given. This will advance our lives, family, church, community and indeed the world. We must be responsible and diligent with our gifts. Ephesians 4: 12-13 emphasises God's intention for our personal gifts, "For the perfecting of the saints, for the work of the ministry, for the edifying of the body of Christ: Till we all come in the unity of the faith, and of the knowledge of the Son of God, unto a perfect man, unto the measure of the stature of the fulness of Christ."

Charge your Worth

It is one thing when people try to mark-down your price, but it is completely a different thing when you reduce your worth and price yourself. Remember there was a young lady (and possibly others) who picked up the bunch of tulips, looked at it, and put it back; even at a measly seventy-five pence price tag. It goes to show that there is no point in putting your life and that which you carry on sale. Some people simply won't choose you even if you're free. Don't be afraid to charge your worth.

Whether it's the cost of your services, the parameters of your relationships, the terms and conditions at your negotiation tables, or who or what you believe you can have! Believe you are everything God says you are and you can do all things through Jesus Christ, so don't be afraid charge your worth, speak your worth, dress your worth, enjoy your worth and place yourself in environments that honour it! Environments matter. I was recently sent this increasingly popular story whose origin is unknown by a friend. It is said that...

> *A father said to his daughter: You graduated with honours, here is a car that I acquired many years ago. It is several years old. But before I give it to you, take it to the used car lot downtown and tell them I want to sell it and see how much they offer you. The daughter went to the used car lot, returned to her father and said, "They offered me $1,000 because it looks very worn out." The father said, "Take it to the pawn shop." The daughter went to the pawn shop, returned to her father and said, "The pawn shop offered $100 because it was a very old car." The father asked his daughter to go to a car club and show them the car. The daughter took the car to the club, returned and told her father, "Some people in the club offered $100,000 for it since it is a Nissan Skyline R34, an iconic car and sought after by many." The father said to his daughter, "I wanted you to know that the right place values you the right way." If you are not valued, do not be angry, it means you are in the wrong place.*

Those who know your value are those who appreciate you. Never stay in aplace where no one sees your value.

It is Time to Change Your Environment

I stayed with the same mobile phone provider for over fifteen years. For more than eight years of those years, I was a dissatisfied customer; feeling undervalued. "Why did I stay so long?" I'm glad you asked. The truth is, I was afraid of change and lacked courage until... Until what? Until I truly believed thatI had options and there were better deals and customer experience waiting for me to arrive and take hold of them. When I decided that I deserved more and that what I desired and deserved were available, I got everything I wanted and more! We will never go beyond what we believe we deserve. This is why we often settle for the status quo, trapped by a subconscious feeling that we don't deserve more. When we raise our standards, we always become and get more. I got more data, a lower price, a handset I preferred and a phone company that operates like it values my patronage. Where in our lives are we stuck, feeling unsure and unworthy of more? Ask for and expect your heart's divine desires to be valued and treated with respect. This is your birthright. Again, God is saying, "You're worth it"!

Self-Concept

Who am I? How we answer this question is a significant factor concerning the quality of our lives. Our self-concept underpins everything! Our self-concept is the cornerstone of our identity. Robert A. Baron and Donn Byrne in their classic book, *Social Psychology,* define self-concept as "an organized collection of beliefs and self-perceptions about oneself."

Based on a study done by Rentsch and Heffner (1994) in which over 200 college students were asked to give responses to one of life's 'big questions' of "Who are you?" The data produced the following 8 components to the construction of the self- concept; in no particular order:

1. Interpersonal Attributes Eg. I am a mother and I take art lessons.

2. Ascribed Characteristics Eg. I am a woman and I am sixty-five years old.

3. Interests and Activities Eg. I love to read and I enjoy outdoor spaces.

4. Existential Aspects Eg. I am beautiful and unique.

5. Self-Determination Eg. I am a Christian and I can become fluent in Spanish.

6. Internalized Beliefs Eg. I like classical music and I am opposed to deforestation.

7. Self-Awareness Eg. I have values and my beliefs are in alignment.

8. Social Differentiation Eg. I am from a Christian family and I am a Jamaican.

As is purported and can be related to, there are many aspects of the way we view ourselves. However, as Christian women we have been given Jesus Christ that provides the most strategic point of reference and transformation that we need to believe of ourselves that which matters most! That is, we are children of God, made royalty by the Blood of the Lamb. God's Kingdom brand costs Jesus' blood. Kingdom self-concept isn't about status and clout, but about surrender. Self-concept in the Kingdom of God isn't about look-at-me nor woe is me. Instead, it's about seeing ourselves through God's eyes and to be always looking to Jesus! Without this sense of security, we will never feel like we are enough…

Yes, You are More than Enough!

Many women love, serve and give from a place of unworthiness. This is born out of a deep sense of rejection; whether conscious or unconscious. Consequently, whatever is done is fear-driven and approval-seeking. This often bears the damaging outcomes of over-giving, over-working and even over-spending. Thus, leading to burn-out and a gnawing sense of resentment.

Loving others without honouring our own boundaries is damaging. We must know our values and boundaries and enforce them. Our time, energy, emotions and money are ours. We are to steward them well; without being imposed upon. We are the teachers of how we desire to be treated. Change the teacher from within and all the 'students' in our lives will adjust.

It is one thing to have mastery of the grace of compassion and faithfulness towards others. However, it also requires a special grace to administer self-care and also to graciously have compassion towards yourself to receive without guilt and shame.

It is true that it is much better to give than to receive (Acts 20: 35). However, the Scripture didn't say it's only good to give and not to receive. Not being able to allow one's self to receive and be loved is a subtle form of pride. It may also be evidence of fear, mistrust and unhealed wounds. Whatever the reason, there is a need for healing and deliverance. Our Heavenly Father is willing, able and delighted to do this for His daughters.

Dry your tears...

If every woman is honest with you, she will tell you that life, with its many ups and downs, has caused her to shed many tears upon her tender cheeks! We have suffered many losses, pain, rejections, abuse, betrayals and hurts which broke our hearts. However, all we had to do was to keep on walking with God or run to God, to realise that some of the tears we cried over these matters were unnecessary! If we could discern, we would have known it was God that was setting us up for deeper, greater and so much more. It's called, 'take-a-licking-and-keep-on-ticking'. It is also called, 'Thank-You-Jesus-for-shutting-that-door!'

The Reigning Woman was born to display miracles, signs and wonders with divine tenacity and courage. Never forget that the joy of the Lord is your strength, so don't let weeping consume your precious days. "Weeping may endure for a night, but joy cometh in the morning" (Psalm 30:5). May I announce to you my precious sister, your season of weeping is coming to an end and astonishing joy is on its way! The brokenness that you had to overcome, or are overcoming, was not meant to break you. It was designed to brand you to display the deliverance and transformation that can only come from Christ, the King. Consequently, who else has your story? Who else has your 'soul print'? And who else has your voice? The broken are waiting for the Chain-Breaker to manifest through you! A. W. Tozer profoundly states:

It is doubtful whether God can bless a man greatly until he has hurt him deeply. God actually rises up storms of conflict in relationships at times in order to accomplish that deeper work in our character. We cannot love our enemies [or simply those who have wronged us] in our own strength. This is graduate-level grace. Are you willing to enter this school? Are you willing to take the test? If you pass, you can expect to be elevated to a new level in the Kingdom. For He brings us through these tests as preparation for greater use in the Kingdom. You must pass the test first.

It is important to know that if we are struggling with persistent tearfulness and other signs of persistent distress for whatever reason, there is always help available. Some levels of brokenness can't be dealt with on our own. We are social beings; we are much better in community. Dependent on the magnitude of our situation, it could be that help is sought from a pastor, friend, counsellor, therapist, coach or medical doctor. Let's not suffer in silence and feel caged by fear, shame and guilt. We must all reach out for the help that we need and we must also be vigilant concerning the wellbeing of those around us. God also promises to be our very present help in times of trouble (Psalm 46:1)!

Leadership: The Changing of the Guards

We must accept and honour God's changing of the guards. When Saul the King disobeyed God's crystal-clear instruction in 1 Samuel 15: 1-3, he was rejected by God for being king. When God signals a change, we must make the transition with Him. Believe it or not, our prolonged mourning can hinder us from receiving new instructions, blessings and the moves of God in our lives, families, churches, communities, nation and world that we pray and long for! We are human beings with emotions, so there is a place for tears. But beyond a certain point, they become liabilities; hijacking God's next transformational moves. Prolonged hopeless crying, procrastination and pointless debates prevent progress. Let's examine our tears. Have they long past their expiry date? "Go forward", I can hear the Lord say. "Go forward", it is a new day!

And the Lord said unto Samuel, how long wilt thou mourn for Saul, seeing I have rejected him from reigning over Israel? fill thine horn with oil, and go, I will send thee to Jesse the Bethlehemite: for I have provided mea king among his sons (1 Samuel 16:1).

Not only did the Lord tell Samuel that He has found Saul's replacement, He gave him instructions on how to participate in the new thing that God was doing. Take note that not everyone will be excited about the new thing that God is doing in you, for you and through you. Can you handle it?

Understanding Opposition

Ironically, opposition is an indication that you are doing something with your life. I grew up in the country part in Jamaica. And believe me when I say that as children, we never gather under an empty apple tree and pelt stones at it hoping for juicy apples to fall. Oh no. We only stoned fruit-bearing trees. We were also very picky; we stoned the best fruit trees. Certain calibre fruits weren't worth our stones, time nor energy.

Could it be that some of the 'stones' you are getting is because you are bearing fruit? And not just any old fruit; but they are juicy and amazing too. So beloved woman of God, know this assuredly, if your life will have great impact, you will experience some level of opposition. These 'sticks and stones' can't be negotiated out of. In fact, they are needful. They provide feedback, keep us humble, prayerful, standing on God's Word and relying totally on His care and protection. Without God we are nothing and we will not thrive. Be not afraid. In Psalm 23 we are reminded that God is with us and He is our Shepherd. His rod and staff will always comfort and guide us. He promises to lead us beside the still water and grant our bruised souls the restoration they need. Therefore, keep bearing fruit and let the name of the Lord be glorified.

Handling Mistakes

What do we do when we've goofed up? When we have made a mistake, we must repent, make amends and then let it go! Never make a tombstone out of your mistakes, nor allow them to be our jail cells. We can't say *yes* to our destiny if we don't recognise that *yesterday* is over! Let's say yes to today. We must truly believe that God's grace is much greater than past mistakes and our heart's condemnation! Here is David's heinous crime against God and man in 2 Samuel 12:9

Wherefore hast thou despised the commandment of the LORD, to do evil in his sight? thou hast killed Uriah the Hittite with the sword, and hast taken his wife to be thy wife, and hast slain him with the sword of the children of Ammon.

David did the right thing by admitting his guilt and said unto Nathan, "I have sinned against the LORD." When the consequence of David's sin faced him, he was understandably heartbroken and terribly overcome with grief for the dreadful sin he committed against Bathsheba, Uriah and not to mention the scandal he brought his reign in as king. And most importantly the reproach he brought on Yahweh. Even though God forgave him, God promised that the child that was conceived would certainly die. David's immediate reaction when he found out that his child was dead, was to get up, sort himself, worship and eat a meal!

> *Then David arose from the earth, and washed, and anointed himself, and changed his apparel, and came into the house of the Lord, and worshipped: then he came to his own house; and when he required, they set bread before him, and he did eat (2 Samuel 12:20).*

It's time to arise from the pain of our failures. We should take off the garment and attitude of self-berating. It is truly time to move on in the forgiveness offered to us through Jesus Christ. And most vital is to decide to worship God in your new-found mental and emotional states of freedom! The profound nature and speed of David's change of emotional state stunned his servants to the extent that they challenged him:

> *Then said his servants unto him, what thing is this that thou hast done? thou didst fast and weep for the child, while it was alive; but when the child was dead, thou didst rise and eat bread (2 Samuel 12: 21).*

David recognised that he couldn't change his past. He knew that if he handles his present moments differently, the future would be different. Importantly, David repented bitterly for his failures and went forward to make some big moves!

> *And David comforted Bathsheba, his wife, and went in unto her, and lay with her: and she bare a son, and he called his name Solomon: and the Lord loved him. (2 Samuel 12:24)*

Being women of surrender, wonder and faithfulness don't mean we won't make mistakes. Too many of us refuse to or have difficulties in honouring our worthiness because of previous mistakes. It's time to put them where they belong; in the sea of forgetfulness where Christ has placed all our sins (Micah 7:19)! Thank God that He is a God of tender mercies and God of a second, third, fourth, fifth and umpteenth chance. This isn't a licence to be presumptuous. However, what we do after our mistakes makes all the difference.

Rachel your Price has been doubled

In Genesis 29, Jacob proved that he was convinced that Rachel was worth his sweat and tears in their intriguing love story. He agreed to work for seven years to get Rachel as his wife.

However, on what was his long-awaited wedding night, Rachel's sister, Leah, was given to him instead of Rachel in a gut-wrenching trickery. Every young man would classify this evil stunt by Laban as treason! Imagine working seven long years for anything, let alone the love of a woman; only to be robbed of the prize. But what did Jacob do? Did he cry, hang down his head, hate Laban and walk away? Absolutely not! He agreed to work another seven years for whom he loved and wanted. In Jacob's eyes, Rachel was worth every ounce of his sweat; including putting up with his conniving father-in-law who changed his wages ten times. I hereby declare to you beloved woman of wonder that you are worth it. Jesus' blood said it and that forever settles it!

WORTHINESS TRANSFORMATION STRATEGIES

1. Know and believe with your whole heart that Jesus believes you are worth it. This is why He died for us all. On this basis, you're totally worth it!

2. Do not compare yourself to others. You are you, there can never be another you!

3. Be loving and lovable. Feeling good about yourself does wonders! Remember to laugh, smile, twirl, dance…just be!

4. Identify the things (whether small or large) that bring you great delight. For example, I love lavender and just a few drops of this essential oil in a diffuser excites me. It makes me feel like I can almost smell heaven! I am curious of what brings you delight.

5. Set and implement boundaries. Become diligent in gently yet firmly teaching others how you would love to be treated.

6. Practice generosity. It is indeed better to give than to receive. Giving sure does give you much needed 'internal and external sunshine'. The practise of generosity ushers you into the space of abundance which boosts self-worth. Let's all set a goal to become a volunteer; even if

it's over the telephone in light of the Covid-19 restrictions.

7. Become conscious of every thought, word and action that erodes your sense of worth. Replace them with ideas that embrace and celebrate your worth. Speak affirming words to yourself. Practise making daily declarations that honour your worth. For example:

★ I'm a masterpiece of God's creation.

★ I'm more than enough.

★ I carry solutions for my family, church, business, joband community.

8. Reframe your struggles. Believe that the brokenness that you had to overcome, or is overcoming, was not meant to break you. It was designed to brand you to display the transformation and deliverance that can only come from Christ the King!

9. Pay adequate attention to your grooming and personal style. Whilst they don't determine your worth, they are indicators of what you believe to be true about your worth.

10. Develop your competencies so that, in addition to your innate worth made in the image of God, you will also have tangible skills to use to add value to people by either solving their problems and helping them to utilize presenting opportunities.

11. Know when it's time to stop mourning. No matter what is happening or has happened, ask

God and people for assistance (or forgiveness) to help you arise and shine for the glory of the Lord has indeed risen upon you! Discern the new season with its accompanying blessings after your period of mourning.

12. Deeply celebrate and intentionally practise joy. The joy of the Lord is your strength. Joy is the birthing place for gratitude. Gratitude is the catalyst for miracles.

13. Be committed to becoming a life-long learner. The more knowledgeable and wiser you're, the more you will be the solution to yours and other people's problems. Problem- solving makes you more indispensable. The bigger difference you make in people's lives, it gives a sense of purpose, meaning and significance.

14. Become a person that is interesting and fun to be with. Try new things, go new places and meet new people and begin to have new conversations!

15. Memorise ten Scripture verses that confirm and celebrate your identity and your self-worth. Here are a few examples: Genesis 1:26-27, Psalm 139:13-14, Jeremiah 1:5 & 29:11 and John 3:16.

As God is worthy, so too, we are worthy through Jesus Christ, our Lord and Saviour. He paid the ultimate price of death to close the wide gulf created by sin. Before a woman of the kingdom of God can live boldly in pursuing and accomplishing the will of God for her life, she must accept her worth. This is not arrogance. This is being humbly, yet boldly, you in Jesus Christ. Like Eleanor Roosevelt said, "No one can make you feel inferior without your consent." As daughters of the King, we must believe that we are the object of God's unchanging affection, kindness and astonishing favour; because He in His sovereignty has chosen us.

You are more than enough! Step out of cloning others; celebrate yourself. The transformed you have no competition and is a blessing to every environment that you enter. Why settle for the cloned version of someone else? In other words, you have greatness in you. I have never met (and I will never meet) anyone that I would exchange myself for, no matter how amazing they are; and I have met some really amazing people. My mother often told me, "Donna, just be yourself in Christ". I totally agree with her. If I were to search this entire planet, there would never be another me in the full dimension of what typifies my distinctiveness. The same is also true for you. There is no other YOU. Not now not ever!

Believe the promises God made to you in the Scriptures and live with God-bestowed confidence that you are made worthy by the Worthy One! There will always be silencing, shrinking and sentencing inner and outer voices! In the end, whose report will you believe? As reigning women that are no longer wandering and will not be contented with waning, we must know, believe and act with the confidence that we belong to the King. And He has made us to be wonders with great impact for our generation and beyond!

WORTHINESS TRANSFORMATION TASK

1. In terms of the Reigning Dimensions regarding *Worthiness*, where are you? (Tick one)

Wonder ☐   Winning ☐   Waning ☐   Wandering ☐

2. Develop a Worthiness Declaration: Eg. I am secure in my sense of worthiness anchored in Christ!

_____

_____

3. Which of the Worthiness Transformation Strategies would give you the maximum impact now?

_____

_____

4. Set a SMART (Specific, Measurable, Attainable, Realistic and Time-bound) worthiness goal.

_____

_____

5. Motivation: Why is this goal important to you?

_____

_____

_____

6. Accountability: Which person or system will hold you accountable?

_____

7. Review Date:

_____

8. Reward: How will you celebrate achieving this goal?

_____
_____

Chapter Five
Transformation Agent #5
WELLBEING

"Keep your vitality. A life without health

is like a river without water."

Maxime Lagace

It's time to get up! Oh, how I hated the early morning shock treatment. In November 2017 I had surgery for the removal of fibroids. I was in pain and didn't want to get up from my hospital bed; at least not at that time. It was too early and the bed was warm. I was alright with the darkness at this time of the day. And who told anyone I was hungry? However, the Health Care Assistants knew that if patients were left to their own ways, we would end up curled up (for those that could even curl) in bed for most, if not all day. I can still remember the pain check question, "Dr. Sherwood, on the scale of 1 to 10, how is your pain today?" I had to think to identify and articulate the level of pain. The pain was off the scale and some days I wanted to choose 11 on the scale of 1 to 10!

This moment our Heavenly Father is like a smiling Health Care Assistant who is opening our blinds and is encouraging us to arise. Whatever we may be going through, He is here to announce to all of us, "It's time to get up! And it's certainly time to be made whole so we can reign now!

If there was ever a time in history that our wellbeing needs keen attention, it's now. In a Covid-19 traumatised world with all its resultant stresses, everyone and women in particular, must prioritise their wellbeing. When we think of the many hats that women wear and the vital roles we play for the adequate functioning of society on every level, wellbeing isn't the latest buzzword, it is a priority!

The *Office for National Statistics* in the United Kingdom (UK) reports that all indicators of personal well-being significantly worsened in the second (April to June) and third quarter (July to September) in 2020 when compared with the same timeframe in 2019. With specific reference to anxiety, the second quarter of 2020 also reports the highest average rating of anxiety on record since 2011 when well-being data started being collected. The average anxiety assessment of 3.39 out of 10 was 4.5% higher than for the previous quarter (3.24) and a 12.5% increase in the same quarter from the previous year (2.97). The trend of decline was evident in the other three indicators too; overall life satisfaction, feeling worthwhile and overall happiness.

The general picture of wellbeing in the UK, and possibly in other countries, is grim. However, the best gifts a woman can give to her world and the world in general, are her wholeness, vitality and energy. If life was a train, then our health would be the train track. Everything rides on it! Let's do a self-assessment for wellbeing based on the four dimensions we have been using.

Wellbeing Dimensions of Reigning

• 1D Reigning: Wandering

Women whose wellbeing is in the 1D reigning category are unaware of the all-encompassing impact that their health has on all areas of life. In some instances, they have possibly simply refused to be intentional about their health. Minimal wellbeing efforts are made. Consequently, ill-health is being experienced in several areas of wellbeing.

• 2D Reigning: Waning

In the Waning second dimension, women are aware of the basics required for optimal wellbeing. However, the care for their wellbeing have been diminishing over time. The healthy practices which were usually done, have been discontinued. This may be a temporary situation or a permanent decision.

• 3D Reigning: Winning

In the 3D Winning realm, women understand that there is a link between the wellbeing of our body, mind, soul and the emotions. Generally, there is a strong sense of health consciousness. Wellbeing is of significant priority. Consequently, they are usually in relatively good health. However, if health issues develop, they are dealt with as a matter of priority. Again, in a general sense, they are usually happy, having done whatever it takes to both safeguard against and deal with anxiety.

• 4D Reigning: Wonder

In the fourth dimension of being transformed into a wonder, health is usually a strong core value. Women in this dimension are usually very intentional about her health and general wellbeing! She pursues a multifaceted healthy living; physically, emotionally, mentally and relationally. Since the quality of our relationships is paramount in determining our overall quality of well-being, hence she is deliberate in building and being a part of healthy relationships.

In this realm, the lifestyle of joy is esteemed which helps to safeguard and help to cope with high anxiety issues. These women are diligent in practising the disciplines of wholistic wellbeing in areas such as rest, healthy diet, stress management, exercise; to name a few. They are also mindful of their environment to which they belong and the physical state of them. They live with a high level of consciousness that almost everything impacts their wellbeing!

Wholeness for Wellness

To a large degree, our bodies are mirrors of the health of our souls. Healing begins on the inside. For many, when they hear the word 'wellbeing', nutrition, sleep and exercise are the areas that readily come to mind. However, spiritual wellbeing is the foundation of all other wellbeing. We can't reign with wonder if we are limping through life; because we aren't healed at the very foundation of our souls.

Unhealed issues impede our spiritual walk, minimise our impact and will threaten our reign! "Beloved, I wish above all things that thou mayest prosper and be in health, even as thy soul prospereth" (3 John: 2). It is evident that there is the prosperity of the soul! Let's talk a selah moment to pause and reflect. On a scale of 1 to 10, where would you put the prosperity of your soul?

Especially in a world such as ours, we can't afford to be busy trying to make our bodies healthy, whilst the core of our souls is broken. As women, we all have pain, problems and pollution of the past (and possibly of the present), we need God to make us whole. Since He has given us all things for life and godliness (2 Peter 1:3), we must take a hold of them and apply them to our lives.

Rahab was a prostitute (Joshua 6:25). Ruth was a widowed heathen worshiper of many gods (Ruth 1:4-5). The Samaritan woman had many previous lovers and at the point of meeting Jesus her current lover was someone else's (John 4:4-19). We all have cobwebs in our cupboards. All of us. We've all been tainted by the stain of sin. Let's repent and turn away from them and come under the cleansing stream of Jesus' blood; and experience the transformation that He alone can give. We need both inner and outer healing.

Here is a love letter from the Father's heart to yours...

Dearest Daughter,

I want you to know that there is great beauty in your cracks; the places you were once broken! Go to any museum and look with observant eyes and you will without fail see the great lengths that curators (managers of cultural heritage institutions such as gallery, museum, or library) go to preserve and display broken vessels and artifacts from the past. Some have been so transformed that their startling beauty makes you catch your breath! I will never throw you away because you are broken. I promise you, that like Kintsukuroi (literally means gold mending) Japanese art, I will fill your cracks with 'gold' to make you more beautiful than you were before!

Don't believe the lies and schemes of Satan, that try to make you think of yourself as an unrepairable, broken and forgotten object! Satan is a liar and the father of every lie. I am the Omnipotent and Faithful God who is the Ultimate Curator who went to the extreme length to permanently mend all your brokenness through the free gift of Jesus Christ. If you let Me, I will make your life an astonishing wonder. Even now, I am knocking on your heart's door. Open up and I will come in and I will make your life a 4D wonder and miracle. Every day you will be like those that dream, your mouth will be filled with laughter and your tongue with singing. I will heal your brokenness. I overlay them with 'pure gold' so that your pain becomes your pulpit, your mess becomes your message and your wounds become your weapon!

Be encouraged, I am the God, who commanded the light to shine out of darkness and hath shined in your heart. Beloved daughter you have great treasure in your earthen vessel, that the excellency of the power may be of God, and not of yourself. You may be troubled on every side, yet not distressed; you are perplexed, but not in despair; Persecuted, but not forsaken; cast down, but not destroyed (2 Corinthians 4:6-10; emphasis mine). So, no matter what you've been through or what you are going through - in fact, because of what you've been through, you owe it to Me, yourself, your friends, family, communities and the world to RISE UP, REIGN and DO EXPLOITS! You are forever my daughter and remember who I am to you; the Lover of your soul and King over everything; including your struggles!

Love and forever Yours,

Dad

Managing Stress

We need stress! The positive side to stress is that, within reason, a bit of stress, keeps us motivated to go forward and to attain the goals in our lives. However, we know that we are over the normal limit when we begin to experience fatigue, unexplained weight loss, excessive hair shedding, insomnia, tear-fullness and general inability to cope and function in day- to-day living. Beyond a certain level, stress becomes damaging.

The hormone called Cortisol is released when the body is stressed. Excess of this hormone can throw other hormones out of balance. Take a break to reduce the cortisol levels in the body with meditation and contemplation. Serotonin hormone positively affects the way we feel. With the complex lives many women live, we must develop strategies to overcome internal and external stresses.

Food plays a major role in how we interact and cope with stress. The body is continuously repairing itself. No matter how healthily we eat, how consistently we exercise, the body is under a lot of stress. It is always present. It is a question of how we manage it. In fact, intentional healthy relationships are necessary for optimal health. In this fast-paced world, quality relaxation won't find us. We must diligently make space in our lives for rest, good quality sleep and relaxation.

Practise Stillness

It is in our stillness that we will know God, ourselves and others! This is a huge contributor to overall wellbeing. Have you ever seen a baby that is screaming and flailing about with hunger and even though the mother is doing everything she can to get her nipple into her mouth, the baby isn't latching on because of the temper tantrum she is having? That which she desires is so near even pointing to her mouth, but alas no connection for sustenance and bonding is being made. Usually, the mother has to strategize to quieten the screaming child. It is only when the child is sufficiently calm that she is able to realise that her mother's nipple is available and lovingly being offered.

Are we that crying child in our difficult wellbeing situations today? Arms flying around wildly and sobbing even though the El Shaddai, the Breasted One, is in our circumstances we can't discern His tenderness, love and deliverance. Let's calm down and experience the 'breast' of God in the midst of our situations. "Be still, and know that I am God: I will be exalted among the heathen, I will be exalted in the earth" (Psalm 46:10).

Detox

Detoxification is the removal of built-up toxins from the body. *Botanical Health* states that the foundation of any effective health programme is body cleansing. This in turn will improve the functioning and efficiency of the organs of elimination, which will also increase the absorption of nutrients from your food. And this helps the body to heal itself naturally. There's a link between the high levels of toxins in the environment and our health. Sadly, environmental pollutants have also entered our food chains such as colourings, flavourings, preservatives and other types of additives. There are several types of detox such as colon cleansing, liver cleansing, kidney cleansing and toxin cleansing. They are done to set the foundation for better body functioning and food absorption.

Carol Vorderman's in her *Summer Detox* book, highlights the following 10 benefits of detoxifying our bodies:

1. Lose excess weight
2. Cellulite will be reduced
3. Have more energy
4. Get fewer colds
5. Get rid of bloating
6. Enjoy better health
7. Possibly lower your blood pressure
8. The skin looks smoother
9. Hair will shine
10. Feel calmer

If you feel that you would want to include a detox programme in your wellbeing transformation, it's wise to do your own research and choose one that is suitable for you in collaboration with the input of relevant health care professionals.

Diet

Proper nutrition is vital for wellbeing. Catherine Geissler and Hilary Powers state that nutrition is about the supply of nutrients, utilisation and the impact on the health of individuals. Diets that are deficient in proper nutrition have unfavourable effects in the short and long term and may eventually lead to sickness and diseases such as coronary heart disease, diabetes, obesity and specific nutrient deficiencies.

Hippocrates said, "Let food be thy medicine and medicine be thy food." As such, aiming to use our diet as an instrument for transforming our wellbeing is vital. Our health span can and should also be equivalent to your life span. The main aim is to eliminate unhealthy processed foods and replace it with healthy whole foods. We mustn't choose healthy foods only because they are advertised and labelled so. Foods marketed as being healthy are sometimes not really the truth. We need to take personal responsibility for our own health. It's never wise to leave this crucial life-impacting decision to experts only. We need to become informed about our health and more importantly not be afraid nor resistant to make life-altering changes. Catherine Geissler and Hilary Powers made the following suggestions:

Hydration: Proper hydration of the body is important for the proper functioning of the body. Excessive water losses from the body lead to dehydration which can be caused by strenuous exercise, severe diarrhoea, excessive sweat loss in high temperatures and abuse of alcohol. The recommended daily water intake for women is 2.7 litres. Make water your main source of hydration. The rest will come from other beverages, fruit, vegetables and the rest of your food intake.

It is important to note that individuals living in extremely hot climates and or engaging in strenuous physical activities need to also increase their recommended water intake.

Sugar: Aim to reduce as much as possible sugar and all its derivatives such as fructose and glucose. These put us more at risk for health conditions; especially for type 2 diabetes.

Fresh whole food versus processed foods: Fresh whole foods have more fibre and are more nutrient-dense than processed food. The latter usually have lower nutrients and less fibre. If you are experiencing any physical ailments, there are usually foods that must be avoided and those that support the recovery from the particular sickness.

The better the quality of our health and the longer we are alive, the more contributions we can make to the kingdom of God and the betterment of humanity in general. We are one hundred percent responsible for every area of our life, including our health. Sometimes the solutions for the ailments for which we pray and fast for deliverance are well within our reach if we intentionally make health-supporting decisions throughout the week.

At times, no sooner the prayer for healing is finished, we make conflicting health choices by that which we put on our plates and in our mouths. If we are asked, on a scale of 1 to 10, how passionate are you about your health? Sadly, we may be forced to admit that we are not serious as we ought to be about our health. Thankfully, we can always start again and make better consistent choices. Let's aim to be mindful of our food intake in terms of the quality, portion size, type and the times that we eat. I've long concluded that consistent lifestyle changes have far more lasting effects than roller coaster dieting which can't be maintained.

Let me share with you some of the changes I have made over the years, but especially after my surgery. These are not recommendations per se, I am only sharing a few of the things that I do in my quest to preserve my health. Regarding one's health choices, you will need to do your own research to be empowered to make wholesome choices along with consultation with your medical professionals. I emphasise that this isn't a prescriptive list. Rather, it is descriptive, simply sharing a few of my current health habits.

1. I avoid soya products.

2. I have significantly reduced my intake of sugar. My preferred sweeteners are molasses, dates and honey.

3. Currently, over 60% of my diet is organic.

4. I consistently eat nutrient-rich foods such as sunflower, flax, chia and pumpkin seeds, raw cacao, turmeric (taken with black pepper to increase bioavailability) wheat grass juice powder, moringa powder, black rice and quinoa.

5. I eat collagen (supported by vitamin C to increase bioavailability) to support the health of my skin, nails and hair.

6. I pay attention to food labels looking out for glucose and unhealthy additives usually highlighted by tongue twister words that I struggle to pronounce.

7. My main form of hydration is water.

8. I take multivitamins and minerals as a food

supplement; vitamin D since I live in London, UK and I don't get enough sunlight, especially in the Winter months. I also take bio cultures with 50 billion CFU to support my gut health.

My next major health goal is to use Inclined Bed Therapy. I will do it by buying bed raisers that will lift the top part of my bed by six inches, which will create a five degrees incline. The proposed benefits are improvements in indigestion (food breakdown), assimilation (food absorption) and elimination (getting rid of waste).

Health decisions are usually made in keeping with the many factors that influence lifestyle changes such as prevailing health concerns, availability of resources, values and others. Whatever changes you make for them to be lasting, they must be made from a place of information, confidence, patience and hope. If not, you will experience conscious and or unconscious resistance. Healthy food needs to be twinned with healthy exercise.

Exercise

No matter how healthy the food is that we eat, without a reasonable level of exercise and consistent mobility, its full capacity will not be maximised. Catherine Geissler and Hilary Powers state:

> *Physical fitness need not be the exclusive domain of the sports person and there is now a wealth of evidence that exercise makes an important contribution to good health and helps to reduce the risk of chronic diseases such as cardiovascular disease and cancer.*

They suggest that exercise needs to be a regular part of our lives at every stage of our lives. It has been recommended to engage in at least 30 minutes of exercise every day. Suitable and adequate exercise can be done by jogging, running, weight lifting, swimming, walking and many others. Exercise has many benefits such as improved sleep, helps to burn calories from the food we eat and can help us to maintain our desired body weight. It also helps to release serotonin, 'happy hormones' that make people feel good. Exercise should be chosen based on personal preferences, health conditions, resources available and the objective of the particular exercise.

Aging with Vitality and Radiance

Aging is inevitable. However, Dr. Michael F. Roizen and Dr. Mehmet C. Oz state that the pace of our aging is directly related to the lifestyle choices we make, especially in the areas of fitness, nutrition and skin care. The aging process isn't an unmanned skating board rolling speedily downhill with us helplessly looking on as the pending crash unfolds. As women we can have a high quality of life throughout our entire lives; albeit to varying degrees. The truth is no matter how anointed we are, if our bodies, minds and emotions are not in good condition, it will impact our focus and capacity to extend our impact. Ill-health is distracting and sapping and will affect the allocation of your time, energy and money. It's possible to live a long healthy and impactful life. Let's think of how beneficial a healthier version of ourselves can be to the kingdom of God, our family, friends, nation and the world.

Declining health as we age is not a given. In fact, we can get healthier as we age as we become more informed and committed to the principles of health. We don't have to limp our way to the finishing line of life. We can get there with health and vigour. Even though we are women of faith, we are also 'workers' because faith without work is dead; of absolutely no effect.

Aging occurs at the cellular level. Drs. Roizen and Oz recommend that it's crucial that we engage in recovering and repairing our body systems as we inevitably age as this is a deciding factor. However, the external factors that impact the aging process must also be simultaneously managed in order to achieve maximum results. For example, how are we managing our exposure to UV rays, stress, sleep patterns, and other lifestyle changes such as exercise? As was previously mentioned, it's wise that we protect our health from the inside and outside. If we are A-star on the internal frontier, but the external frontier is neglected, this is to the detriment of our health and the rate of our aging.

Little health problems here and there have a compounding effect over time. So, by no means should we ignore the small health problems because they aren't really debilitating. Think of the stacking effect when one illness is stacked unto another; referred to as co-morbidity. We've all experienced health issues. A significant percentage of the rate at which we age is within the scope of our day-to-day choices. Largely, the rate of our aging is in our hands. Our health decisions without fail will determine the quality of our lives.

Mental Wellbeing

Since the lockdown arising from the pandemic, loneliness, depression and suicidal thinking are on the increase across all age groups. This results in physiological changes in the body. Brené Brown, social researcher aptly says, "In the absence of love and belonging, there is suffering." Mental anguish. And oh, how some of us have suffered. Self-care is vital in every facet of wellbeing. Treat yourself like royalty. Treat yourself like the beloved princess Jesus died for. Treat yourself like a lady that is of infinite value. Treat yourself like the possessor of much worth; worthy of a second chance, worthy of forgiveness. Treat yourself as the creative value producer that you are. It's unreasonable to expect others to treat you better than you are willing to invest and treat yourself! Love thyself. Put on your oxygen mask first.

Let's pause to pray the *Serenity Prayer*:

> *God, grant me the serenity to accept the things I cannot change. Courage to change the things I can, and the wisdom to know the difference. Living one day at a time. Enjoying one moment at a time. Accepting hardship as the pathway to peace. Taking, as He did, this sinful world as it is, not as I would have it. Trusting that He will make all things right if I surrender to His will. That I may be reasonably happy in this life, and supremely happy with Him forever in the next. Amen.*

Now pause with me for a while and ponder the implication of this truth...how are we providing love and belonging for our spouse, children, employees, business customers, church members, teammates, community members, 'tribe' and even the very person we are meeting for the very first time! Remember without love and belonging, everyone, no exception, experiences suffering. Let's volunteer to go on a mission as love ambassadors to others; especially to those who are hurting. Enlist today.

Being Fully Present

On my first holiday from Jamaica to London in 1996, I asked a flight attendant if I could be shown the cockpit. That was before 9/11 when such a request was considered normal. The main thing that left an indelible impression on my mind is that the pilot, Matthew, was able to have a conversation with me while everything, at that point, was being accomplished in autopilot mode! Could it be that like Matthew, the pilot, we are accomplishing a lot, but we are still on autopilot mode. How much of our lives are on autopilot mode? What would we become and achieve if we were to learn to become more present with whatever we do? Learning the skill and having the consciousness of recognising the condition of our internal and external states are vital. How would our marriages, friendships, businesses, continuous learning, churches, communities, personal worship change if we were to become more aware and fully present in our lives?

At the basic level, we experience our world through our senses. Through the power of the Holy Spirit, intuition and discernment, we can have access to a greater realm of awareness. Being intentional about focusing on our present moments would radically change our lives. We would feel more, connect deeper, rise higher and learn more. When we move from automatic mode to intentional living and being fully present, new portals of awareness open up and bring us into a space of greater depth and possibly better quality choices. Our minds are vital tools for wellbeing. Hence, they need special care including rest and good food. With greater consciousness and deliberate focus and attention, our everyday routine activities of life can become enriched by us being fully present and enjoying and feeling the moment. Suddenly, the everyday activities can be transformed into oceans of creative experiences such as cooking, feeding a child, taking a shower, eating, walking, singing, praising and speaking. We then become the master of how we choose to respond to our experiences. We are then better able to label our feelings and emotions. As a result, we would be better able to articulate and notice our triggers. This heightened level of awareness would help to transform our relationships.

Relational Wellbeing

Healthy relationships lead to greater fulfilment and significance. One of the many deceptions Satan uses on women, is that he tricks us into believing that we can't get along with other women! Often, you'll hear a woman make the comment, "I get along better with men than women". Consequently, they consciously and unconsciously repel other women; instead of being their mutual buddy and cheerleader. Words can't adequately capture the remarkable blessings that other women can bring to our lives! Ask God for divine connections with women (and men too) that will inspire you to become a better reigning woman and committed citizen of the kingdom of God!

The Holy Spirit will assist you in discerning the people who belong in your life. Inviting the wrong people into our lives is the deadliest mistake we can ever make! I can truly say that my life has been significantly enhanced by some ace women from all over the world. Alas, I also know the pain of deep injury from my own gender too. The power of relationship capital can't be over-estimated. Therefore, let's not allow relational wounds by anyone; whether males or females to allow us to go to the extreme of cheating ourselves of the wonders of beautiful friendships. They are worth the while, I promise you! As such, let's invest in our growth and development that will equip us to bring our A+ game to others in sacred friendships. John and Stasi Eldredge assert that:

> *Friendship is a great gift. One to be prayed for and not taken for granted. If you don't have the kind of friendship you long for, ask God to bring it into your life, to give you eyes to recognise it when [H]e does. When God gives a friend, [H]e is entrusting us with the care of another's heart. It's a chance...to be a Lifegiver, to help someone else become the [person they were] created to be... Friendships need to be nurtured and guarded and fought for.*

By the way, let's not be too quick to say, "ashes to ashes and dust to dust" over all our broken friendships. Could it be that the bare trees that you see, are friendships' Winter waiting for the warmth of Spring? Could it be that this friendship is simply gone to sleep, and when it's rested it will awaken at dawn? But no matter what, we should rejoice, celebrate and be grateful for all God's gifts called friends.

Environmental Declutter

It is without question that our environments affect everything about us! They impact our mental state, emotions, moods, capacity to think, self-esteem, relationships and even future possibilities. Therefore, it's vital that we do everything possible to improve the quality and harmony of our environments. One of the main ways to gain environmental wellbeing is to declutter. Clutter is a reflection of a state of mind than it is even about the physical surroundings. Where there is clutter and disorganization, there usually silent stress, chaos, time wasting, underutilisation of that which can't be found, increased spending to buy that which is already owned and possibly some level of shame.

If clutter gets to the extreme, it may even lead to social isolation and social phobia; not wanting anyone to see the state of our surroundings. The list is almost endless regarding the negatives of an unhealthy environment. So, let's declutter, physically, mentally, emotionally and even relationally. This will make room for space, beauty, harmony, peace and mindful living.

Ill-health... Enough is Enough!

There comes a point in every woman's life when she has to make an "enough is enough" declaration and be prepared to make some bold moves. If you don't disrupt the status quo, you become nothing, do nothing and have nothing! As you reign, are your hopes and dreams being hijacked by disruptions to your wellbeing? I can hear many answers in the affirmative. I have been there, struggling with health problems can be very debilitating but our stories don't have to end there. God's healing can be so comprehensive that you have to really try to remember what you have been through. God's healing ushers in freedom! Beloved sisters, it's time we get our health back!

There was a woman in Luke 8: 43-48 who had a major health issue; she was bleeding constantly. Some women can relate to this woman only too well. This means she was very tired and her hair, skin and nails would not have been at their best. In addition,due to the nature of her condition, she was at the fringes of society and her relationships would have been strained because of the isolation. But she had simply been around her health mountain long enough (for twelve long years) and was sick and tired. She needed deliverance. She had spent every penny she had and was still sick. As such, this woman who wasn't even given a name in the Scriptures, strategized for her healing. Even though she was very tired and was still bleeding, she dared greatly. She pressed through the crowd and touched Jesus. What an audacious faith!

She knew she was breaking the rules by being in the crowd in her bleeding state. But she knew that what the doctors could not do, Jesus could…with just one touch! And so, she touched Him and she was made whole immediately. In one moment, she shattered the imprisonment of societal norms and got her healing. Jesus is the transformer and lifter of women! She went for healing but she also got comfort and was called "daughter". When a woman is rightly aligned to the Fatherhood of Christ, it's a big deal. It ushers that which is transformational into your life and it marks and moves you. Do you know who your Daddy is? What is in our lives that we need to decide to touch Jesus? Jesus is passing your way right now. Capitalise on the "fierce urgency of now"! Let's touch Him.

WELLBEING TRANSFORMATION STRATEGIES

1. Let's not be strangled by the negatives of our past. Repent and accept the forgiveness (and give it too) that comes only in Jesus Christ. This wholeness of the soul is the foundation for our general wellbeing.

2. As was mentioned in Chapter 2 on Worship, practise a lifestyle of prayer, fasting, and the Word which has a positive effect on wellbeing.

3. Choose the best quality food that is possible in your situation and be intentional with your food combinations and timing of meals.

4. Get adequate good quality sleep and rest. If you are struggling with insomnia, a sleep journal is more about using the art of journaling to clear your mind of clutter and allowing sleep to come. You might notice patterns emerging that allow you to adjust your life to improve your mental health and your sleep. Seek medical intervention, if needed.

5. Ensure you get adequate sunlight and intentionally spend time outdoors.

6. Take time for silence and meditation.

7. Prioritise your health. Pay keen attention to food labels looking out for preservatives and additives.

8. In spite of the lockdown due to Covid-19, we must deliberately seek opportunities to connect with other people. Since face-to-face contacts are restricted, let's think of creative ways of keeping in touch. For example, instead of making regular telephone calls to those we would love to meet up with, we could make video calls so that there is a seeing element to the contact, rather than only the hearing dimension.

9. Be intentional in creating beautiful moments of wonder befitting the royalty that you. Schedule

recreation that brings you joy and delight. Be intentional in preserving these moments; a picture, a stone, a piece of jewellery, a signed note, a card, a potted plant, a dried flower...whatever. Let's ensure when we have collected our memorabilia to help us savour the moments of wonder, let's not bury them in boxes and cupboards where they are out of sight and often out of mind. Instead, put them where they can be seen, enjoyed and continue to inspire us to go create more moments of wonder.

10. Consistently do routine check-ups such as mammograms, eye testing, cervical smears, glucose levels and vital body functioning. It is important that we do our due diligence in researching and consulting with the relevant medical and other professionals concerning our health. Depending on where you live and what your health needs are, ensure that you have adequate medical insurance for yourself and your family.

11. Set SMART (Specific, Measurable, Attainable, Realistic and Timebound) wellbeing goals (Record your priority goal).

12. Become committed or even more committed to serving others, especially the less fortunate. Generosity is life- giving.

13. Make a conscious effort to be respectful of the environment in ways such as recycling, practise water conservation and shop locally, where possible. As we live in dominion we

ought also to seek to live in harmony with the rest of creation.

Our wellbeing is like a plant, it requires watering and nurturing. If we put our health on automatic self-care mode, it will not work. Soon we will find our health becoming broken not in spite of what we are doing to maintain our health (that does happen at times) but because of neglect. Our mental, physical and emotional health need consistent care in order to thrive.

One of the prerequisites of reigning in the ultimate dimension of wonder is being healthy enough to do so. Good health is invigorating. It transforms and impacts all other areas of life. Your health is the track on which every other area of your life runs. It is much harder and in some cases near impossible if you, when it's within your power to do so, neglect and impair your health. Invest time, energy, money and love in attaining the highest level of health within your reach.

Health is a great wealth capital. If we don't give our bodies the attention they need, we will regret the consequences later. Nowadays, we want everything fast and easy. And when it comes to food, we usually make the wrong choices when we depend so much on things we can order at a click of a button. Let's choose healthy and natural food that's good for our body and soul. Exercise and engage in activities that will contribute to your physical, mental and emotional wellbeing.

Let health transformation be intentional, sustainable and consistent. Build a healthy version of a life that is possible, building a strong foundation, brick by brick, one healthy habit at a time. Wellbeing and health transformation start from the inside out. There is no point in adding a lot of expensive lotions and potions externally, if our internal health is neglected or given a half-hearted attempt to experience the transformation in our health that is possible and that which we can do. The inner healthy you are then able to create the outer healthy you. And the overall healthy you then in turn are in a position to chart the course of creating a healthier life in general.

WELLBEING TRANSFORMATION TASK

1. In terms of the Reigning Dimensions regarding *Wellbeing,* where are you? (Tick one)

Wonder ☐   Winning ☐   Waning ☐   Wandering ☐

2. Develop a Wellbeing Declaration: Eg. I am aging gracefully and I am in the best health of my life!

_____

_____

3. Which of the Wellbeing Transformation Strategies would give you the maximum impact now?

_____

_____

4. Set a SMART (Specific, Measurable, Attainable, Realistic and Time-bound) wellbeing goal.

_____

_____

5. Motivation: Why is this goal important to you?

_____

_____

_____

6. Accountability: Which person or system will hold you accountable?

_____

7. Review Date:

_____

8. Reward: How will you celebrate achieving this goal?

_____
_____

Chapter Six
Transformation Agent #6
WARM-HEARTEDNESS

"Warmth, kindness, and friendship are the
most yearned for commodities in the world.
The person who can provide them will never be lonely."

Ann Landers

A glowing fire was started by only a spark. Your warmth is that spark that will cause amazing things to happen for yourself and others. Your warmth is the fragrance of your servant's heart that is saturated by divine love. This quality makes an individual loving and lovable. Warm-heartedness ought to be a permanent code of conduct because if ever a time that we must be intentional about exhibiting consistent warmth, it's now when the world is gripped by a pandemic-induced social distancing and what feels like the prison bars of personal protective equipment. With gloves, masks and space firmly in place; things we took for granted- to touch and be touched, to speak and be clearly understood, to hug and be hugged, to smile and be seen to be smiling, are all now feats! The world all over would do well with some warmth! But what is the temperature in your world? You have the thermostat in your hand, turn it up!

On New Year's Eve 2021, I was already snuggled up in my warm bed when I got a call from my beloved brother, Richard, saying that he would be coming over. I was rather happy, so I went downstairs, to await his arrival. On reaching downstairs I realised that the temperature had dropped. It wasn't warm and cozy like I was feeling under my duvet. So, I turned on the heating. When he arrived, we had tea and the usual laughter. After some time, he suggested that I put the heating at a set temperature and keep it on consistently rather than turning it onas and when needed.

In surprise, I asked him if he wasn't warm enough and he assured me that he was (because if I were warm enough it means that everyone else would be warm enough too) since my ideal temperature is usually most people's sauna. He said he could tell by the frost on the skylight portion of the kitchen roof that the temperature wasn't consistent. Can you imagine that the air in the house was warm enough, but the skylight wasn't satisfied with the amount of warmth it was getting! Wow. How insightful. I have since acted on his advice and what difference it has made.

In a similar manner, everyone that enters our lives will know the difference between a woman that is consistently kind and affectionate and one who have just turned up the 'charm temperature' just for the moment! The observant will know. Let's all ask ourselves, are we consistently warm-hearted to everyone we meet, or are we 'turning it on' as a reaction? As the skylight gave away the fact that my heating wasn't on for a long time, what is revealing that our friendliness, curtesy, kindness, compassion, joy and magnetism aren't our 'lifestyle temperature'?

Let's look closely at where we are in the warm-heartedness dimensions…

Warm-heartedness Dimensions of Reigning

• 1D Reigning: Wandering

1D warm-heartedness is a wandering way to live. Thus, surrendering the capacity to reign that will be impactful. Being closed, resistant and withdrawn is the 'coldest' manner in which to live. Although sometimes people may appear withdrawn, it's not because they aren't necessarily warm-hearted; but because they don't know how to respond to warm-hearted interactions. They don't know what being likable looks and feels like. And since it's hard to build a rapport where there is very little trust, they may give the impression of wanting to be left alone. Consequently, they struggle to give and receive love and kindness. And as such, they feel safer to simply withdraw and become closed. It could also be that there are unresolved issues which are creating the blockage to the friendliness that is possible. In some cultures, random acts of kindness can be met with much suspicious or outright rejection.

However, whatever is causing barriers to being warm-hearted, we are one decision away from becoming the God-ordained 4D wonder version of ourselves which gloriously showcases the divine nature of the King!

• 2D Reigning: Waning

The friendliness and happiness of the 2D warm- hearted woman have deteriorated and she is characterised by moodiness. Therefore, the manner in which she interacts with people is largely determined by what mood she is in. Everyone needs and desires to be treated with consistent respect and compassion. Consistently, having evident mood swings makes a woman unpredictable. People don't know how to interact with us since they have no idea what mood we will be in.

This 'see-saw living' prevents a woman from truly living a values-centred life where the standards act like an anchor and compass for living. A reactionary life is rather disempowering. Life is now the case of if people are agreeable and the circumstances favourable then the positive version of the individual shows up. Vice versa. The influence is being greatly exerted on them rather than they influencing those around them. They are usually not strong leaders and trend-setters due to their significant mood swings. The temperature in their environments is like a moving swing up and down. Moodiness is a reactive way to live.

• 3D Reigning: Winning

A 3D warm-hearted woman is committed to winning. She is polite and friendly. This is why the warm-hearted 4D woman of wonder stands out head and shoulder above the crowd! Sometimes you get the "Hi, are you alright?" greeting, and you know that it's primarily a formality; not necessarily a heartfelt genuine care. In 3D warm-heartedness, women are friendly enough. But only just enough. It doesn't have the depth of compassion and the commitment to love no matter what.

Another distinction between 4D and 3D warm-heartedness is that the former loves and does goodwill to all; exerting much effort to be inclusive as a 'love ambassador'! The latter may be selective of those she extends her care to. In addition, her sense of 'reaching out' is not that intentional and inclusive as the woman of wonder.

• 4D Reigning: Wonder

Being a wonder, a 4D warm-hearted woman is amazing to behold and experience! Women who are diligent in their wellbeing are more likely to be able to operate at this 4D in the warm-heartedness division as a lifestyle by design. Your personal health, quality of relationships and self-image have a huge effect on the affection that is displayed in the world! Well-being supports 'warmth-being'.

When a woman genuinely loves people, she becomes irresistibly magnetic. Hence, people are generally attracted to her! She creates a positive magnetic pull with consistent warmth; not an on and off unpredictable version! This woman is on a mission to be God's 'love ambassador' as is described in 1 Corinthians 13. She is aware that without love she is absolutely nothing. Without love, we are all reduced to noise.

A 4D warm-hearted woman has a pleasant 'sound'; certainly not noise! Just as Jesus wept in John 11:35, she is also deeply touched by the realities around her. Her heart is a wellspring of compassion for everyone in her environment. In keeping with the strand of *contribution* in the Reigning DNA, she is always ready to be a distribution channel to people who are in need. She is certainly not a proverbial 'ivory tower'. She is ever so willing to go beyond her comfort zone to extend the touch of God to all.

The 4D woman who exudes throne room grace, love and mercy. She may say the very same words like others, but she exemplifies a deep compassion and genuine care. She is a rare brand of God's transformational touch! With 2D, one minute you're happy and the next minute you're cold. This is why joy in the 4D level is a state of mind and decision; whilst happiness is largely based on what our circumstances are.

There's nothing quite like when a woman knows her God, is strong, exudes confidence and has divine joy. She is likable, good-natured, peaceful and courteous. Consequently, no matter the looks of her physical features, something about a warm-hearted woman of wonder makes her an absolute knockout to both men and women, boys and girls, friends and foes!

DIVINE NATURE

Our behaviour is always in alignment with whatever is enthroned in our hearts. Godly women are conscious that they are mandated to be salt and light in a world that would certainly benefit from some flavour and light; not to mention preservation! Their mindset and deportment are consistently in keeping with their royal status. The 4D woman of wonder uses Jesus Christ as her perfect template to both experience and exemplify His divine nature. Let's briefly examine the divine nature of God to be informed about the depth and character of warm-heartedness.

The Nature of God

- God is Light. 1 John 1:5

- God is a Spirit. John 4:24

Page 190

- God is love. 1 John 4:8

- The Lord is Peace. Judges 6:24

- The heavenly Father is perfect. Matthew 5:48

- He is the anointed Holy One. 1 John 2:20

- Holy, Holy, Holy, is the Lord of hosts. Isaiah 6:3

- God is compassionate, gracious, longsuffering, merciful and truthful. (Psalm 86:15)

- The Lord is slow to anger and is good to all! Psalm 145:8-9

- Great is God's faithfulness. Lamentations 3:22-23

This list makes us realise that the mandate to be warm-hearted carries a weight of demand that can't be executed by a light commitment in the flesh. "Be ye therefore followers of God, as dear children; And walk in love, as Christ also hath loved us" (Ephesians 5:1-2). It can only be consistently and satisfactorily done when we are soaked in the anointing of the Holy Spirit. It's a call to look like Jesus through and through. Being warm-hearted isn't about being just a 'nice woman' or having a certain personality. It's for everyone. And it requires that we know the love of Christ beyond mere head knowledge and to be filled with all the fullness of God (Ephesians 3:19)!

In light of the divine nature of God, we ought to be filled with the Spirit of the Lord, compassionate, merciful, gracious, faithful, in control of our emotions, longsuffering, holy, peaceful, gentle, light carriers, loving…truthful. Wow! The reigning woman models well the sweetness of surrender and service! Only God Himself can make us this 4D brand of reigning women. Our best efforts will fail. We need therefore to make our minds up that we will yield our lives totally to Christ and do whatever it takes to allow Him to work in and through us; transforming us daily to be more like Him.

Let's observe a selah moment and pray. O blessed Lord, turn up Your reigning temperature in my life. Take away every trace of inconsistency, moodiness and whatever else that mars Your glory in me. Lord, help me to be totally led by Your Spirit and infused with Your love. Father grant me the grace not to be weary in doing that which is pleasing to You, because You are the God that neither slumber nor sleep and nor is there any shadow of turning in You. Let it be O Mighty God that the 'flag' of righteousness is flying high from the castle of my heart; declaring that You, the King, is in residence there! Hear my heart's cry. In Jesus' name. Amen.

Positive Mental Attitude

A positive mental attitude is having a strong sense of optimism and confidence; especially in difficult times. It's the habit and attitude of seeing the glass half full, rather than half empty. A positive mental attitude doesn't exclude a balanced measure of reality. Rather, it refuses to be stuck in the doom and gloom that so many get caught up in.

It's often said that, "Your attitude determines your altitude." If this is the case and it is, we must urgently detox all our bad attitudes and replace them with great ones. To allow attitude toxins to take over our lives is to sabotage our transformation, derail our impact and damage our reign! Let's identify attitude toxins and purge them from our lives. Here are 7 major toxins:

Dealing with Attitude Toxins

1. Indecision

Not to decide is indeed a decision. We might as well make up our minds. If not, they will drift aimlessly without a target. This evening a gentleman boarded the bus. He was spoilt for choices for empty seats to occupy; since we are having a third lockdown in England. And as such, it's mainly key workers who are still out and about. So, as he stood there in the valley of indecision to simply choose a seat, the only thing he was achieving was being tossed about by the movement of the bus!

Similarly, while we take forever to make up our minds, the world is on the move just like the bus! Everything is on the move, which includes our spouse, children, job, parents, business, friends, community, church...ideas. Let's make up our minds. Now.

This is not the same as hasty and unwise decision-making. However, forever is not given to anyone to decide. Make a decision. Your 'bus' is moving. "But let him ask in faith, nothing wavering. For he that wavereth is like a wave of the sea driven with the wind and tossed. For let not that man think that he shall receive any thing of the Lord. A double minded man is unstable in all his ways" (James 1:6-8).

2. Constant Criticism and Complaining

If we've become criticism and complaining specialists, it's time to change our lens! There are so many wonders in the world, including ourselves, life is too short to be stuck on finding faults. We are alive, there is a roof over our heads, food in our cupboards, we have our brothers and sisters…and above all a God that promises never to leave us. What's there to constantly criticise and complain about? I will pause to acknowledge that there are millions who are really struggling; some homeless, bereaved, hungry and all sorts. So, we respectfully empathise.

Therefore, even more so, we are the change that needs to happen about the things that gripe us and to lend a helping hand to those who need it! We are change-agents and wonders with impactful solutions. Let's be transformed and stop our pointless criticism and complaining and go change our world! "Do all things without murmurings and disputings: That ye may be blameless and harmless, the sons of God, without rebuke, in the midst of a crooked and perverse nation, among whom ye shine as lights in the world" (Philippians 2:14-15).

3. Insecurity and Jealousy

Do you know who God has called you to be and who He says you are? If you can answer yes, it means you have absolutely no reason to be unsure of yourself and envious of others. So, let's stop making pointless comparisons. It will either inflate, deflate or stagnate us! It serves no good. "For we dare not make ourselves of the number, or compare ourselves with some that commend themselves: but they measuring themselves by themselves, and comparing themselves among themselves, are not wise" (2 Corinthians 10:12).

4. Revengeful

We are not omniscient, hence can't rightly execute justice. Let's take our hands off the 'R' which belongs to God only (revenge), and let's focus on the 'R' for our Reign. Revenge is crippling and distracting. Let God be God, let

Him take over our cases and we put our heads on the soft pillows, while we allow God to do His job. "Dearly beloved, avenge not yourselves, but rather give place unto wrath: for it is written, vengeance is mine; I will repay, saith the Lord" (Romans 12:19).

5. Fearful

Fear is popularly referred to as "False Evidence Appearing Real." Every area of life involves some degree of taking risks. Whether in business, relationships, health decisions, or as simple as getting on a plane, requires pushing past our comfort zones and reaching beyond. Our desired results and rewards are usually located beyond our comfort zone and in the stretch zone. Fear is a sabotaging and paralysing spirit. Let's cast it down and drive it out. And let's go forward and take some informed risks. Just jump, our wings will emerge during the flight! "For God hath not given us the spirit of fear; but of power, and of love, and of a sound mind" (Timothy 1:7).

6. Resisting Change

One of the only things which is certain in life is change. Therefore, to be resistant to needful changes without a rhyme nor a reason and most of all without a better solution is exhibiting a toxic attitude. "Behold, I will do a new thing; now it shall spring forth; shall ye not know it? I will even make a way in the wilderness, and rivers in the desert" (Isaiah 43:19).

7. Blaming

This is relieving yourself from being responsible for a fault or a mistake. When we assign blame to another, we give away our personal power to that which we blame. It's like sitting in a rocking chair but it gets us nowhere. Always remember that we are one hundred percent responsible for the quality of our lives. Listen how woeful blaming is and sounds... "And the man [Adam] said, the woman whom thou gavest to be with me, she gave me of the tree, and I did eat. And the Lord God said unto the woman [Eve], What is this that thou hast done? And the woman said, the serpent beguiled me, and I did eat" (Genesis 3:12-13).

Instead of displaying attitude toxins, let's embrace great attitudes for which we'll be tremendously blessed!

Great Attitudes for Impact and Blessings

In the sermon on the Mount in Matthew 5: 3-12, Jesus outlined the transformational Beatitudes that should characterise the lives of all believers! The *'Be Attitudes'* are remarkable lifestyle principles which guarantee that women (and men too) will exude divine warmth and give them a strong platform from which to reign! A poor attitude equals a poor reign; and the suffering of the people in our sphere of influence. Great attitudes equal great blessings both for *now* and throughout *eternity*!

The Beatitudes

ATTITUDES	MEANINGS	BLESSINGS
1. Poor in spirit	To have a servant's heart and to honour and prefer others.	Possessing the kingdom of heaven.
2. Purposeful mourning	Responding with deep emotions for the loss, hurt, and mistakes for yourself and others.	Receive comfort and cheer.

3. Meekness	Being humble and will adjust and sacrifice to serve others; not prideful.	Inheriting the earth.
4. Hunger and thirst after righteousness	Aiming wholeheartedly to do God's perfect will according to His perfect Words.	Being filled and satisfied with the righteousness of Christ.
5. Merciful	Not quick to execute punishment nor condemn; rather isgracious and forgiving.	Obtaining mercy.
6. Pure in heart	Look at things through God's eyes and think the best of others.	Seeing, experiencingand being like God!
7. Peacemakers	Isn't quarrelsomeand will do whatever it takes to seek peace and pursue it (Psalm 34:14).	Being called the children of God.
8. Persecuted for righteousness' sake	Is persistent in doing the right thing. Isn't easily put off from being and doing good!	Inheriting the kingdom of heaven. Having extravagant joy and gladness!

Fruit Check, Fruit Check; 1 2 3

Consistent genuine warm-heartedness is an ever-green evidence in a woman's life when the Fruit of the Spirit is present. "But the fruit of the Spirit is love, joy, peace, longsuffering, gentleness, goodness, faith, meekness, temperance: against such there is no law" (Galatians 5:22-23). Take note of how similar the Fruit of the Spirit is to the divine nature of God! Likewise, notice that love is first on the list of the aspects of the Fruit of the Spirit. "This is my commandment, that ye love one another, as I have loved you. Greater love hath no man than this, that a man lay down his life for his friends. Ye are my friends, if ye do whatsoever I command you" (John 15: 12-14). In addition, meekness and peace are both Beatitudes and parts of the Fruit of the Spirit!

Having the Fruit of the Spirit isn't optional, it's a requirement. Jesus' severe reaction to a barren fig tree in Luke 13:6-9 should make us realise that not having the Fruit of the Spirit in its fullness shouldn't be taken lightly! Jesus strongly dislikes barrenness. Consequently, His expectation of every living thing (of which we are the apex of His creation), is that it bears fruit. Mankind has the mandate to reign and have dominion. Jesus cursed the fig tree that wasn't bearing fruit as was expected. Will He ignore it if we are devoid of the essential life-transforming Fruit of the Spirit? Absolutely not. "Herein is my Father glorified, that ye bear much fruit; so shall ye be my disciples" (John 15:8). The Father is glorified when we bring forth fruit that showcases Him, the indwelling King! And the most excellent way and greatest evidence of transformation is love!

Vulnerability: Courage to Love

Will we take the plunge and choose to love? The fear of failing, getting hurt, or being rejected can be crippling. To love deeply and effectively requires vulnerability. As we continue in the love of Christ, we must intentionally give love to everyone, but especially to those who are hurting! As we are unique, so is our perception of what it feels like to be loved most effectively. We all have a preference in the way we desire to be loved. For some, this truth is still unrecognised.

The longing for connection is a universal desire in the heart of everyone; there is no exception. The why, how and wherefore may differ, but we all long to belong to somewhere and someone. It takes great and fierce faith to 'walk across the room' with a decision in your heart to love someone. It takes courage. It presents the possibility of huge risk but also huge rewards. Brené Brown in her book, *Daring Greatly*, states forthrightly the consequences of not daring to be vulnerable:

> *When we spend our lives waiting until we are perfect or bulletproof before we walk into the arena, we ultimately sacrifice relationships and opportunities that may not be recoverable, we squander our precious time, and we turn our backs on our gifts, those unique contributions that only we can make.*

In attempting to love, to try to eliminate the possibilities of all pain, disappointments, sadness, loss and sorrow, is a futile effort. These and other emotions can convert themselves into different disguises that will squeeze through the cracks and windows, while we are busy closing the door on our feelings. In addition, as we attempt to close the doors to that which we perceive as negative emotions, we will simultaneously close the door to love, joy, delight, anticipation and all that is sweet. Corrie ten Boom in her masterpiece 'The Hiding Place' said:

> *Do you know what hurts so very much? It's love. Love is the strongest force in the world, and when it is blocked that means pain. There are two things we can do when this happens. We can kill that love so that it stops hurting. But then of course part of us dies, too. Or we*

can ask God to open up another route for that love to travel.

We need all the multifaceted sides of the emotion coin to truly feel, truly have and give compassion. Be prepared to love even the unlovely. They need our love the most. What is the point in loving only those who are lovely and who love us in return? Being active participants in the ministry of reconciliation requires grit and commitment; loving and serving against the odds and opposition. What if a hurting 1D woman who is cold, withdrawn and distant is awaiting your 4D heart of warmth and cheer? Emmet Fox insightfully captures the power of love when he said,

> *There is no difficulty that enough LOVE will not conquer, no disease that enough LOVE will not heal, no door that enough LOVE will not open, no gulf that enough LOVE will not bridge, no wall that enough LOVE will not throw down, no sin that enough LOVE will not redeem.*

It is no wonder that God Himself is love! If only we could take the risk to love ourselves and every living thing purely and deeply, more than half of what ails us would dissolve and we would live in divine and triumphant power! Deciding to share the warmth and compassion of your soul may be risky, but it is well worth it.

Are You Feeling My Love?

It is one thing to know that we should love people and even make the effort to do so, but it's a very different thing if people feel loved by our efforts. Dr. Gary Chapman's epic work called the Five Love Languages, has completely revolutionized the relationship space. It may be viewed as being empowered to love with Emotional Intelligence and with greater accuracy. The greater our self-awareness is in any area of life; it has a compounding effect that improves all other areas of life. It is wise to heed the instruction to make every effort to intimately know ourselves. As a result, we are better able to love ourselves and teach others to do the same. And if everyone invested time, energy and effort to intentionally and intelligently love our spouse, children, grandchildren, teammates, employees, church brethren, neighbours and others, what a world this would be!

The 5 Love Languages are as follows:

1. Words of affirmation: Affirming individuals with words.

2. Receiving gifts: These individuals feel particularly loved by receiving gifts.

3. Quality time: Give these persons special attention; which takes time to do.

4. Physical touch: For these individuals, appropriate touch connects and speaks volumes.

5. Acts of Service: Show these people love, not so much as telling them.

Everyone receives love in a blend of all five languages but to varying degrees. However, everyone has what Dr. Gary Chapman calls a "Primary Love Language". My primary love language is "Words of Affirmation". It is almost 15% ahead of my second-place love language, which is "Quality Time". This insight has been transformational! Not knowing your Love Language has grave implications. For example, if my best friends consistently buy gifts for me but hardly ever say kind words, I wouldn't feel loved even though they are going to great lengths to love me. Love for me is spelt, "Words of Affirmation". Even though I appreciate gifts, for me to feel loved, affirming words are what make my heart sings. Think of children that you know are struggling, do we know their love language? If not, how then can we deeply love them, inspire them and effectively help them on their own journey of transformation?

Dr. Gary Chapman has made available Love Language quizzes for singles, couples, children, teens, men and the military. He also provides an Apology Language quiz. The full details of these tools can provide much value in our quest for transformation and becoming women of wonder with great impact.

The Gift of Forgiveness

Nothing dampens the warmth of love quite like unresolved issues and mounting resentment from unhealed hurts. Nothing. Unforgiveness will either turn our souls into blocks of ice or raging infernos; neither of which is befitting of reigning women! As we navigate the field of love and endeavour to sow love's hopeful seed, it is without fail, that we will fail and wound the very people we want to love the most. For the flowers of love to consistently bloom, we must be diligent in uprooting the weeds of hurt, disappointment, abuse and betrayal. If this isn't done, the weeds will, over time, choke the tender plants of love; leaving them sapped of all the nutrients needed for them to flourish.

Every day we must decide if we will nurture love or will nurture unforgiveness. We don't get to do both. They are equally powerful forces; the former for good and the latter for evil. No matter the hurt, we ought not to let our brokenness break us. We will forgive, do the hard work of healing, and will, with the engagement of the will, let it go. As we have been graciously forgiven, we commit to doing likewise. It is often said, "Forgiveness is a gift we give ourselves more than it is that which we give to others." Unforgiveness is a prison that will gladly award a life sentence to our souls. Today is our parole date; the day of our freedom. Let's pray as it is recorded in Matthew 6:9-15:

> *Our Father which art in heaven, hallowed be thy name. Thy kingdom come, Thy will be done in earth, as it is in heaven. Give us this day our daily bread. And forgive us our debts, as we forgive our debtors. And lead us not into temptation, but deliver us from evil: For thine is the kingdom, and the power, and the glory, forever. Amen. For if ye forgive men their trespasses, your heavenly Father will also forgive you: But if ye forgive not men their trespasses, neither will your Father forgive your trespasses.*

Lord today, I deeply acknowledge that forgiveness is part of Your will. As such, I choose to forgive, myself and others, as You have lavishly forgiven me! I will obey Your instruction to forgive. I refused to be strangled and defiled by bitterness (Hebrews 12:15). Forgiveness is the fertilizer for love. I chose to love and be free.

Loving the Invisible Through the Visible

We are told in Matthew 25:40 that whatever we do to the least of God's children is viewed as being done to God Himself! The Shunamite woman in 2 Kings 4:8-37 modelled warm-heartedness excellently. She was described as a "great woman". What a compliment! Could this be said of us? Let's find out the character traits that made the Shunamite woman great. She was great because she was:

- **Perceptive:** She discerned that Elisha was a holy man of God.

- **Extravagantly generous:** She didn't simply allow Elisha to use her guest room, she extended her house to accommodate him! She also paid attention to detail as she thoughtfully furnished his room with everything she knew he would need; a bed, table, stool and candlestick!

- **Very caring:** She wasn't content to be enjoying her above-the-average lifestyle selfishly, she cared for others.

- **Grateful:** She was appreciative and content that she was living amongst her own people. Indeed, she was selfless and thankful.

- **Humble and respectful:** When Elisha called her, she didn't enter his room (even though she was the one extending her hospitality) she stood in the doorway! What respect and honour.

- **Nurturing:** Her son was taken to her when he had a terrible headache.

- **Tenacious with radical faith:** She knew exactly what she wanted. She didn't want the attention of Elisha's servant, she needed Elisha's help. Even though her son was already dead, she believed that Elisha was able to bring him back to life! And because she knew what she wanted, she got it!

- **Decisive:** In what is likely to have been the greatest test of her life, she refused to panic and was able to problem-solve and make strategic decisions to get the outcome she desired.

- **Manages her emotions well:** She knew how to give a measured response even under extreme pressure and in much pain. Her words, "It is well" have become a mantra for many.

Let's learn some more strategies that will transform our lives with the warmth that we need and which this world longs for.

WARM-HEARTEDNESS TRANSFORMATION STRATEGIES

1. Embrace the truth that the highest evidence and reward of transformation is love! Take a minute to think about this. Yes, it is the agape love of the Father which empowers us to value and add value to people. All people. If we are warm only to people that live like us, look like us, worship like us, vote like us and think like us; it's not love. I will admit I don't know what it is, but I'm sure that it isn't the divine, evergreen and all-encompassing love of God. Remember without love we are nothing (1 Corinthians 13: 2)!

2. In our current context and within our means, intentionally practise the lifestyle of radical generosity and humble servanthood like the Shunamite woman. Live in sync with the reigning DNA of abundance and contribution and develop the mindset of a giver.

3. Go on a detox to remove negative attitudes that don't support you becoming a woman of wonder that will have positive influence in your environments.

4. Practice the law of honour. That is, acknowledging, deferring and preferring others.

5. Find out your Love and Apology Languages. Also do so for the significant others in your life (Eg. spouse, children, teammates and employees). This insight will revolutionise your relationships. Dr. Gary Chapman's work can be found online and in his many books.

6. Let's make up our minds to be salt and light. The world is flavourless and dark. Shift into the 4D dimension of wonder and begin to shine that the Father will be glorified and men and women, boys and girls and even babies on the breasts will know somehow that a woman of wonder is reigning with the King of glory in their environment!

7. Be willing to sacrifice for the wellbeing of others. A woman of wonder has come to recognise that she is a love ambassador, called to bring love, joy and hope to everyone she meets.

8. Let's go beyond our comfort zones to extend warm-heartedness to everyone. We don't have the luxury to pick and choose who we minister to. We are instructed in Galatians 6:10 to maximise all our opportunities to do good unto all, but particularly those who are of the household of faith.

9. Be prepared to be rejected sometimes. Not everyone will accept the warmth that you offer

to them. And others will repay you evil for the good you have shown them. But be encouraged and don't get weary in doing the right thing. Rest assured; you'll be rewarded by your Father who is faithful. Whoever gives to the poor lends to God (Proverbs 19:17) and whoever waters the lives of others, will be watered too (Proverbs 11: 25)!

10. Be empathetic to the feelings and needs of others and aim to be the answer to what ails them and or refer them to those who can. Warm-heartedness raises the temperature in its environment with love. And love always finds a way to get answers and go forward!

As reigning women, let the divine nature of God saturate our lives like well-marinated food ready to be served to the hungry. Let's be the spark to start the revolution of radical love; especially to those who are hurting and those who are difficult to love. They are usually the ones who need God's touch through us the most. Let's be willing to lovingly share our warmth with depth and "the fierce urgency of now". May we allow Christ to soak us with His grace to be 'toasty wonders' which are a joy to be around.

As such, a woman who will reign in the fourth dimension recognises that all the toxic attitudes need to be detoxed by the Spirit of God through His Words as she totally surrenders to His Lordship. She willingly replaces the attitude toxins with the Beatitudes. Thus, she becomes an impactful wonder and is tremendously blessed. The Fruit of the Holy Spirit is always abounding day by day in her life as she follows to know Christ and to make Him known.

The 4D reigning woman is committed to love radically. Therefore, she doesn't practise 'lazy loving'. Rather, she exerts time, energy and vulnerability to love others and herself with insight, integrity and wisdom. As such, she freely gives and receives forgiveness. And like the Shunamite woman, she loves deeply for the sake of it and to lift the King of glory higher!

Practising warm-heartedness in the 4D realm makes women irresistible with great and lasting impact. We are living in a world that is chilled to the bone by the freezing temperatures of hurt, pain, loss, needs, financial distress, apathy and shattered dreams! What a time and an opportunity to have a heart that is ablaze with the love of Jesus. Let's not talk about love, let's be and do love; even as God our Father is love!

It truly only takes a spark, you and I, to start a blazing fire of love. As we have been tremendously loved, let's arise and spread the fire of God in the earth; touching one heart at a time. And the time to begin is *now*!

WARM-HEARTEDNESS TRANSFORMATION TASK

1. In terms of the Reigning Dimensions regarding *Warm-heartedness*, where are you? (Tick one)

Wonder ☐   Winning ☐   Waning ☐   Wandering ☐

2. Develop a Warm-heartedness Declaration: Eg. I am a love ambassador and as such, I intentionally love everyone I meet!

_____

_____

3. Which of the Warm-heartedness Transformation Strategies would give you the maximum impact now?

_____

_____

4. Set a SMART (Specific, Measurable, Attainable, Realistic and Time-bound) warm-heartedness goal.

_____

_____

5. Motivation: Why is this goal important to you?

_____

_____

_____

6. Accountability: Which person or system will hold you accountable?

_____

7. Review Date:

_____

8. Reward: How will you celebrate achieving this goal?

_____

_____

Chapter Seven
Transformation Agent #7
WORK

"Concentrate all your thoughts upon the work in hand.
The sun's rays do not burn until brought to a focus."

Alexander Graham Bell

Work is one of life's greatest joys. Without it, we might as well call a funeral home and inform them of our own death and the day we desire to have our official farewell! Rabindranath Tagore explains the nobility of work succinctly when he said, "I slept and dreamt that life was joy. I awoke and saw that life was duty. I acted and behold duty was joy". To be truly alive, we must work. To be reigning women who are impacting our own world and the world at large, we must, by necessity, place a high value on the work we do. And since work is so vital to our sense of spirituality, wellbeing, productivity and contribution, we must take great care in selecting the work that we expend our time and energy committing to.

Who is the Servant?

One Friday afternoon, as I was doing my cleaning chores, I was listening to one of Bill Johnson's insightful messages.

He made this profound comment, "If God is your servant, He will frustrate and disappoint you forever, but if you are His servant, you will constantly be amazed". I immediately had to repent profusely as I faced the reality of the dreadful truth that we sometimes treat the Lord as if He was our servant. We often expect that He will do this, that and the other for us as a matter of urgency. As opposed to we His children showing up to do our work with urgency, and as a matter of priority in the assurance that He will work as He promised and if we let Him! Unconsciously we've made God our servant, rather than being fully convinced and appreciative that we were made to be His servants.

How often we lament like a squeaky machine in need of being greased, complaining about the business or the job that we are presently doing, pleading for bigger and so-called better ones. At the same time, we haven't been the best servants for the Lord, customers nor bosses. Our work should be seen as God giving us an opportunity and a platform from which to labour to see what we allow the job to make of us, and we in turn, to make of the job.

Let the King Do a Work

Before we run off to begin to work on ourselves and on our income-generating endeavours (whether jobs, investments and or businesses), it's critical that we allow Jesus, the Chief Architect, to do a work in our hearts and lives in general. Indeed, it's critical that before we set out to *do* God's work, we first must *become* His handiwork!

Have you ever thought about why God made His Spirit move upon the earth before He began to work on it? If the earth needed the movement of the Spirit of God, what about us, His daughters? If we run ahead and begin to work without wisdom our work won't work, nor will it have the desired impact we want. Who would be the best person to tell us what work to do, how, where, when and even to give us the reason for doing it, like the Omniscient and the Omnipotent One? Here is what God said about Bezaleel from the tribe of Judah in Exodus 31: 3-5:

> *And I have filled him with the spirit of God, in wisdom, and in understanding, and in knowledge, and in all manner of workmanship, to devise cunning works, to work in gold, and in silver, and in brass. And in cutting of stones, to set them, and in carving of timber, to work in all manner of workmanship.*

So, before we do any work, let the Miracle Worker and Holy Spirit of God rest on us and endue us with power, might, knowledge and exceptional understanding so that the works of our hands will be blessed. I don't know about you, but I am tired of hitting and missing, floundering in the dark. I declare that this is a new season and that everything we put our hands to do will prosper for the express glory of the name of Christ, the service of humanity and our advancement.

Oh Lord, do a work in us, for us and through us your daughters that will totally transform us and all that we do. We believe it will be exceedingly, abundantly and above everything, we could ask and think in alignment with His power at work in and through us (Ephesians 3:20). So, shall it be in the mighty name of Jesus! Now we can partner with God and work on ourselves...

You: Your First Work

Many women work so hard on their jobs or even businesses that we forget to work on our own lives. Jim

Rohn offers this insightful advice, "Learn to work harder on yourself than you do on your job. If you work hard on your job, you can make a living. If you work hard on yourself, you'll make a fortune." This by no means is a suggestion that we should be sluggards on our jobs and in our businesses. Rather, it is a useful advice that we shouldn't lose sight of the need to ensure that we engage in working on ourselves and not be short-visioned in only working for a living. It's when we work on ourselves that we become truly become alive, so that we can fulfil our jobs with the excellence and empowerment that rested on Bezaleel; wisdom, understanding and multi-skilled! I would suggest working hard at both ourselves and our work; both will help us in the creation of our fortune!

The need to consistently work on ourselves cannot be overestimated. There are multitudes of ways to work on ourselves: seminars, webinars, workshops, read and listen to books, ask intentional questions, schedule thinking times, engage the service of mentors, coaches, enrol in masterminds, travel...observe. Other transformation strategies will be examined later in the chapter. Growth is one of the characteristics of all living things. The moment we stop growing, we officially begin to die.

Relating to work, which dimension are we in?

Work Dimensions of Reigning

• 1D Reigning: Wandering

In the 1D reigning category, work is seen as a drudgery and a painful necessity to pay the bills. Yes, we need to work to honour our commitments. However, work can be and was meant to be so much more. Oftentimes we are deceived into believing that this negative mindset and attitude towards work will improve when we get our dream job, earn more money, relocate or get a promotion. These and other desired factors aren't satisfactory cures for poor work ethics and mindset. We will always take ourselves into the new contexts that we envision as the cure to that which ails us in our work. I am sure you will agree that nothing will work and nothing will change until we work and change!

Some women refuse to work because the work opportunities we've been given are less than what we considered to be our ideal. However, what are deemed as small opportunities are oftentimes empires in disguise! We are advised not to despise the day of small beginnings (Zechariah 4:10). Inactivity and an unwillingness to work will inevitably lead to economic and social exclusion and hardships in ways such as begging, borrowing and even stealing!

Why live a life of wandering? Whatever our hands find to do, we ought to embrace it as an opportunity and then put our all into it.

• 2D Reigning: Waning

In the 2D *Waning* dimension, this woman has settled for mediocrity. She is off-course; which is the opposite of living a purpose-centred life. Life is meaningless, painful and boring without a discovered and refined purpose. Purpose gives direction and gets us out of bed in the mornings with a pep in our step and a bounce in our ounce. One of the worst things to see and to do, is to try to get good at what we are bad at. It is trying to achieve what we aren't wired nor gifted to do. Misguided passion and efforts waste energy and time. This can cause harm and destroy our personal economy; since the remuneration we receive will always reflect the quality of the value we offer. It is of utmost importance that we get really good at what we do. When we are struggling to discover our purpose and to be good at that which we do, the rates of incomplete tasks is normally high. People are usually only ever paid for the tasks that they finish!

• 3D Reigning: Winning

The woman working in the third dimension (3D) is focused and purpose-centred. She knows what she was born to do and she is committed to doing it. She is hard-working and goes above and beyond the call of duty. She has a very strong work ethic. The 3D winning dimension of work focuses on *what* needs to be done; results, bottom line and goal achievements. She is very committed and usually has a sense of what is motivating her such as family, self-actualization, helping people and to execute a mission for life.

• 4D Reigning: Wonder

A woman becoming a *wonder* in the fourth dimension of work, will execute her work with a servant heart disposition. At the African Regional Convention in Offinso, Ghana, in August 2018 one of the presenters, Whaid Rose said, "We will know if we are servant-hearted by our reactions when we get treated like servants!" This thought left an indelible impression on my heart. I have used it many times to evaluate my reactions. Are we real servants? Lord give us servant hearts indeed.

Women of wonder, work in the centre of their 'sweet spot'! Max Lucado, in his excellent book entitled, *'Cure for the Common Life'*, defines the 'sweet spot' as a God-given "zone, a region, a life precinct in which you were made to dwell. He tailored the curves of your life to fit an empty space in His jigsaw puzzle." Indeed, God has given everyone an endowment of greatness by His Holy Spirit and amazing grace. "The manifestation of the Spirit is given to each one for the profit of all" (1 Corinthians 12: 7).

Not only should we work from our 'sweet spot', but also completed with intentional excellence! This is so because work is seen as worship to the King as we make our contributions to our environments. A woman of wonder is not content to leave her work incomplete. She is a finisher. She is also aware that an individual is only rewarded for work that is completed. Our influence and wealth are directly dependent on our ability to complete that which we've started! What are the incompletions in our lives?

When a woman operates in the 4D category, she deems it an honour to assist in the transformation of other people's lives. This helps in building of a thriving network as she delights in adding value to people's lives through the high quality of her work. Consequently, she consistently thinks of and seeks best practise strategies to improve the value she offers to God and the people she serves. The focus of this dimension is the reasons behind the work that is done. It is about making Christ known and expanding His kingdom!

Pre-wired and Hard-wired for Purpose

Work that is effective and impactful is always tied to purpose. In terms of work, what is your specialist area?

What is your 'one thing' that you do very well? When we discover our 'one thing', we are second to none. Not knowing our purpose makes a mockery out of setting goals; unless the first goal is to find our purpose.

When we live our purpose that is attached to an overarching mission, we become influencers; with or without the label. When we don't live our purpose, we become possessions; owned by the agendas of others. We shouldn't be content with a life of imitation. George Sheehan states this declaration with much insight, "I am - just as you are - a unique, never-to-be-repeated event in this universe. Therefore, I have - just as you have - a unique, never-to-be-repeated role in this world." Blaze a trail beyond the much-trodden path. Live in such a way that you will never be dismissed as trivia. When we reign from the centre of our purpose for purpose, everything about us exudes a presence beyond our physicality. We will radiate joy, energy, love, harmony, a largeness of heart (1Kings 4:29) and hope.

When you work from a correctly aligned stance of your purpose, you have centeredness that stabilizes you in the inevitable storms of life. Before we were even born, everything possible that is needed for our purpose was already assigned to us. "Before I formed thee in the belly, I knew thee and before thou camest forth out of the womb I sanctified thee, and I ordained thee a prophet unto the nations" (Jeremiah 1:5). Jeremiah was called to be a prophet. What are we called to do? All we have to do is to show up with our 'Purpose ID' and touch the 'magnetic strip' of heaven, through Jesus Christ, and all that is beyond will open for our admittance.

Preparation

Your discovered purpose will require preparation! When a woman allows God to take her through the process of preparation, there is no limit to who she'll become and what she can do. It's undeniably true that purpose plus preparation equals miracles! God works wonders with a woman that is fully surrendered to Him and is willing to make the investment to be prepared. The anointing doesn't replace preparation! Learning is a crucial part of preparation. Time spent in preparation will undoubtedly yield great return on investments.

When you're prepared, you'll eventually be sent for. Your gifts will make room for you and bring you before men of distinction (Proverbs 18:16). It is vital that we explore our unique gifts because they will make the biggest difference in our lives and give us an advantage and distinction. Our gifts will make for us a platform from which we serve people and meet their needs. Our gifts strip away every boundary of imposed or perceived limitations of geographical location, educational background, ethnicity, political persuasions, disabilities, special educational needs, tribal origins...rank. Excellence in your gift will defy all odds and create a place for you around the table of the greats. Honour God and serve people well with your gifts. In time, without fail, people will send for you.

The story of Esther speaks volumes about the necessity of a woman to be prepared before going before a king. Although Esther was a stunningly beautiful young virgin, she simply couldn't rush in the presence of Ahasuerus, the king. Esther had to undergo extensive preparation with twelve months of beauty treatments for the opportunity to spend a night with the King! In the end, she found favour with him (Esther 2:9-13).

After a while, Jews living in Persia were earmarked for extermination by a wicked man named Haman. The riveting story climaxes with Esther's bravery when she decides to approach the king without an invitation. She said, "If I perish,". Again, Esther took the time to prepare by fasting and praying. Esther solicited help from the people of the provinces and requested supernatural kindness from God. This led to the saving of the lives of her people (Esther 8: 7-14). Until today, Purim is celebrated by Jewish people around the world to mark this monumental time in their nation's history. God sovereignly used a beautiful woman to turn pending tragedy into amazing triumph.

As you prepare, don't be short-visioned nor half-hearted in your preparation. Instead, adopt the advice in Isaiah 54: 2-4 (NIV):

Enlarge the place of your tent, stretch your tent curtains wide, don't hold back; lengthen your cords, strengthen your stakes.

For you'll spread out to the right and to the left...

Don't be afraid; you'll not be put to shame.

Don't fear disgrace; you'll not be humiliated.

Workers Needed!

After preparation, there is always work to be done! Moses' life typifies how God strategically prepares and then uses individuals in the building of His kingdom. God's people were crying for a deliverer. God planted the seed of deliverance in Moses' heart. Moses grew up in the household of Pharaoh, the king. However, his allegiance was towards the true God of his Hebrew mother. So, when he saw an Egyptian and an Israelite fighting, he was concerned enough to intervene. Albeit, using a less than noble method, but he did care, hence, he killed the Egyptian. Consequently, he had to run away. In time, he got himself a family and was busy making a living to provide for them by looking after his father-in-law's cattle.

When the Lord visited Moses in the Midian desert, he didn't speak to him until He saw that he, *"Turn aside to see"* (Exodus 3:4). Have you ever seen a group of youngsters playing and someone from the group says (with shoulders and head rocking from side to side and with a raised palm) and says, "Look at my face, do I seem bothered"? Are we bothered by the things of God? We must be concerned about the things that concern God. There're lots of bounties in the presence and Word of God. But it's critical that we show interest and make them our priorities. They'll not just fall on our laps.

We need to turn aside from excessive watching of television, idle telephone conversations, endless internet browsing and updating our profiles on social media platforms, countless addictive shopping expeditions and whatever else that can be added to this list! Take note of the word excessive. These things aren't wrong per se. However, the excess of anything robs it of its potential value! As women of God, we need to live our lives with balance and purpose. A good thing can become a bad thing. We can't be glued to the trappings of this transient life and simultaneously hear what God has to say and see His glorious wonders.

There are many people who are crying to God from the bondage of their addictions, pain, low self-esteem…whatever their circumstances. They're waiting for the 'deliverer' whom God will send. As God did with Moses, He has prepared you as a woman of wonder. He longs to call you by your name, reveal Himself to you, and commission you to use what is in your hand. God wants to use your heart, hands, feet, intellect… your entire life, to help to break the shackles of sin from people's lives so that they are free to worship Him (like He did for the children of Israel). He wants your life to become exemplary for His glory. Woman of God, it's truly time to rise up and reign and to do great exploits!

Is it Working?

Recently I took up a pen to highlight a section in the *Believe Bigger* book by Marshawn Evans. Alas, the pen wasn't working. Where can you find a pen that can actually work when you need one! It was then that I remembered that my colleague said, "It wasn't working". However, as I held the pen in my hand examining it, I could see that the pen had all the capacity to work. I realised that it was relatively new. I could see through its transparent casing that it was filled with ink! How can a pen that was almost brand new and filled to peak capacity with ink be not functioning?

So, I decided to do what most people would do I began to scratch the ball-pointed pen across a sheet of paper. This carried on for some time without the desired outcome. All I got was indented streaks across the paper but no blue ink. I paused and again I looked at the tube of unused ink. And I made a decision. This pen had the capacity to work and work it will! Consequently, I returned to scratching the pen across the paper, but this time I was scratching with two times the force I used before. Again, it refused to work. I thought let me try one last time. So, again I began to mark across the paper; but this time it was with all my might. After a few moments, guess what happened? The pen started to work! Hip hip hooray! As women, even though God has worked in us, we have worked on ourselves and we know our purpose, why are we not working as we ought to?

LESSONS FROM A PEN

LESSON #1

We have everything we need to function inside us! Precious woman of God, you have everything to function in your greatness. But just like the pen had a full tube of ink and the ball of the pen was spinning smoothly, but the ink was dormant. Are we fast asleep with our 'full tube' of gifts, talent and latent purpose? It's now time to wake up so we can reign, become a wonder and have good success!

LESSON # 2

Like the pen was labelled by my colleague as "not working", as women we are oftentimes labelled by our temporary moments of brokenness. This labelling can be very crippling, in so much that, the temporary labels are regarded as the permanent truth; which can abort our potentials. We must allow the Life Giver to breathe His life-giving Spirit upon us and wake us up from our slumber. Whose report will you believe? The labels people put on you? Or what God says about you in His Word and to you personally in divine encounters?

Your Maker has called you as royal, peculiar and chosen (1 Peter 2: 9). And your capacity is unlimited. You can do everything that you were born to do through Jesus Christ! Let God alone label you. He is the only One qualified to do so since He is the One who made you fearfully and wonderfully and knows exactly what He has deposited in you!

LESSON #3

Don't give up on God nor on yourself! Could it be that ink 'heard' when my colleague said that the pen doesn't work? And as such, it went on strike to live up to the inaccurate label placed on it! What if the ink said, "They said I haven't been working for so long, I believe what they say about me and I'm going to behave according to my label, so I refuse to work so you can write!" Is that why we are not working to birth the treasure contained in us? Is that why we have lost our drive, imprisoned in the wrong job, the wrong ministry, the wrong ministry role and the wrong industry?

LESSON #4

It took repeated and increased efforts and force to get the ink to flow and the pen to work! What is God doing in our lives that is similar to being rubbed against paper to get us to use the 'power ink' He has given to us? Socrates wisely said, "The unexamined life is not worth living." Again, what are we going through that we are calling "attacks from the Devil", while it's really God trying to wake us up? Let's not resist. Yield.

LESSON #5

On further inspection, the pen was labelled BIC and the capacity was clearly displayed as "MEDIUM" point. Just as how the manufacturer identified this pen's capacity, God has done thesame thing for us so that there will be no guessing and trial and error. Here are a few questions for us to ponder:

- What is it you are called to do in the body of Christ?

- What problem are you assigned to be the answer for?

- What impact are you destined to have on a world that is waiting for *you*?

- What are your YOU-nique gifts, talents and experiences that will change lives?

- How can you use your wonder-packed story for God's glory?

Let's do a refresher study on spiritual gifts according to 1 Corinthians 12: 28-30. Indeed, there is a specific place for every worker on the mission field of the Lord. Oh, may we find it!

LESSON #6

If I had left the pen to its own device, it would never have worked! So it is, if God and the people He has divinely placed in our lives, leave us alone, we will never fulfil our calling, accomplish our assignment, make an impact, embrace our destiny and not to mention reigning eternally! He is birthing something huge through us. Thankfully, He will send us midwives and destiny helpers. We've tried it alone, now it's time to get a team.

LESSON #7

God's will and manifesting miracles, signs and wonders are never in the comfort zone. It takes courage, discipline, boldness, perseverance and wisdom. Therefore, by necessity, we must reach beyond our grasp to do whatever it takes.

Your 'water' has broken, wake up. It's time to birth the God-ordained version of yourself and represent the King of kings with purpose, excellence and abundance. You are destined to be a great kingdom contributor.

> *Arise, shine; for thy light is come, and the glory of the Lord is risen upon thee...but the Lord shall arise upon thee, and his glory shall be seen upon thee. And the Gentiles shall come to thy light, and kings to the brightness of thy rising (Isaiah 60: 1-3).*

So, grab a hold of God's hand and PUSH. The discomfort and the stretching will be worth it...

What is Your Deeply Desired Work?

Don't be afraid to own your desire for more. Oftentimes women's 'more' can be so large and different from our present realities that we allow ourselves to be overwhelmed, frightened and even threatened by the sheer size of the desire and dream. If we've allowed ourselves to be purged of self and selfishness, then we can trust God that what we desire is for the sole purpose of making His name great and for His glory.

Beloved sister, it's OK to embrace your desire for more and for the possibility of where you can be! Here is our encouragement in Psalm 37: 4, God is committed to giving us the desires of our hearts. However, we must first delight in Him totally.

Think about the imposing and super-sized desires that you have for God. He Himself is going to grant you the grace so He can give it to you, so that you can then give them back to Him. Wow. What are the desires of your heart? Write the vision and make it plain (I use two vision boards to do this, one for my personal desires and the other for ministry). One of the major desires of my heart is to have the time freedom to engage in focused ministry to serve the needs of women globally on a full-time basis! Remember we have to own them (admit and embrace them) before we can actually own them (experience the manifestation of them).

However, here is a caveat, before we run off with some self and devil-engineered desires of a deceived or distracted heart, let's go back to the foundation of God's word. Ask yourself, are these desires and ambitions in alignment with God's Word? In addition, prayerfully and wisely share your dreams and desires with the authority figures in your life (Eg. Husband, pastor, mentors, parents). Firstly, this is practising the law of honour. Secondly, we all have blind spots, so they help to keep us safe.

God only honours God-approved dreams and desires. And they are the only ones we should work on too!

Self-employed...No Matter What!

Those who do extremely well in life and are distinguished in terms of their achievements always take one hundred percent responsibility for the quality of their lives! Brian Tracey in his insightful book *21 Success Secrets of Self-made Millionaires* states that the top 3% of the wealthiest individuals see themselves as self- employed no matter how they generate revenue and who it is that pays them!

He encourages us to adopt the belief that no matter where we work or what we do we are working for ourselves! This shift in mindset is empowering. It makes us realise that we are always 'self-employed'. In effect, I am the President of the Donna Services Limited. If you are Lucy, then you're the President of the Lucy Services Limited. The point being made is, this is so no matter where you work! Therefore, it's time to declare your 'self- employment' status. I am the _____

This mindset will increase our creativity, responsibility, productivity, entrepreneurial thinking and certainly our earnings! It is often said that there are three types of people in the world. "Those who make things happen, those who watch things happen and those who wonder what happened." It is without question that the mindset of thinking like a 'self- employed' (not necessarily being one) helps to make things happen.

THE SUCCESS CYCLE

Source: This illustration is based on Dr. John C. Maxwell's presentation at The LEADUK Transformation Leadership Conference (Birmingham, UK. 2020).

If we are to become skilled at being in charge of our work life with the mindset that we are 'self-employed' (that is, being fully responsible, no matter what), The Success Cycle by Dr. John C. Maxwell is a useful tool. It will help us execute becoming the 'President' of our services and the necessary growth plan to assist us become reigning women of wonder.

We will need to try a lot of new things and walk the path less trodden. It is wise to know from the outset that some of our ideas will succeed and others will not! Let's unpack The Success Cycle:

1. **TESTING**: We must continually test new ideas for improvement. We should be adventurous to go where we've never been before. Pause and answer this question, "When was the last time I did something for the first time?"

2. **FAILURE:** People think that failure is the opposite of success. It's not. Failure is the twin sister of success! They come as a package. The more ideas we test, the more some will fail. Equally true, the more ideas we test the more likely that some will succeed.

3. **LEARN:** The value of failure is learning from it. Ask often, "What did I learn?" If we learn from our failures, they become assets. If we don't, they are liabilities. And this is the only time that we've truly failed...when we've learnt nothing! Dr. John C. Maxwell aptly said, "Experience isn't the best teacher, evaluated experience is." It's time to begin to, "Fail Forward"!

4. **IMPROVE**: For every idea that we test, we need to evaluate them and get better, faster, more cost-effective, more impactful and efficient.

5. **GET BACK IN THE GAME**: We should never quit when we encounter failures. However, don't be too quick to brush yourself off and rush back into the game without learning. Don't get back up until you've learned and improved. Then and only then should you get back up and re-enter the game!

It will take strategic thinking to help us learn from our mistakes to help us to re-enter the game. It's time to think!

Think for Work to Work!

It has been often said, "The definition of insanity is doing the same thing over and over and expecting different results."Putting in sheer high volume of hard work without intentional thoughtfulness and evaluation, is like pouring water in a bucket with holes. To get the answers that will transform our work and all other areas of our lives, we must become skilled and consistent thinkers! Thinking is one of the strategic ways we sharpen our blunt axes! Dr. John C. Maxwell purports the following eleven thinking skills:

1. Seeing the wisdom of big-picture thinking

2. Unleashing the potential of focused thinking

3. Discovering the joy of creative thinking

4. Recognising the importance of realistic thinking

5. Releasing the power of strategic thinking

6. Feeling the energy of possibility thinking

7. Embracing the lesson of reflective thinking

8. Questioning the acceptance of popular thinking

9. Encouraging the participation of shared thinking

10. Experiencing the satisfaction of unselfish thinking

11. Enjoying the return on bottom-line thinking

Let's spend some time thinking about these thinking skills. If we infuse them into a planned thinking schedule, they would certainly help us on the journey of becoming wonders; being super-efficient, effective and impactful. We would find there are gaps in what we do, they are better ways of working, there are people we need to strategically partner with and others. However, these life-accelerating thoughts won't intrude into our rat-race lives. We need to recognise our need for them, plan for them, invite them in, provide an optimal space for them and efficiently capture them. Then our high-quality thoughts will grace and transform our lives and help us to become reigning women who will go forth to change the nations, one life at a time!

Now that we have thought about it, it's now time to go ahead and *do it*…

Self-Discipline

If we are dreaming *big* dreams to have great impact, we must practise self-discipline. It's basically doing what we are supposed to do, when we are supposed to do it; even if we don't feel like doing it. This is what separates the *talkers* from the *walkers*! It is critical that when we fail, and we will, that we don't see ourselves as failures. This is important, if not, we will not be able to get back up and go conquer the mountains for God! When weare defeated in our minds, we can't exercise self-discipline.

Brian Tracy in his book, *The 21 Success Secrets of Self-Made Millionaires*, asserts that every act of self-discipline will help to support and strengthen other disciplines. When we practise self-discipline in small things, we are more likely to be able to do so in the greater opportunities and challenges in life. He further states that everything in life is a test to see if we are able to do the things which are most important and persist until they are completed. Every self-discipline test that we pass we upgrade ourselves in life. This improves our self-respect; causing us to like ourselves even more. Notice how lovely we feel when we are able to tick off the attainment of a special goal.

The work required for women to reign in the dimension of wonder and have great impact require great self-discipline. We are called be disciples of Jesus; which makes us His students. And every accomplished student will tell you that the process wasn't a stroll in the park! It took commitment, effective time and emotions management, perseverance and what Sir Thomas Buxton calls a "fixity of purpose" to achieve the set goals. These attributes are built upon the foundation of the Word of God as directed and empowered by the Holy Spirit. It's worth noting that the greatest benefit of setting goals is not so much the thingsthat we will achieve per se. However, of far greater value is what the process of their achievement will make of us! The attainment of our worthy goals changes us deeply and irrevocably. This is what the trophy should be awarded for.

Transferable Skills

In today's world, there is fast becoming no such thing as a job and even a career for life. It's an era where we must become skilled at pivoting at critical junctions. Therefore, it's vital that we are intentional in building up our skill set to meet the demands of our current work situations, and vitally to best position ourselves for the highly likely work transitions and changes throughout our careers. Upskilling and continuous learning are necessary in all areas of life.

Transferable skills are worth their weight in pure gold. In fact, this is what can give you an edge and advantage when you position yourself in a different sector and target market. But we must start somewhere. As long as you are learning and contributing somewhere, it can never be deemed a failure.

There are many tests to help us identify our personality, leadership traits, wealth tendency, gifts and talent and others. These tests that can be very useful in helping us to navigate the meandering path to finding out how and where to position ourselves in offering our uniqueness to the world. Mentors, sponsors, internships can assist in the process too. In the workplace in most sectors, women experience a glass ceiling effect and often downright inequality and discrimination. However, don't be afraid to aim high and make changes.

Lasting Work: Evangelism

Work that will last must include evangelism; in whatever form that is suitable for that context. The Great Commission isn't the 'Great Suggestion'. Doug Fields, author of the *Purpose Driven Youth Ministry* states that, "Evangelism isn't a program; it's a process- a process of a person modelling his or her transformed life to someone in need of God's transformational grace." I really love this definition of evangelism because it includes transformation; which highlights its power and impact. So, as we work tirelessly to put bread on our tables and the tables of others, we must equally, if not even more so, practise sharing the Bread of Heaven to souls that are hungry for the only Bread that lasts and truly satisfies! Let's do it with our might.

The woman at the well in John 4:1-25 was ignited by and for evangelism. Jesus saw the brokenness of her life and broke protocol and made a date with her to catapult her into her divine destiny. Today the Lord wants to do the same for us whereby He will meet us in the midst of our pain and greatest need and bring lasting transformation and blessings. The woman at the well must have thought here we go again another man with the same-old-same-old chat up lines and intention. But it was soon revealed to her that this man was a King, a man of nobility that had only impeccable intention towards her, who wouldn't waste her time and would never ever abuse her. Jesus always leaves those He encounters better…always. How can we keep this gospel to ourselves? Let's go be it, do it, tell it, and defend it!

The Proverbs 31 Woman

The Proverbs 31 woman is characterised by several distinctive qualities. However, one of the highlights is that she "worketh willingly with her hands". Let's learn how to improve our work by examining her work ethics.

1. **Trustworthy:** To excel as a worker, the people in your environment must be able to be secure in knowing that you have their best interest at

heart. Can our bosses, clients, ministry colleagues and community members trust us?

2. **Goal-oriented:** She knew she wanted to make clothes for her household and beyond and so she needed to get wool and flax to make them. If we don't know what we want to accomplish, we won't know the ingredients to get! Do you know what it is that you want to do and the thingsrequired to do it?

3. **Right attitude:** She not only did her work well but her attitude was right; she was willing. Have you ever seen someone doing a task but they hated it and certainly didn't want to do it? What a torture it is for everyone to cope with an unwilling worker! Let's look in the mirror and ask the obvious question, "How willing am I to do what I'm doing?" Let's do an attitude check-up.

4. **Sacrificial:** She is willing to sacrifice greatly to attain her set goals. There isn't a lazy bone in her body; she works tirelessly and does whatever it takes. She is likened to a merchant ship that brings her trade ware from far flung regions. How impressive!

5. **Visionary:** She is a visionary and is able to forecast worthy investment ventures and take actions to attain her desired outcomes. Importantly, she is also able to evaluate her work; which is necessary for growth and development. This visioneering trait makes her prepared to handle the demands of crisis by her ability to plan ahead and strategize for life's

eventualities. Do we have a life emergency strategy for the different areas in life such finances, health, parenting, marriage, business, jobs and accommodation?

6. **Resilient:** A woman of wonder is strong! To be resilient, we need the tenacity to carry on in spite of the difficult odds stacked against us.

7. **Refined in taste:** She had very fine taste. Hence, she doesn't settle for mediocre quality.

8. **Entrepreneurial:** She wasn't content with only being a consumer. She diligently engages in meeting the needs around her and solves their problems in exchange for compensation.

9. **Honourable:** She is typified by honour, grace, excellence and goodwill. What a compliment. Is this true for us?

10. **Impactful:** Her work, attitude and kindness made her very influential. And people around her responded to her accordingly.

WORK TRANSFORMATION STRATEGIES

1. Finding Self-Expression

Everyone is great at something! Work is a wonderful platform that enables you to serve people from your 'sweet spot'. Have you identified what you are great at doing? What one skill that if you should make that decision to totally focus on it with your time, energy and money would totally transform your life? I believe my one skill is communication with the strands of writing, speaking, coaching and training.

2. Commit to Excellence

Work that is worth doing, is worth doing with the spirit of excellence. It doesn't matter what you are called to do, as long as it's done with all your might (Ecclesiastes 9:10). Make a commitment today to be the best at what you do. Your life will never be the same the moment you commit to being the best rendition of the God-ordained version of yourself. Only high competence twinned with excellence will be rewarded with the best of everything.

3. Positive Attitude

Not only should we work with excellence but also with a positive attitude. Set a positive intention every day. We can learn a lot from the Book of Nehemiah about work. Nehemiah was in captivity; yet his attitude was of such a high standard that it showed on his face! He served the King with joy and a gladsome countenance to the extent that the day he appeared before the King sad, it was noticed. Practise joy no matter what.

4. Going the Extra Mile

Develop the foundational mindset for long-term strong work ethic. This will inspire you to give extraordinary value with all your heart. Practise the habit of going above and beyond the call of duty. This will make you memorable and head and shoulders above the competition because so many people are happy to get by with the bare minimum of effort and commitment. Distinguish yourself by over-delivering on the expected standard of value.

5. Purpose-alignment

Work from the standpoint of your uniqueness and what you are called by God to do. It is painful to work your way to the topof a self-assigned work only to find it was leaning again the wrong wall! Whether it's a project, business, job or career, every effort must be made to ascertain that what you are working on isin alignment with the call of God on your life and who He has hard-wired you to be and do. This is when work becomes a high note of worship!

6. Time Blocking

Greatness requires focused time. In order to consistently take massive actions in alignment with your purpose and goals, it requires quality planned blocks of time. For example, I could decide that I will write five days per week for at least ninety minutes from 7pm-8:30pm (devoid of every distraction including my phones). We can't do work that matters, have a huge impactand that will leave a strong legacy by doing it in an ad hoc fashion.

7. The 80:20 Principle

According to Edward Russel-Walling in his book, *50 Management Ideas*, The 80:20 Principle (otherwise called the Pareto Principle), was initially discovered by the renowned Italian sociologist and economist Vilfredo Pareto. Essentially, it states that 20% of our efforts will produce 80% of our results. Thatis, 80% of that which you achieve will be as a result of 20% of thework that you do! The wonderful thing about this principle is that it is highly transferable and can be effectively applied in different organisational structures, industry and job functions.

To help us operate in the 4D dimension with regards to work, ask ourselves, "What is my 20% essential work effort and what are my priority work tasks?" Once we have accurately done this, we will become unstoppable in attaining our desired results.

8. Outsourcing

For many people, this concept is readily associated with business. But guess what our lives are businesses. We are always operating at a loss or profit. Outsourcing is usually given to those who provide specialist high quality and efficient goods and services in the area of our needs. As a reigning wonder operating at the 4D level, let's not try to do everything for ourselves. A popular piece of advice is to, "Stay in your lane."

9. Diligence

It has been often said, "Too many people stop working as soon as they get a job." We are advised in Ecclesiastes 9:10 that whatever our hand finds to do, we should do it with all our might; for there is no work, nor device, nor knowledge, nor wisdom, in the grave, where we will eventually go. There is a timeframe to do our work and we must be committed to it.

10. Thoughtful Work

Schedule time to think. Make this a part of our daily work tasks. We must sharpen and excavate the wonderful contents of our minds. This will help us to embrace change and become what is popularly deemed 'thought leaders'. Without scheduled time to think about the work that we do, we will relegate ourselves to chasing established trends rather than being trend-setters.

11. Focus Focus Focus

Focus is concentrating single-mindedly on the attainment of an established goal. It requires being present in the moment without any form of distractions. Focus increases productivity, quality and efficiency by which tasks are accomplished. Brian Tracy said, "Throughout my career, I have discovered and rediscovered a simple truth. It is this: the ability to concentrate single-mindedly on your most important task, to do it well and to finish it completely, is the key to great success, achievement, respect, status, and happiness in life."

12. Build a Strong Team

No matter how amazing we are, we can't accomplish great things in great numbers by ourselves. We need others to safeguard our 'strength zone' so we don't kill it with the demands of that which will distract us (even though it may be a good thing). A great team also covers our weaknesses. Why struggle to do that which we aren't gifted to do? We can't be great at everything. It is impossible. In fact, God designed it this way to create loving and fruitful interdependency.

We cannot reign as wonders if we aren't convinced and committed of the necessity of efficient hard work. Unproductivity is one of the traps and snares of the Devil which may even result in other greater snares such as theft, fraud, gambling, lifestyle-begging, lying; to name a few. Work is a significant part of our lives. The dignity and blessing of work is a command from God for all His capable children. And those who can work will be compensated both by God and those we create value for. In Ephesians 4: 28 we are instructed to be engaged in wholesome labour, working with our own hands at good things and in turn, we will have to give to those who are in need of help. We must discover and use our giftedness for God's honour and perpetual praise on the earth!

Again, let me impress upon women everywhere to invest whatever it takes to discover our purpose. It is worth repeating, that indeed the woman that knows her God will be strong and do exploits (Daniel 11:32, emphasis mine)! When a woman gets to that place when she becomes convincingly aware that she is unique and that she is intentionally and exceptionally prepared for a unique kingdom assignment she becomes incredibly useful in God's hands and is unstoppable. She is also a 'dynamite' against the kingdom of Satan and its stronghold.

Finally, we must allow Christ to make us His workmanship so that we can effectively work for Him. Those who are committed to becoming wonders and reigning with great impact, will be richly rewarded. You're entering your time of refreshing and God-sized blessings for your work at such a time as this. You will be experiencing a new dimension of transformation for productivity and fruitfulness. God has already given you your amazing future now; in seed form. Work it, your abundance will flow. And above all else our work must help to win the lost at any cost!

WORK TRANSPORMATION TASK

1. In terms of the Reigning Dimensions regarding *Work*, where are you? (Tick one)

Wonder ☐   Winning ☐   Waning ☐   Wandering ☐

2. Develop a Work Declaration: Eg. My work is valuable and it prioritises soul-winning!

_____

_____

3. Which of the Work Transformation Strategies would give you the maximum impact now?

_____

_____

4. Set a SMART (Specific, Measurable, Attainable, Realistic and Time-bound) work goal.

_____

_____

5. Motivation: Why is this goal important to you?

_____

_____

_____

6. Accountability: Which person or system will hold you accountable?

_____

7. Review Date:

_____

8. Reward: How will you celebrate achieving this goal?

_____

_____

Chapter Eight
Transformation Agent #8
WEALTH

"No man becomes rich unless he enriches others."

Andrew Carnegie

Abraham, the father of the Christian faith, was a heavyweight champion in wealth. So beloved daughter of the Most High God we can be godly, surrendered and wealthy all at the same time! Wealth is God's desire for us. As such He gave us the power to create great wealth (Deuteronomy 8:18). Wealth is an all-encompassing word that means experiencing abundance, prosperity and great riches. However, in the context of this chapter, personal finance will be the primary focus. Personal finance addresses how we manage our money and the financial plan we implement for our future. Every financial decision we make will have a direct and indirect impact on our financial well-being both short-term and long-term. If there was ever a time that every woman must take control of her financial wellbeing, it's now! In a world economically ravaged by Covid-19, how must a woman respond to the financial crisis and opportunities?

Let's address the elephant in the room. After a decision, there needs to be a definite goal to be attained. How can we aim for and achieve bullseye a target which was never set? Many women don't have a financial goal because they think that money is evil and ungodly. This is the juncture in the money conversations where some women, passionately yet inaccurately, quote 1 Timothy 6:10 that "money is the root of all evil." They may even add a hallelujah for good measure after the wealth-blocking rendition of this Bible verse. This is one of the most misquoted verses in the entire Bible. All the while, Satan who wants to destroy us, is blocking us from having this vital kingdom expanding tool in our toolbox! It is *the love of money* that is evil; not money per se. All we have to do is to look at creation and God's original paradise in the Garden of Eden and we will most likely conclude that scarcity and corruption were never God's idea! Never.

At this stage of our journey in becoming *The Reigning Woman* of wonder, it's imperative that we have chosen the King. Jesus is our King; the highest 'wealth currency' known to mankind! In Matthew 6: 33 an instruction is given, that if it's heeded, will set us apart for the rest of our lives! It will cause us to reign, both *now* and for *eternity*. "But seek ye first the kingdom of God, and his righteousness; and all these things shall be added unto you." Our highest goal and 'gold' (pardon the pun) is Jesus Christ and His kingdom!

Now we can go forth boldly and unapologetically to unpack the essential Transformation Agent of wealth; in the financial sense of the word.

Source of all things...

If we ignore and treat lightly the instruction in Mathew 6:33, the Lord takes it as a personal insult when His children live without acknowledging Him as the Source of everything. All good and perfect gifts come from God, the Creator of Heaven and earth (James 1:17). In essence, everything of worthwhile value comes from God! To believe and live out of alignment with this truth, is to do so to our own peril. In the futile attempt to gather wealth apart from the Source is to court and marry loss and eventual ruin.

Can you remember the story that started this book by Theodore Effiong from his book, *Why Certain Men are Poor, Remain Poor and Die Poor*? Let's give a brief recap. The King in India invited the poor people of his province to come to his palaceon a specific day. They were given permission to take anything they wanted. And anything really meant anything! Whether it was a diamond ring, a gold necklace, a silver goblet and so on. Many people came and took whatever the luxurious items they wanted. Then there came a wise woman and when she double-checked if she could really get anything she wanted, she was assured by the king that it was indeed the case. She then made a decision that not only changed the immediate contents in her purse, it changed everything; including ensuing generations! Guess what, she chose the king!

What results have our decisions concerning our wealth given us so far? Now let's have a look at our wealth standard through the lens of the four dimensions of Wonder, Winning, Waning and Wandering.

Wealth Reigning Dimensions

• 1D Reigning: Wandering

In the 1D *wandering* category, there is a wanna-be (want-to-be) mindset. Mindset acts as an anchor that gives a sense of groundedness. Hence, not knowing who we are, can possibly lead women to make all sorts of unhelpful and or destructive decisions regarding their wealth. Women in the 1D category are usually indebted without a debt elimination goal and complementary plan. It isn't so much the presence of debt that is the deciding factor. It's more so the handling of the debt. There is no plan to get out and sadly sometimes no intention to honour the debt. Many have treated debt responsibly and have even used it as a leverage. (We will revisit this later in the chapter).

Due to the indebtedness, they are usually struggling to cope financially. Consequently, they are likely to become overly dependent on benevolence for their survival. We all need the generosity of others. However, the Transformation Agent of work is a necessary component in the wealth equation. God has an expectation of every individual, when possible, to be conscientiously engaged in the joy and duty of work! If an individual is wandering to the degree of not being gainfully working, even though it's possible, then the weight of their upkeep is placed on other entities such as family members, the state, church or charitable organisations.

It must be noted, that receiving help from individuals and institutions isn't wrong where there are genuine needs. However, if these needs exist because of a deliberate refusal or half-hearted commitment to work, this would be an infringement on the principle of work as is revealed in

Scriptures. God's radical stance is, if we don't work, we mustn't eat (2 Thessalonians 3:10); as basic as this essential need is!

• 2D Reigning: Waning

In the 2D Waning Dimension, women are barely surviving financially. Consequently, they find it difficult to practise the kingdom lifestyle of generosity; experiencing hesitancy to share. At the 2D Waning level, women see the act of blessing others and even tithing as a risk to their already struggling finances. This has led to a sense of scarcity rather than one of abundance.

• 3D Reigning: Winning

Women in the 3D category of wealth are winning in the area of their finance. Generally, they are thriving and are financially free. Admittedly, financial freedom looks differently for differentindividuals. Everything is connected to values and purpose. However, in a general sense, financial freedom is having the ability to maintain a desired lifestyle without financial anxiety. There are individuals that believe that this should be done on a passive income for it be considered financial freedom. The debate rumbles on. The main point being made is being able to handle one's financial affair without shortage, struggle and stress!

• 4D Reigning: Wonder

In the fourth dimension, women have become wonders and are experiencing a wellspring of abundance in the area of their finances! They have found astonishing favour with God and man. They live the lifestyle of covenant wealth, which is consistently and generously giving to God and to

His people. Women of wonder know that they are blessed to be impactful philanthropists for their generation and beyond. They believe that to whom much is given, much is also required (Luke 12:48). Radical generosity is their mindset and lifestyle. As they have been blessed, they're committed to blessing others.

In Genesis 12: 2, God made a covenant with Abram and He said, "And I will make of thee a great nation, and I will bless thee, and make thy name great; and thou shalt be a blessing." Just as God expected Abram to be a blessing, it certainly goes for us too. The Abrahamic inheritance of blessing comes with rights and responsibilities.

Women in the ultimate fourth dimension of reigning are very intentional in setting up generational legacy for their children (where applicable) and much further afield in ways such as leaving a Will, setting up Trust Funds, charities, Foundations, thriving businesses and others. The Reigning DNA of Purpose, Excellence, Abundance and Contribution is practised lavishly. They are modern day Dorcas (Acts 9: 36).

What is God's intention for wealth?

My brother Richard, shared this useful illustration with me concerning wealth. He said, if you were the head of a government, and were looking for a charity to distribute crisis relief in different parts of the world, you're more likely to choose a charity that has a wide distribution channel such as Red Cross International; rather than a small local one without an established distribution channel and a track record of generosity. In a similar way, God is more likely to give money and other resources to whom He knows will find a way to get that which is intended for the people to the people. Why should God give us wealth if we truly aren't committed to being a blessing to others? If all we are interested in, is to hoard the resources and make ourselves rich, without the mindset of being a consistent contributor, it defeats the purpose. What would be the point?

Simply put, God's purpose of wealth (in all its multiple facets) is to share the real love! "For the love of money is the root of all evil: which while some coveted after, they have erred from the faith, and pierced themselves through with many sorrows." (1Timothy 6:10). Loving the wrong thing will prevent us from loving the right thing. An excessive love for money will derail our ability to love God and His children.

Money is a store of value. And our handling of money is also a graphic indicator of our own value system. Some people love the resources, but they don't want to do the will of the Master; the serving, the giving and the sacrificing! Sadly, some are only interested in the 'frills and fancy' parts that come with having great wealth. We must have the mindset of radical generosity and be prepared to give to others. We shouldn't think of keeping it all for ourselves. We must be minded to partner with God for the ethical and generous management of our wealth.

Strategic parenting, mentoring and equipping of children are invaluable parts of one's wealth base. If we are involved in the lives of children, we must prepare them to be godly stewards of wealth! The quickest way to lose money is to pass it on to unprepared heirs.

When God instructed Solomon in 2 Chronicles 1: 7 to ask Him for whatever it is that he wanted, he didn't ask for the obvious. Can you imagine being given a blank cheque from the El Shaddai, the God of all abundance! Most people would make some lavish requests. In modern times, God would be 'shopping' for some top-end crazily priced luxury items that would make His 'head' spin! But not Solomon. He asked Him for wisdom, knowledge and discernment to reign over God's great people! It's worth taking some time to examine and reflect on the answer that God gave Solomon and its implications in 2 Chronicles 1: 11-12:

> *And God said to Solomon, because this was in thine heart, and thou hast not asked riches, wealth, or honour, nor the life of thine enemies, neither yet hast asked long life; but hast asked wisdom and knowledge for thyself, that thou mayest judge my people, over whom I have made thee king: Wisdom and knowledge is granted unto thee; and I will give thee riches, and wealth, and honour, such as none of the kings have had that have been before thee, neither shall there any after thee have the like.*

The real wealth is to have all that we have (to whatever degree), and to still know and live with the consciousness that God is and forever will be the ultimate Source and Lord over all! Our money ought to be on a mission for the advancement of God's agenda.

The question for all of us now is, "Can we wisely steward great wealth! To be an effective custodian of wealth takes training, preparation and godly surrender! God's wisdom supersedes riches. God blessed Solomon with a desire towards Him and wisdom to be of value to people. It was only then he could be trusted with great wealth.

We need adequate funding for stable family life, executing one's purpose and carrying the weight of other responsibilities for the expansion of God's kingdom.

The data is clear how destructive 'sudden millions' are to some people who win the lottery or other similar means.

> *But you have exalted yourself against the Lord of heaven; and they have brought the vessels of His house before you, and you and your nobles, your wives and your concubines have been drinking wine from them; and you have praised the gods of silver and gold, of bronze, iron, wood, and stone, which do not see, hear or understand. But the God in whose hand are your life-breath and all your ways, you have not glorified. (Daniel 5:23).*

This is a serious charge against those who exalt the stuff that money can purchase above the Almighty God who is the Giver and the real Gift! For life to be well with us, we must live with balance. We shouldn't make an idol of wealth, neither should we demonise it.

Rain for the Reign

Money answers all things and it sure is a defence (Ecclesiastes 10:19, 7:12)! Without adequate funding on every level and in every context, it creates suffering. Sadly, for some, it may even lead individuals to compromise their faith.

Even though many parts of the world are still experiencing the curtailment of face-to-face interactions, money is still exchanging hands every minute of every day! According to the *Office for National Statistics* (UK), "The proportion of shopping carried out online reached record levels in January [2021], to 35.2% of all sales. This is an increase of 5.6 percentage points compared with December 2020, and an increase of 15.7 percentage points compared with January 2020." God has created us to be problem-solvers. When you solve pertinent problems for people in an excellent manner, for a large number of individuals, you will be compensated for it.

We serve an unlimited God who wants us to thrive in financial dominion. Dr. Mike Murdock in his thought-provoking book *Why Men Stay Poor* states the following concerning the pointlessness of poverty:

❑ *It is unwise to be poor.*

❑ *It is unnatural to be poor.*

❑ *It is unscriptural to be poor.*

❑ *It is unnecessary to be poor.*

Reading these statements may have stirred within you some discomfort, as it did for me. But the reality is clear that far much more can be accomplished for God and His kingdom with wealth, and we would be hard-pressed to find comparable benefits of poverty.

However, the greatest poverty isn't a lack of money. It is the absence of God, life-giving relationships, discovering one's purpose and joy. The truth remains that God has given us the power to get wealth. Have we efficiently stewarded the power or is the power untapped? Poverty is a 'voice silencer' as in the account in Ecclesiastes 9:14-16.

> *There was a little city, and few men within it; and there came a great king against it, and besieged it, and built great bulwarks against it: Now there was found in it a poor wise man, and he by his wisdom delivered the city; yet no man remembered that same poor man. Then said I, Wisdom is better than strength: nevertheless the poor man's wisdom is despised, and his words are not heard.*

Let not our voices be silenced by poverty. Because it is our voices that will forever be the missing piece of the symphony of conquest and dominion in earth's dark night. Without our unshackled voices the world's brightest light will still have a void and Satan's darkness be made to roam freely! Ithiel in Proverbs 30: 7-9 made a request that is worth modelling. He said:

> *Two things have I required of thee; deny me them not before I die: Remove far from me vanity and lies: give me neither poverty nor riches; feed me with food convenient for me: Lest I be full, and deny thee, and say, Who is the Lord? or lest I be poor, and steal, and take the name of my God in vain.*

Wealth, if correctly administered, positions us for impact and influence. It is a life and values amplifier. Our wealth can reach the four corners of the world, parts of which our feet may never reach. Let's put some structures in place to enlarge our capacity for great wealth with a Godly purpose, excellently harnessed, abundantly shared and strategically contributed.

Empowered Wealth Mindset

You may have read the foregoing descriptors of the four reigning dimensions (Wonder, Winning, Waning and Wandering) of wealth and may feel overwhelmed. You may have said, "It's too late for me." It's never too late to make a change for the better. As long as our hearts are still beating and we have the courage to change, then we have what it takes to attain astonishing victories in our finances!

Admittedly, the journey of wealth creation is best started early in life. (Let's empower our children and young people with financial literacy). If you have this book in your hand, it means you're not in the grave, thank God. So *now* is always the best time to begin. Jaachynma N.E. Agu said, "Wrong thinking will take your life the wrong way, channelling your thoughts to the right direction will cause you to soar in life." It does not matter our ages or how grim our finances may be at the moment; we can learn to get better than we were yesterday. So, whether we are seventeen, twenty-seven, forty-seven, sixty-seven, seventy-seven or even ninety-seven without a penny in our purses; it is never too late to create a brighter future for yourself, those you love and those you choose to serve and add value to! Let's begin to go forward…with adequate help.

Wealth and Our Words

If we want more financial empowerment, it is a huge mistake to speak maliciously of the rich. We won't learn from wealthy people, let alone implement their suggestions and instructions if we believe negative things about them. On a much deeper level, why would the compass of your life guide you to the money destination that you despise? If we speak things such as "Rich people are evil and greedy", "Rich people climb on other people to get to where they are" and "Rich people sacrifice their families to get money". The truth is some rich and poor people can be evil, if they choose to be so. It is not the money that makes people evil or not, people simply make a decision to be evil or not to be.

Farrah Gray wisely states, "Money doesn't change who you are; it magnifies who you really are." There are countless rich people who are humble, godly, amazing, smart, hardworking, generous and have lovely functional families. The same can also be said of poor people who choose to be so. Be truthful, which would you prefer to be-have all of the aforementioned admirable qualities and be poor or have the same admirable qualities and be rich? I know the one I would prefer, hands down! Let's tell the truth and shame the Devil. The patriarch of our faith, Abraham, has modelled integrity whilst having great wealth.

Don't forget, money is one of the tools (other tools are time, energy, skills, personal qualities) in people's hands to accomplish their purpose, impact the world, leave a legacy; all of which bring God much glory. Again, let's neither deify nor demonise money. It is what it is- an option currency. We all get to choose what we do with it. It can be used for much good or much evil. Just like if you constantly speak negatively about another woman or anyone for that matter, after a while the relationship breaks down and she doesn't want to be anywhere near us. So it is with money, if we speak maliciously about money, it will repel us. Money must be 'courted' before it can be counted.

Wealth and Work

There is a labour dimension for the creation of wealth that will have an impact and that will be generational. Proverbs 14:23 states, "In all labour there is profit: but the talk of the lips tendeth only to penury." The NIV version puts it this way, "All hard work brings a profit, but mere talk leads only to poverty." To become all that God designed us to be in having sufficient wealth to fulfil our purpose, make a significant impact and to leave a generational legacy we must arise, reign and do exploits!

To thrive financially, we must exercise our minds consistently whilst simultaneously feeding it with the correct 'diet'. Embracing the "get rich quick" mentality is a recipe for unscrupulous behaviour that will short-circuit our integrity. Are we spending some time each day doing something to move in the financial direction that we desire? What are the tangible and intangible skills and attitudes that we are deliberately entrenching in our 'Reigning DNA'?

Let's all answer Earl Nightingale's insightful wealth survey questions. Firstly, "What are your plans for increasing your income, how much do you want to earn?" Secondly, "How much money have you decided to be worth by the time you are sixty-five [or retired, whichever comes first]?"

It is without question that if we will succeed at moving from where we are to where we want to be in our finances, we must be prepared to work diligently and make the required sacrifices. Excuses are unacceptable at this stage of our lives.

Honour God with our Wealth...First

Our first responsibility in terms of giving is our privilege and duty to return the tithe to the Lord. At the core of every sin is a sin of dishonour. Therefore, withholding the tithe is a sin of dishonouring God and His explicit instruction in Malachi 3: 10 to"Bring ye all the tithes into the storehouse, that there may be meat in mine house, and prove me now herewith, saith the Lord of hosts, if I will not open you the windows of heaven, and pour you out a blessing, that there shall not be room enough to receiveit." Does this sound like it is optional? Does this sound as if it should be done when it is convenient?

God says not returning our tithes and offering, amounts to robbing Him. He also states that robbing Him creates a wide-open door in our lives to be cursed. "Will a man rob

God? Yet ye have robbed me. But ye say, wherein have we robbed thee? In tithes and offerings. Ye are cursed with a curse: for ye have robbed me, even this whole nation." (Malachi 3: 8-9). Imagine not only robbing God but also robbing the nations. Withholding our tithes and offering is an assault on loving the nations through evangelism. We certainly don't want to be living under the curse of God Almighty.

Let's delete the crippling lie of Satan; the deception that we can't afford to tithe. The truth is we can't afford not to consistently and accurately tithe. Think of El Gibbor, God as Warrior and Champion, on your team rebuking every devourer that dares to come near you and yours. The most reputable solicitor in town can't come anywhere near the sheer protection that comes from the courts of heaven on your behalf. Let's honour God and watch Him work for us. Better still, honour God with our tithes and enjoy unprecedented joy in our souls, pep in our ordered steps and confidence in our mouths.

Just like God said, "Prove me now if I will not open the windows of heaven and pour you out a blessing" (Malachi 3:10). Let's pause and appreciate three vital life- changing words in this promise. Firstly, "I will". When God Himself makes a promise, it's yes and amen. Victory won. Case closed! Secondly, "windows" will be opened. In every house there are more windows than doors. God will open the windows of heaven! Thirdly, "Pour out". This suggests that there is an abundance; not a trickle that is barely coming down. Pour means to flow outward, spurt, surge, spout, burst forth, ooze, spew and gush out! The tithe is sacred, let's not tamper with it. Like I've said before, we can always start where we are, there is always mercy and forgiveness with God!

Relationship Capital

Everything that we desire in life is encompassed in our relationships; including our wealth. We are only one relationship from great wealth in every area of life. Our associations are a graphic picture of who we are becoming! The impact and potential of our associations can never be overestimated! In business, connections are priceless! One person can change your life forever!

Think about it, everything from creation to eternity is all about relationship! God is a genius at relationships and He is the only One we are permitted to be a copycat of. If we are serious about going forward financially, we by necessity, must become intentional about creating, maintaining and contributing to healthy relationships.

To get to significant wealth means we have to genuinely loveand serve people without any hidden agenda. Love and serve people well. Solve their problems and we'll be renumerated. Another thing, not all currencies have a symbol before it! They oftentimes have greater rewards than the dollars and sterling. This currency is RELATIONSHIP! One phone call can open a door that having a million pounds can't.

Relationship is the highest currency. It's in relationships that we learn about all other currencies and how to harness the capital of wealth to do our part in the end time move of God in the earth! When we are on our death beds, when everything gets stripped away, it is the quality of our relationships that will determine the quality of our lives.

Multiple Sources of Income

Having only one source of income is a dangerous financial reality. It is like living on a knife's edge. All it takes is for a boss to call you in his office and give you whatever version of his I-am-so-sorry-but-we-have-to-let-you-go speeches. This conversation usually takes less than ten minutes. In fact, this is usually a monologue; with little to no room for negotiation. Covid-19 has made this truth indisputable. You can have all sorts of fancy qualifications and still lose your job. Or you can have only one thriving business and it can go under.

Operating our financial lives on a single source of income; especially on a long-term basis, is an unnecessarily high-risk financial behaviour. It takes just one major sickness, one company restructuring, one decision maker's dislike to pull the financial rug completely from under our feet. Ask yourself, "What else can I trade other than my time?" Ensure that much thinking, research and implementation are done to have multiple sources of passive and active incomes. Active income is when you're exchanging your time for financial compensation. In passive income, after the initial setting up of the income-generating strategy, it is largely (by no means totally) done on autopilot.

According to the *Office for National Statistics* (UK, February, 2021), "Both coronavirus and EU [European Union] exit-related uncertainties may have caused some employers to reduce staff. Redundancies have increased faster during the coronavirus pandemic than during the financial crisis of 2008 to 2009". Many lost their jobs; some were furloughed and some got not so much as a penny. Let's begin to implement multiple streams of income to help safeguard our financial wellbeing.

Saving

One of our major financial responsibilities and priorities is saving. We grew up hearing the advice to, "Save for the rainy days." We need to also save for the sunny days so that when financial and other opportunities come our way, we can respond in ways that favour us. Not putting aside money for future opportunities and emergencies is unwise.

Financial health must include consistent savings. Let's aim to save a minimum of ten percent of what we earn. If we are able to save more, why not, the more the merrier! However, if at this season in our lives we can't save the desired minimum of ten percent, be consistent with whatever we can do. The important thing with saving is first developing the discipline so that when our finances improve, we will already be in flow and we simply increase the percentage.

Emergency Fund

An Emergency Fund is a readily available source of assets that is accessible to help people to handle financial crises such as sudden major health problems, house and vehicle repairs and loss of income. The function of an Emergency Fund is to have a portion of cash and other extremely liquid assets (A liquid asset is an asset that can be easily converted into cash in a very short time.) that are readily available to pay the expenses for financial emergencies. It provides a financial short-term safety net in a financial emergency. Importantly, it reduces the likelihood of incurring debts at exorbitant interest rates, provides financial privacy and safeguards making financial decisions with negative long-term consequences due to the pressure and urgency of a temporary situation. For example, cashing in a fixed-term ISA (Individual Saving Account) or withdrawing from retirement portfolios.

Financial advisors recommend that individuals establish an Emergency Fund to meet the living expenses for three to six months. However, the extremely harsh global financial realities for many during the pandemic suggest strongly that we need more than six months. Ideally, saving eighteen months living expenses would be a welcomed financial safety net and would go a very long way in alleviating financial stress.

Investing

Saving is a critical strategy for financial wellbeing. However, if this is not coupled with investing its ability to propel us forward to financial freedom is very limited; especially in light of the all-time paltry interest rates offered by the banking systems around the world! Very few wealthy people got there by only saving. The majority made their wealth from investments.

In most countries, interest rates on savings are minimal in light of inflation, the cost of living and global economic realities such as we've never seen before. Think of the financial effect of the Coronavirus. In the United Kingdom on March 26, 2020 interest rate fell to an all-time low of 0.1% (Trading Economics, 2020)! If we thought only saving money was not the best return on investment prior to the pandemic, now we can categorically say it is unwise. Not only is it inefficient money, but the value is actually being eroded by the higher Consumer Price Inflation rate of 0.9% in January 2021 (*Office for National Statistics*, UK).

It is important for investment portfolios to be diversified to safeguard and minimise risks. However, initially, a primary investment strategy can be selected to be the focus before attempting to put many irons in the fire all at once. Before investing, ensure that you are sufficiently informed about the investment ventures and have at least some genuine interests. If needed, seek the guidance and services of financial experts that will give you the informed, detailed and bespoke support that your unique financial situation needs.

Money Tracking

Like wisdom, money is a defence. Without adequate money, we are vulnerable. As such, we need to be aware in great detail about the inflow and outflow of every penny that we earn. This is referred to as Money Tracking. It is a vital money habit of using a method (whether hard and digital templates or apps) to consistently be aware of our income and expenses and other money-related matters throughout a given period of time.

Money tracking is an essential activity for wealth creation. It is impossible to achieve, maintain and secure great wealth without keeping track of your money; all of it. Do you budget? Do you know how much money you spend per day, week, month, quarter, year and from which category of your budget? When we track our money, we will almost always find areas where we can be more frugal. For as long as I can remember, we were given the advice, "Don't hang your basket where you can't reach it." In other words, don't be wasteful and live beyond your means. To be great in any area of life, we have to master the discipline of delayed gratification. If we practise spending on a whim, it will be difficult, if not impossible, to accumulate great wealth. Intentionally reduce your living expenses and increase your income.

The best way to track your money is the way that works for you to provide consistent information about your financial matters.

1. Do you presently track your money?

2. What method do you use or plan to use?

3. What can you do to improve your consistency with regards to tracking your money?

Make the declaration, "I am an excellent tracker of my money and I do so consistently!" Now let's make goals and plans to complement our declaration.

Know Your Net Worth

To truly reposition yourself financially, you must know your net worth. When you know your worth, you will not settle for living a life of being oblivious of your exact financial location. Net worth is essentially the sum total of an individual's assets (owned) minus all the liabilities (owed). If you have more assets than liabilities, then you have a positive net worth, vice versa.

For example, if all your assets are valued at £360, 000.00 and your liabilities are valued at £400,000.00. You would have a negative net worth of £40.000.00 (Owed). On the other hand, if your assets were valued at £200.000.00 and your liabilities valued at £80.000.00, you would have a positive net worth of £120.000.00.

Playing the guessing game with our finances is a sure recipefor financial failure or underachievement. Would you be happy with the mechanic that guessed how much air he is putting in your tyres? Would you be amused with the nurse who guessed the weight of your baby girl at birth? Would you be pleased with your accountants if they were simply guessing when doing your tax returns? Would you find it funny if your medical doctor guessed that your blood pressure was high? Well, well, well- we wouldn't tolerate guesswork from anyone. Right? Right. Why are we tolerating guesswork from ourselves concerning such an important area of life as money?

Money Tracking can be done with the old fashion pen and paper or Excel spreadsheet way by listing the value of all your assets minus all your liabilities. It can also be done with the help of apps, other technical aids or the help of a chartered accountant. However, not knowing our financial situation isn't going to make us into financial wonders. The only thing that it will accomplish is cause us to wander and live in financial bondage.

Demolishing Personal Debt

In essence, personal debt is spending that which we don't have. It is spending tomorrow's harvest today. It must be acknowledged that many have used debts strategically and with discipline. In fact, many people attribute their strategic use of debt for the creation of their wealth. However, be this as it may, God's stance on debt throughout the Scriptures is very clear, it's not the ideal way to live; full stop! We are told categorically to owe no one anything except to love him (Romans 13:8) and that the borrower is the slave of the lender (Proverbs 22:7)! Financial debt is slavery and every slavery is extremely damaging!

Debt creates financial anxiety which is compounded since it's usually serviced at high interest rates. Wherever we have debt, let's set a SMART goal and also make a definite plan to become debt free as a matter of urgency. Those who are debt free or have been debt free would say, it's a wonderful feeling and it causes you to live life in a whole new way. It gives a sense of freedom, having greater options and not to mention the joy of being able to help on a greater and more impactful scale.

The Debt Snowball Method is useful strategy by Dave Ramsey that can be used to eradicate debt.

1. Record ALL your debts in order from the smallest to the largest.

2. Pay the minimum payment on ALL of your debts.

3. Put any extra money towards paying off the smallest debt first.

4. Once the smallest debt is paid off you roll that money over towards paying off the next smallest debt.

5. Continue doing this till all your debts are paid off.

The opposite of this method is called The Avalanche Method whereby you go from biggest debt to the smallest. Continue doing this till all your debts are paid off.

WEALTH TRANSFORMATION STRATEGIES

1. Develop a healthy Christ-honouring and effective mindset about wealth. God gave His children the power to achieve wealth (Deuteronomy 8:18). And when it is surrendered to Him, it can be a very useful tool in His hand. Paradoxically, although wealth is possible and is useful, we must always remember that all is absolute vanity and proper

vexation of spirit. Our highest priority is living for God!

2. Become (or continue to be) a consistent tither. "Bring ye all the tithes into the storehouse, that there may be meat in mine house, and prove me now herewith, says the Lord of hosts…" (Malachi 3:10-11). Here is a suggestion, set up a Standing Order to pay your tithes automatically to your local church. (Remember to reference it with your name.)

3. Practice a life of simplicity. In our pursuit for wealth let there be much contentment.

4. Set financial goals. Without financial goals, we would be wandering in the dark. If we don't know where we are heading financially, we can never thrive. Wealth is not accidental nor is it random. Wealth is intentional.

5. Make and observe a budget. It is a distribution system of how you intend to allocate your finances under pre-determined categories.

6. Begin to save consistently. Automate it. Start at the percentage that you can afford now; with the intention to increase it when possible. Save an Emergency Fund first.

7. Practise radical generosity to be a blessing to all (not only money; but advice, time, skills etc.). It is truly a blessing to give (Acts 20: 35). It is a universal principle. As you water others you will be watered and God promises to satisfy your soul even in drought (Isaiah 58:11)!

8. Financial Automation is a very powerful strategy so you do not have to rely on self-discipline and memory. Also use financial apps to assist!

- Set up automated savings, investing and bill-paying functionality with your financial institutions to improve your finances.

- Set up balance notifications to help you track your financial accounts balances.

- Set up 'minimum payment' or 'pay in full' instructions on all your credit card accounts to avoid late or missed payment with its accompanying interest costs and damage to your Credit Score.

9. If indebted, make a plan with a deadline to come out of debt as fast as you can!

10. Live frugally. God hates waste. Jesus instructed the disciples to pick up even the very "fragments" (Matthew 14: 20).

11. Negotiate everything. Get several estimates and do adequate research (especially needful when spending large sums of money). The art of negotiation is viewed as a second income!

12. Begin creating generational wealth and legacy. "A good man leaves an inheritance to his children's children" (Proverbs 13:22).

13. Practise gratitude to God and the connections He has given you. Thankfulness produces increase in every area of life. We are commanded to be thankful unto Him and bless His name (Psalm 100:4). A gratitude journal can help you to

practise being grateful by entering every morning or evening at least five things you are thankful for.

14. Seek financial mentorship and successful connections. It is often said, "Success leaves clues." When you are given sound Biblically based instructions, follow them. The fragrance of success will inspire you.

15. To prosper you must be willing to invest time, money and energy for your financial advancement. Read, Read, Read! Become a learner, ignorance is not bliss. Executed financial information and ideas will revolutionise your life. There are multiple ways to become more financially literate- ask questions, listen to useful YouTube videos, buy books, attend seminars and conferences, join a library and download free useful material.

The lack of financial wherewithal to meet the demands of life can be very demoralising, distressing and if not handled well may lead to one's demise. Money is indeed a defence (Ecclesiastes 7:12). Wealth is what it is; a tool in God's hand (if welet Him). It is also a currency to give us the capacity to buy options and in doing so we can intentionally design our lives, rather than live by financial default. We need adequate finances to execute our purpose, live with excellence, abundance and to become a contributor for the glory of God, the service of humanity and to enjoy financial and general wellbeing.

Money is a useful instrument in the hands of women who have made a rock-solid decision about who their Source is and have made Christ the Lord of their lives. They have surrendered everything, including their wealth to Him. Being fully aware of God's intention for wealth, they have become distribution channels to display God's might and love in the earth.

Wealth mastery requires diligence and us doing our share to partner with God in becoming wonders in our financial lives. We are to develop an empowering wealth mindset. In addition, we must know assuredly that our words and work have significant impact on our wealth dimension positioning. By necessity, we must honour God with our wealth, first. A rich reward is promised for obedience. Likewise, grave consequences will result in the lives of those who choose to live otherwise.

Importantly, we need healthy relationship to serve, love and grow, if we are to become great financially. Relationships are our most valuable currency! If our financial lives are to be transformed, we need to save, invest, track our wealth, budget, become debt free and become students of finances. These and other transformation strategies will revolutionize our wealth and greatly impact the rest of our lives.

WEALTH TRANSFORMATION TASK

1. In terms of the Reigning Dimensions regarding *Wealth*, where are you? (Tick one)

Wonder ☐ Winning ☐ Waning ☐ Wandering ☐

2. Develop a Wealth Declaration: Eg. I'm highly compensated for the valuable goods and services I bring to the marketplace.

_____

_____

3. Which of the Wealth Transformation Strategies would give you the maximum impact now?

_____

_____

4. Set a SMART (Specific, Measurable, Attainable, Realistic and Time-bound) wealth goal.

_____

_____

5. Motivation: Why is this goal important to you?

_____

_____

_____

6. Accountability: Which person or system will hold you accountable?

_____

7. Review Date:

_____

8. Reward: How will you celebrate achieving this goal?

_____

_____

Chapter Nine
Transformation Agent #9
WARRIOR-STANCE

"He will never fail us, even in the face of trials and hindrances."

Linda Evans Shepherd

The war is on. As such, a warrior-stance is necessary. This stance is to live with the conviction and consciousness that we are soldiers of the Lord. It is also joining in the teamwork and camaraderie of the fellowship of the saints as God's end time army! When you have yielded yourself to the Lordship of Jesus Christ and allowed Him to make you into a vessel of honour and wonder, you're automatically placed on the assassin list of Satan and his troops.

However, we can take great delight in the fact that where there are great treasures, there is always top-notch security! Our God is a wise investor and He will do everything to safeguard His children. Let me repeat, we must partner with God and have the mindset that we are soldiers in the army of the Lord. A laissez-faire posture on the battlefield will cause the death of the greatness we carry, which may put our very lives at risk. As Alysia Helming said,

> *Strong women aren't simply born. We are forged through the challenges of life. With each challenge we grow [spiritually], mentally and emotionally. We move forward with our head held high and a strength that cannot be denied. A woman who's been through the storm and survived. We are warriors!*

The reigning woman is a kingdom royalty but she is also a warrior for Jesus Christ. She doesn't shirk her responsibilities and is not missing in action from the battlefield. With much commitment, she shows up...as a daughter, wife, mother, sister, auntie, committee member, choir leader, prayer partner, friend, coach, mentor, business owner, philanthropist...to name a few. With convincing courage, she asks, like the valiant warrior David, "Is there not a cause" (1 Samuel 17:29)?

The reigning woman exercises dominion even in times of war. Indeed, the war is on, but the reigning woman knows that she is always royalty. She is forever royalty because she is conscious that Jesus Christ is her Lord and Saviour! Always. At no time can we afford to abandon our CROWN (Christ-like Reign Over Worldly Norms) and start fighting like the heathen that knows not nor fear God. Even in the turmoil of war, we are reigning kingdom royalty whose primary job description is to be an ambassador of love and peace and the minister of reconciliation.

The reigning woman is gracious and peaceful. However, don't be fooled she isn't passive, nobody's doormat and is a million miles from being a wimp. Take note much beloved lady, you're a warrior champion. Do not be afraid. You're more than able to possess your 'Promised Plan' (Jeremiah

11:29), just like Israel did their land of Canaan. Say it out loud with confidence, "I am God's warrior champion!" Repeat this truth for good measure. "I am God's warrior champion!" This is so because your God is your Father and He has never lost a battle. He is ambidextrous and has a multitude of strategies. Some of them may defy logic and others appear to be downright ridiculous; but they never fail. Israel was promised Canaan, but that didn't mean there weren't giants there.

In a similar manner, we have to fight to possess our inheritance. Our warfare isn't carnal, because if we fight the battles having the wrong mindset and with the wrong strategies, we will suffer major losses. "Fight the good fight of faith, lay hold on eternal life, whereunto thou art also called, and hast professed a good profession before many witnesses" (1 Timothy 6:12).

However, where are we in the warrior-stance dimensions?

Warrior-stance Dimensions of Reigning

• 1D Reigning: Wandering

In the *Wandering* 1D reigning dimension of the Warrior-stance, this woman is MIA (Missing in Action)! She hasn't shown up to the battle even though she is in a battle and the world at large is at war! This woman is paralysed by fear. In 2 Timothy 1:7, we are reminded that "God hath not given us the spirit of fear; but of power, and of love, and of a sound mind." Without this soundness of mind, love and power, we will, without fail, go about life wandering; living in the minimal 1D realm. We need the perfect love of Christ which drives out every known fear whether big or small (1

John 4:18). Where there is fear, it is usually accompanied by discouragement and inaction.

When the arch-enemy and our enemies sense our fear, it's game over. Defeat is imminent and being devoured is highly likely.This dismal fate is not our portion, in the name of Jesus! To be merely existing in the 1D realm has huge negative outcomes in both the time and eternal phases of The Reigning Timeline (See the Introduction). Fear forfeits our ability to reign now and forever! Did you know that the fearful is classified with all the others that will be eternally lost? In Revelation 21:8 it states categorically that, "The fearful, and unbelieving, and the abominable, and murderers, and whoremongers, and sorcerers, and idolaters, and all liars, shall have their part in the lake which burns with fire and brimstone: which is the second death." Lord, we ask You for Your help in conquering fear. We surrender every trace of fear right now. Oh great King, we ask You to transform us and transport us from being a wandering 1D warrior. We heed Your call to Rise up, Reign and Do Exploits for You, build Your kingdom, serve humanity and awaken our souls in You. Make us into *wonders* oh Lord, no more will we *wander*!

• 2D Reigning: Waning

In the *Waning* 2D reigning dimension of warrior-stance, we are usually limping and our wounds still need healing. It is also the case where the wound and the wounding become a crutch or a case for needless wars because there is difficulty in healing. Sometimes we simply refuse to be healed despite the administering of 'treatments'. Wounds that refuse to be healed cause pain, are unsightly, break focus, may even be 'smelly'. And the longer the wounds persist, is the greater likelihood of disfigurement. The vital work of healing and deliverance still need to be done with much urgency.

In any area where we've been injured, to falsely believe that time will take care of it, is to invite gangrene of the soul. Ask many amputees (especially those who had diabetes which makes wound healing more difficult) and they will tell you that it was a wound that wasn't addressed in time and or wasn't treated properly that eventually led to loss of limbs. How incapacitating. How tragic. Let's all pause and ask, where in our lives are we still wounded, and or refusing to be healed? Have we caused needless 'amputations' in our families, churches, businesses, friendships, committees, communities and nations? Oftentimes we aren't sufficiently intentional about being healed of past hurts, traumas and dramas; hence we are limping permanently. What intentional healing and deliverance are we going to seek for that which still ails us? Gracious Lord, we ask that You heal us today and let Your healing start within; so that when we are healed, we can help to heal others!

• 3D Reigning: Winning

In the *Winning* 3D reigning dimension of having a warrior-stance, this woman is a confident and healed warrior. There is no shame nor blame attached to the scars. She sees them as testimonies. She is confident and knows that God is for her and that He will make her victorious. She believes one hundred percent that she can do all things through Jesus Christ; even winning the battles of life.

• 4D Reigning: Wonder

The ultimate reigning dimension is becoming a 4D *Wonder!* A 4D woman of wonder knows that she is defended by a host of heaven's army and there's nothing to fear! There is a realm in God when His daughters become fully aware that they operate under heavy-duty protection of the heavenly hosts which are at their full disposal. This gives a sense of protection and confidence in God that negates being fearful and a warmonger. She knows that not every battle is an invitation to fight. Therefore, she chooses her battles carefully.

In this dimension, you are highly protected. Even when you're at war, you stand still and let God fight your battles. This stance, by no means, is a lazy cop-out! On the contrary, it's becoming a skilled warrior trained in God's army, that your power is under much control and you're sensitive to God's moves, strategies and timings. So you know when it's time to do 'nothing'. You know that the battle is already won in Christ.

In this 4D warrior-stance realm, you are a healed warrior. However, it's not good enough to be a healed warrior, but your battle scars become your testimonies and exhortations. Wounds are injuries that are unhealed and still require spiritual attention. However, scars are evidence of healed wounds. So yes, there were injuries, but she is no longer oozing from leaking issues. No pun intended. Four-dimension warriors have scars, but they have been to their Father's surgery and have been made whole.

Frontiers of the Fight

A wise soldier knows that the first frontier to conquer in any war is the inner self! Long before we go traipsing off to conquer frontiers wider afield, let's conquer them on the intimate grounds of our inner self. Charles Spurgeon said, "Beware of no man more than of yourself; we carry our worst enemies within us." It is truly the enemy within that we must contend with most fiercely. Until we have conquered this ground, we will never truly win the battles without; let alone to thrive in triumph and the miraculous and becoming a wonder! Until this essential victory is won, every semblance of external victory will be reduced to a mirage that isn't real and can never last.

Again, we come to the place for the need of integrity. We must be alert, it is the enemy within, which presents the greatest difficulty to fight and is of greater threat to our desire to reign both *now* and *eternally*. Paul acknowledges the war of moral deficit and the war on the internal frontier in Romans 7:18-24. He said:

> For I know that in me (that is, in my flesh,) dwelleth no good thing: for to will is present with me; but how to perform that which is good I find not. For the good that I would I do not: but the evil which I would not, that I do. Now if I do that I would not, it is no more I that doit, but sin that dwelleth in me. I find then a law, that, when I would do good, evil is present with me. For I delight in the law of God after the inward man: But I see another law in my members, warring against the law of my mind, and bringing me into captivity to the law of sin which is in my members. O wretched man that I am! who shall deliver me from the body of this death?

Beloved sister, the reality of the internal war is fierce and frustrating. However, be encouraged, "But the people that do know their God shall be strong, and do exploits" (Daniel 11:32). We thank God that we don't have to fight this war in our flesh, nor do we do it alone. Jesus Christ, our Lord, is our answer to the war within and without. And He is in us the sure hope of glory and victory!

The Motive and Focus for the Battle

The motive for the fight must be thoroughly purged of that which is tainted and self-exalting. The objective of legitimate warfare is the expansion of the kingdom of God. Before we rush into battle, ask ourself, "Whose honour and glory am I fighting for?" It was said of David that he fought the battles of the Lord. The one time he was going to fight because of feeling insulted by Nabal, the fool, Abigail was assigned to him to remind him of his destiny; that he couldn't afford to abort it because of a fool! Let's be honest, we can all remember being drawn into battles because of foolish people who injured our egos which had nothing to do with our kingdom assignment nor the agenda of the King of glory! We simply fought because we consciously or unconsciously believed we could.

God is issuing a Cease-and-Desist Order on pointless battles right now! In these battles, there are no spoils to gain but much to lose. They only bring disrepute on the name of Christ, damage our priceless good name and give us a spiritual bloody nose! Why fight for nothing? Why fight for the wind? The truth is when we begin to have dominion and mastery in spiritual maturity, even when we have every reason to rage war, we won't even bother. We will simply hold our peace or engage at the least combative level. The reigning woman's first duty is to seek peace and pursue it (Psalm 34:14).

The faith of our fathers is under seize in this sin-darkened world and often entertainment-driven church! Therefore, if there is only one battle to be fought, it would be for the faith of our fathers. The precepts of the doctrines built on Jesus Christ are worth living and dying for. Let's not be deceived. If Satan can get us so distracted that we are busy walking around with a fire extinguisher, putting out what amounts to petty fires, he knows he has won. If Satan can get us to be constantly fighting, derailing our time, energy and emotions from the real fight that matters; then he will be having a party at our expense.

Be aware that not all distracting and destructive battles will come with 'guns blazing'. Some will come under stealth and appear to be legitimate. For example, Nehemiah was invited to stop his kingdom assignment of spearheading the repair of the wall in Nehemiah 6: 2, to meet with the scheming enemies of God, Sanballat and Tobiah! Yeah right…an innocent meeting. No. This meeting and others like it are ploys of Satan to get us to fight foolish battles with the haters of the cross of God, rather than doing what God has instructed us to do.

On the other side of the coin, there are times when there are legitimate problems to be addressed but not by us, as is seen in Acts 6:1-8 in the early church. The disciples were making a lot of progress; the numbers in the church were increasing and then… "There arose a murmuring of the Grecians against the Hebrews". When God's kingdom and yourself are making progress, be extra vigilant not to get swept up in the demands and or battles of the moment. Ask yourself, "Am I being distracted to leave my kingdom-assigned post?"

Even though the needs of the Grecian widows were urgent, it was not the divine priorities for the disciples! With much wisdom, the disciples said unto the multitudes, "It is not reason that we should leave the word of God, and serve tables... But we will give ourselves continually to prayer, and to the ministry of the word" (Acts 6: 2, 4). Let's do an evaluation of our lives (ministry, career, family, finances, relationships) are we busy "serving tables"; engaging in tasks that are distracting us from our assignment?

As reigning women of wonder, it's important to ensure that we are not fighting battles because of our wrong motives, wrong assessments and wrong foci!

Learning from a Soldier!

According to Private Gayle, an ex-soldier in the British army, the aim of the training in the army is to remove your civilian mindset. It breaks you down and builds you back up. Does this remind you of being in God's army? It removes our carnal fleshy mindset and gives us the mindset of Christ. The Queen is the head of the British army and the regiment is a royal regiment. As such, you take on the royalty of the Queen under the royal regiment. From the outset in the British army training, you 'lose' your first name and you take on the Queen's identity. For example, if your name is Susan Brown and you're being trained as a trooper. Your new name would be, Trooper Brown. Your training replaces your first name.

In a very similar manner, Jesus Christ is the head of the church. And as enlisted soldiers in His army we are broken down and built back up in Him! We are even surnamed by Him too like He did for Jacob and Israel! "For Jacob my servant's sake, and Israel mine elect, I have even called thee by thy name: I have surnamed thee" (Isaiah 45:4). Presuming that we have said "yes" to Christ, what have we lost in order to take on the identity of the King of heaven?

A soldier that does well and stays alive must be prepared to take orders; with no questions asked! Soldiers are trained to take orders. There is no place in the army for those who are hard-headed and disobedient. Being active in the British army, you are paid 24/7 by the Crown; you are technically not your own; you live for the Queen and country. Are we living for the King and kingdom advancement? Jesus not only takes care of us 24/7, but He also bought us twice with His very life. Who are we living for? Are we still our own? Or are we truly surrendered to the total will of God? "Jesus answered and said unto him, if a man love[s] me, he will keep my words: and my Father will love him, and we will come unto him, and make our abode with him" (John 14:23).

Private Gayle said that to be on time in the army is considered to be late; they must be five minutes early at all times! Lateness is not tolerated. The reigning woman must become known for being punctual. The late entry has been glamorized by many. The woman who reigns in the 4D realm has mastered being punctual. Things do happen, but to be known to be permanently late is not a flattering reputation. Most of us need to improve in this area. And congratulations to those who are almost always on time!

The motto that is in operation in the British army is that of leaving no man behind. You may not be the fastest nor the strongest at whatever the task may be, but you have to possess a very strong and determined mindset. Don't give up when you encounter obstacles. This is a distinctive mark of a seasoned soldier; persistence and tenacity. When you lose focus, that is the time that the enemy strikes. A soldier is trained for combat and hence must be vigilant. These are the same principles of persistence and tenacity that we must embody, if we are to have the victory in and for Christ! Courage isn't only needed for combat, but also to stand up for that which is right; a type of moral combat. Discipline is everything and to carry out order. Respect for others, loyalty, commitment and integrity are vital traits of a soldier.

Soldiers have specific jargons and language that help to keep themselves and their peers safe. For example, watch your 6 and your 12, means to watch your back and your front respectively. It's abbreviated and coded so it is concise and conveys a meaning that is unmistakable; because it's not lost in a lot of crisis-influenced language. This increases safety, secrecy (you don't want your opponents knowing your business), wellbeing and a sense of security because there is far less room for miscommunication, misunderstanding and death.

Every country's army operates with certain core values. It is the intention that with adequate training and growth over time, those that are committed will become the embodiment of the identified core values. Are we committed to the core values of the kingdom of God and our personal core values? When your values become your lifestyle, your life will go to the next level and ultimately become a wonder in the hand of the King and for the King!

In the army, if you are not disciplined, you die and cause the death of others. As in God's army, we shouldn't fight amongst ourselves, we oppose the common enemy! A soldier never stops training. Skilled soldiers don't go about discharging their weapons randomly! What about you? Do you start 'firing' at the slightest thing? Sometimes winning a war simply means not fighting one!

Self-discipline is of the uttermost importance in the army of the Lord. As a soldier of the cross, are we waning and causing the death of others by our lack of discipline? Or are we reigning with the consciousness and commitment that we are soldiers of the cross? Training comes in phases and there is a recognition of accomplishments as progress is made. When we said "yes" to Christ, we didn't become a wonder in its fullest dimension overnight. Greatness cannot be microwaved, it's a slow cooker process. But rest assured that you are going from glory to glory.

Characteristics of God's Warriors

To thrive in any noble endeavour, we need to *be* before we *do*! Before we can successfully and adequately address warfare strategies, we need to explore the characteristics of the warriors. Who have we allowed ourselves to become? The kind of warrior we are at our core, will greatly impact the outcome of the war. The battle is not won so much on the basis of engaging weaponry. Rather, the battle is primarily won when God's children become a processed sword in His mighty hand. As God said of Israel, so He is saying to you woman of God, "Thou art my battle axe and weapons of war." (Jerimiah 51:20). Notice that *you* are the battle axe and weapon of war. The emphasis is on who we allow ourselves to *become* and to a lesser degree what we *do*.

An untrained and undisciplined soldier does not advance the agenda of the battle. She is a danger to herself and her comrades. Let's make the main thing, the main thing; becoming rather than doing. Whilst no wise soldier goes to war without weapons (strategies) but more importantly, none goes to war without being in a ready state for the war. There is no end to what God can do with a life that is surrendered and equipped to the degree of becoming God's battle axe and weapon of war. Here is what was said of Israel in Jeremiah 51: 20-23 and parallels can bedrawn for us too as we go forth to secure comprehensive victory through God and for God!

> *For with thee will I break in pieces the nations, and with thee will I destroy kingdoms. And with thee will I break in pieces the horse and his rider; and with thee will I break in pieces the chariot and his rider. With thee also will I break in pieces man and woman; and with thee will I break in pieces old and young; and with thee will I break in pieces the young man and the maid. I will also break in pieces with thee the shepherd and his flock; and with thee will I break in pieces the husbandman and his yoke of oxen; and with thee will I break in pieces captains and rulers.*

Warrior-stance Characteristics

Here are some characteristics that should typify a life that is God's prepared and authorised battle axe and skilled soldier:

Focused Follower

A kingdom soldier comes under the Lordship and leadership of the Army General, Jesus Christ. She possesses the mindset of submission and her heart is fixed trusting in and yielded to the Lord (Psalm 57:7, 108:1).

Fed

To go into war hungry and devoid of heaven's manna is to court being taken out by the sniper of Satan and his agents of mass destruction. Our hearts, mouths and lives must be filled with the Word of God. Job said He loved God's laws more than his necessary food (Job 23:12)! Imagine that. Our lives would be totally transformed if we begin to be more passionate about God's Word more than food. God's truth is the only safe and accurate strategic manual to safely engage the enemy. We are advised to let the Word of God dwell in us richly. There is a food that is above all other foods. "It is written, Man shall not live by bread alone, but by every word that proceedeth out of the mouth of God" (Matthew 4:4). To be 'malnourished', is spiritual suicide on the battlefield.

Fearless

When there is absolutely no fear in your heart except for God, you are dead and at the same time too alive for Satan to handle. Peace is a necessity to be fearless. Psalm 119:165 states, "Great peace have they which love thy law: and nothing shall offend them." Peace is the presence of God in all situations, not the non- existence of war. We can have peace and be fearless even in the midst of the battle. There is a time to play and have fun. But when it is wartime, it is just that, wartime. It is suicidal to have a weak mindset and resolve when going into war and engaging the enemy. "And from the days of John the Baptist until now the kingdom of heaven suffereth violence, and the violent take it by force" (Mathew 11:12).

Faithful

To be missing in action in any army is a criminal offence. Thisis even more so in the army of the Lord. We are called to radical faithfulness. "But he that shall endure unto the end, the same shall be saved" (Matthew 24:13). We can't recant, so help us God. Our faithfulness will determine the outcome of our eternal destiny.

Fit

To be enlisted and thrive in the army of the Lord we must be fit. And to be fit requires disciplined training for reigning. This involves consistently studying the Word of God, praying, fasting and being in fellowship. It is never safe to be flabby and out of spiritual shape.

Finisher

We serve a God who is Alpha and Omega. I wonder why He isn't just Alpha only. What is the importance of God being Omega? Many great things have been started: marriage, projects, businesses, books, schools... ministries. Alas, many never finish. May the Finisher's anointing rest on us, even now. Let's never, never, never quit. Some battles are long and intense. Nevertheless, we must be committed to finishing that which we have been commissioned to start!

Friendly

Being a soldier is not the same as being a warlord! The pathway of peace is a priority protocol. Our default setting must be that of peace. Before you engage in warfare double-check that it's not a self-assigned, misinterpreted and unduly costly battle that you have no business fighting. Warfare is not for trigger-happy fighters who are too immature to assess the need for war, let alone having an appropriate strategy! When we are not to fight and we do so, we make ourselves odious (extremely unpleasant and repulsive) like the children of Ammon in 1 Chronicles 19. Wouldn't it have been better to send a thousand talents of silver to David as a peace offering rather than using it for war? As wise women of wonder, the priority is a peaceful solution, not needless wars.

Freed

Entering the battle with the excessive weight of sin (whether committed or omitted), will cause defeat. There is absolutely nothing as freeing as knowing that all our sins (past, present and future) are totally forgiven at Calvary and is placed in the sea of forgetfulness. We too must forgive all sins done against us and forgive ourselves for what we've done against others. Both are too heavy for a warrior to drag into battle. Therefore, it is imperative that we are blood-washed and Word-washed to be effective warriors.

Faith-filled

Having unshakable faith is being confident that El Gibbor, the Warrior Champion God, is more than able to be and do what we desire according to His will. Therefore, we must then lift up the shield of faith to quench the fiery dart of the arch-enemy of our souls. To be faith-filled requires action; moving the shield of faith in whichever direction the doubts, fears and debilitating arrows of Satan may come from. Every believer has a measure of faith. However, warriors believe wholeheartedly that the Lord of Host is with them and that the enemy is already defeated and under their victorious feet. They're confident that they will possess the gates of the enemy and his agents. They are already convinced that no weapon that is formed against them will prosper. We need confidence in God and a stance of absolute trust.

> *And what shall I more say? for the time would fail me to tell of Gedeon, and of Barak, and of Samson, and of Jephthah; of David also, and Samuel, and of the prophets: Who through faith subdued kingdoms, wrought righteousness, obtained promises, stopped the mouths of lions. Quenched the violence of fire, escaped the edge of the sword, out of weakness were made strong, waxed valiant in fight, turned to flight the armies of the aliens. (Hebrews 11: 32-34)*

These verses graphically capture the critical role of faith for being triumphant in the battles of life. Indeed, faith is the catalyst for resounding victory!

Fresh

Yesterday's anointing and battle strategy can't win today's war. We must always have a 'now word' before going into battle. Let's ask God to grant unto us a sensitive ear in the realm of the spirit so that we can be accurately positioned and repositioned based on the latest instruction from heaven's Headquarters. It's vital that the same anointing of knowing their times which was upon the tribe of Issachar, also be upon us. Ask God to equip us with what I call the 'Issachar anointing'. This tribe understood their times and hence knew what to do (1Chronicle 12:32). As soldiers in God's army, we need to be relevant and strategically up-to-date with what God is saying and doing *now*. As such, we must be flexible in battle by operating in the new wineskin (See Mathew 9:17).

Fellowship-centred

The kingdom of God and its complementary royal army is the brotherhood of the saints. Therefore, lone rangers don't embody the kingdom army's mindset. Fellowship-centred warriors value family, local community and the ecclesia.

Filled with Joy

We need joy to reign and to engage in God-assign battles. A crushed spirit is a distraction and energy drainer. This state puts our lives and that of our fellow kingdom soldiers at great risk. Let's seek healing and deliverance when there is a wound or struggle that is depleting our joy. We will need joy to win in our battles and to thrive in life in general. Joy is the birthing place for miracles, the musical notes for faith, the glow of a cheerful face and tonic for our strength. Joy and a crushed spirit are both infectious. The former is life-giving and the latter is death-giving. Do everything to preserve your joy!

Fulfilled

We shouldn't go into battle carrying a lot of trinkets to keep us satisfied, they will only weigh us down. In Christ alone is true, lasting and noteworthy satisfaction. Every warrior must be purged to the extent that we have come to a place of total surrender and completion in Him. Every demi-god must be torn from our hearts so that God alone is enthroned. "For where your treasure is, there will your heart be also" (Luke 12: 34).

Fervent in Prayer

Prayer is not only a strategy of warfare (which we will address in the next section) but it is the headquarters of fellowship that births precision in knowing God's mind and hearing His voice. This makes us relevant, efficient and effective in battle and life in general. Loving God's presence is key. Intimacy with Him is a prerequisite for an overcoming life. Relationship is the foundation for effective warfare.

Now that we have a knowledge of the transformation that is required of us, let's take a look at the strategies at our disposal for the battle.

WARRIOR-STANCE TRANSFORMATION STRATEGIES

A strategy is a plan of action using specific tactics and weapons to secure the victory in a battle. As we engage in the battles that life will inevitably throw at us, always remember we are not fighting for victory. We contend from a place of victory and citizenship. We are beloved daughters of God. When you know your identity in Christ, when entering the battle, you shouldn't panic and worst of all, employ incorrect weaponry.

> *For though we walk in the flesh, we do not war after the flesh: (For the weapons of our warfare are not carnal, but mighty through God to the pulling down of strong holds;) Casting down imaginations, and every high thing that exalteth itself against theknowledge of God, and bringing into captivity every thought to the obedience of Christ. (2 Corinthians 10: 3-5)*

1. Put on your Warfare Armoury

We ought to enter the battle from a stance of strength and power that comes only from God. It is suicidal to go to war against the arch-enemy of our soul and not be wearing our full battle armour. If any piece is missing, we are at extreme risk and we could be taken out by an enemy's sniper! We are told clearly in Ephesians 6:10-18 to put on the entire armour of God, that we may be able to withstand the cunning schemes of the devil so thatwe are able to stand! The armoury kit is as follows:

    A. The belt of truth

    B. The breastplate of righteousness

    C. The gospel of peace

    D. The shield of faith

    E. The helmet of salvation

    F. The sword of the Spirit

    G. Prayer

Importantly too, we are instructed in Romans 13:12 to put on the armour of light! The armour of light is often a forgotten piece of the soldier's armour because it appears to be a little-known battle gear. But once you do, it makes perfect sense that light is a part of a soldier's armoury. We would be dead as a dodo going to battle without being able to *see*. For those of us that can remember, we'll tell you how unsettling and inconvenient power cuts were. For many, it's still a current-day experience. If we ever get caught in a power cut without our lamps, torches, generators, or whatever it is that we rely on to guide us in the dark, it's both frightening and painful; hitting yourself against something that you did not remember was in your path.

If we can feel such disorientation being in the dark in a familiar environment, can you imagine the dangers we expose ourselves to, to be in unfamiliar enemy territory without the armour of light? We must be able to *see*, to be able to fight effectively. Darkness is a sure recipe for defeat or possibly death. Let's live and wage war in the light. Jesus is the Light!

2. Employing the Word of God

The Word of God is both an offensive and defensive weapon for being victorious in life. What foundational weapon to have like God's Word which is spirit, life, truth and light! Studying and declaring God's truth with confidence is a super-charged weapon of mass destruction! God's anointed Word must be activated by the Holy Spirit and always be in our mouths. We must also ponder on them day and night. Here is a portion of God's words in Joshua 1:5, 7-8 to encourage us to stand.

> *There shall not any man be able to stand before thee all the days of thy life: as I was with Moses, so I will be with thee: I will not fail thee, nor forsake thee. Only be thou strong and very courageous, that thou mayest observe to do according to all the law, which Moses my servant commanded thee: turn not from it to the right hand or to the left, that thou mayest prosper withersoever thou goest. This book of the law shall not depart out of thy mouth; but thou shalt meditate therein day and night, that thou mayest observe to do according to all that is written therein: for then thou shalt make thy way prosperous, and then thou shalt have good success.*

The power of the Word is critical in deliverance, healing and vanquishing the arrows of the enemies. Strategically confess the Scriptures in alignment with the specifics of your warfare situations. For example, in July 2011, I became extremely claustrophobic. The suddenness and dire intensity took me by surprise. But I remember clearly knowing that it wasn't a medical matter, but a destiny assassin attack from hell. It was even further complicated because my sleep pattern had not returned to normalcy since I had only recently completed my doctoral studies and my body had been trained to survive on very little sleep over the years of studying. So, can you imagine the sheer scale of the terror of the combination of insomnia and extreme claustrophobia? Take my word for it, it was absolutely frightening. One of the strategies I employed for my gradual yet resounding victory was repeating healing scriptures over the situation. These two were the 'Word Lifeline' that I doggedly held on to.

1. *"He giveth his beloved sleep." Psalm 127:2*

2. *"For God hath not given us the spirit of fear; but of power, and of love, and of a sound mind."* (2 Timothy 1:7)

I repeated these verses morning, noon, night and in-between. If these Scriptures had backs, they would have been very sore! The Word works if we work it. I am certain that these and other scriptures were instrumental in my deliverance.

3. Wisdom

In warfare, without wisdom we are naked and at great risk to the attack of the enemy. "Blessed be the Lord my strength which teacheth my hands to war, and my fingers to fight" (Psalm 144:1). We will need wisdom to know what to do in a particular situation. For example, Joshua got directives for the battle and he told the children of Israel to march around the wall of Jericho for six days without so much as uttering one word and then shouting on the seventh day. Imagine a large group of people remaining totally silent for six whole days (Joshua 6:14-16)! What a battle strategy! But as long as it's God's wisdom, it will always work.

4. Worship

This has been addressed in Chapter 2. However, it is still worth a brief mention in the specific context as a battle strategy. Suffice it to say that worship intimidates the enemy. You are a warrior worshipper. Praise is a warfare strategy (both offensive and defensive) that we can use to call upon the Lord to be saved from the attacks of our enemies! "I will call upon the Lord, who is worthy to be praised: so shall I be saved from mine enemies" (Psalm 18:3).

Charge your atmosphere with the presence of the King using God-exalting triumphant music, dance, silence and confessions! Music affects our emotional and mental states. Also, make declarations about the worthiness of God. Use the names of God to evoke His presence. For example, El Gibbor, Lord of Host, The Almighty God and so much more! When we do this, it reminds us that we belong to Him who has never lost a battle.

5. Prayer

Prayer is the act of going to God through His son Jesus in reverence and confidence according to His will. Effective prayer is always a dialogue, not a monologue. This is particularly necessary in warfare situations when hearing God's instruction is vital and its absence could be fatal. Prayer also provides the opportunity and context of becoming soaked in the presence of the King of glory. At its very core, prayer is about relationships; and relationships are about love and communication.

Use the Word of God as our language of prayer. We shouldn't complain about our problems and magnify Satan's antics, and then call it prayer. This is not prayer. The Bible is already laden with many ready-made prayers and prayer templates.

Before going into any battle, we must go to the control tower of heaven for instructions for the answer to the vital question, "Do I fight or do I be still?" Whatever the answer, always ask God for His strategy. God will never send His children into battle without a battle plan. If you hear or sense no instruction, then do nothing. This is the time to stand still and be in readiness mode. We must wait for our Commander's vital instructions!

As women, it is critical that we are consistent in our prayer life. There will always be things and people demanding our attention for our time, energy and emotions. However, we must ensure that we don't give to our Sovereign King the left-overs. We must strategize to find time to pray.

6. Ministering Angels

Activate the ministry of angels. Angels aren't fairy tales, but real present-day help in the kingdom of God. There are many Biblical accounts of angelic encounters, but what of ours? Angels are spirit beings who are very active in the realm of the spirit and whose assignment is to help us live victorious lives for God's glory.

Our awareness and deployment of angels will without question shift our lives to a more intimate, productive and victorious level. Let's ask God to dispatch angels to assist us as we fight on His behalf. Let's no longer leave the innumerable angels with nothing to do! They long to get busy on our behalf. Give them their job description and watch them help us become signs and wonders in battle and assist us to become all that we are meant to be.

It is a promise to us in Psalm 91:11, "For he shall give his angels charge over thee, to keep thee in all thy ways." Notice that the deployment of angels is not reserved for warfare but is profitable in "all thy ways". The well-known angels, Michael and Gabrielle are prevalent in scriptures. Women of God it's time to begin to reign in dominion with the assistance of angels that excel in strength that obey the commands of the Lord; including the perfection of those things that concern us! "Bless the Lord, ye his angels, that excel in strength, that do his commandments, hearkening unto the voice of his word" (Psalm 103:20).

7. Personal Silence

This strategy will prove to be very difficult for many! It is a popular saying that "women have the gift of the gab". I have deliberately decided not to unpack the accuracy and challenge the stereotype of this comment, so as not to digress. Silence is a masterful strategy; when a woman can go through major pressure and unexplainable pain and intentionally say nothing. Nada. Button up those trembling lips that could say so much but know that this is not the time nor the place to speak. Not speaking conserves energy, preserves focus and confuses Satan. Beloved sister, have you ever realised that your silence can't be misquoted? It may be misinterpreted, but never misquoted.

As with divinely ordained words, there is much power in divinely appointed silence. Why do we often surrender the power of silence for hasty ill-advised and ill-timed words? Be reminded that it is, "In quietness and in confidence shall be your strength" (Isaiah 30:15). Be confident and courageous to be silent when it serves to advance the victory for kingdom building and personal advancement.

Rahab would have forfeited the deal with the spies if she had spoken about their business (Joshua 2:12-14). Similarly, we shouldn't inform everyone about our dealings. It can cancel our favour. Esther was also instructed by her uncle, Mordecai, not to say anything about her kindred association. It was her silence about her family background that was instrumental in the pending defeat of hateful Haman who plotted to annihilate the Jews (Esther 2:10, 20). My sister, Lois, told me many years ago a profound thought she told her students- "In silence you think and in silence you become great!". We will never be great and victorious if we don't master the weapon of personal silence.

8. Corporate Silence

The victory over Jericho was already assured in Joshua 6: 2 from the outset. "And the LORD said unto Joshua, See, I have given into thine hand Jericho, and the king thereof, and the mighty men of valour". However, the victory was contingent on the rather strict terms and conditions. "And Joshua had commanded the people, saying, Ye shall not shout, nor make any noise with your voice, neither shall any word proceed out of your mouth, until the day I bid you shout; then shall ye shout" (Joshua 6:10). The church as a whole appears to struggle with practising silence. Our church services are packed to the breaking point of their allotted time with one activity after another. How often we hear the saying, "Brethren, time is against us". Let's listen more and do as God instructs.

9. Uncommon Faith

It is impossible to please God without faith (Hebrews 11:1). Hence, it goes without saying that a woman can't effectively reign without faith; neither can she become a wonder! A Christian woman without faith is powerless to overcome the ensnaring schemes of Satan and his demons! It is truly impossible to please God without this vital weapon. We need both faith and action to be a mighty kingdom warrior. Both sides of the coin- faith and action, are needed to make it a viable kingdom currency.

Playing life safe in the lane of doubt and fear should not be passed off as waiting on and trusting in God. Be confident to take God-sized actions. One of the tactics of Satan which he uses against women is the three-pointed dagger of delay, distraction and discouragement. Therefore, we must develop and use dogged faith-fill determination to destroy his ammunitions! We need to heed the instruction in Deuteronomy 1:29-30, "Do not be terrified, or afraid of them. The Lord your God, who goes before you, He will fight for you."

10. Empowerment of the Holy Spirit

To reign as a kingdom queen, you must by necessity be *filled* and *led* by the power of the Holy Spirit. We will need God's power to tread on the serpents lurking in our lives. The importance of the Holy Spirit was underscored by Jesus, when He instructed his disciples to wait in the Upper Room for power and presence of the Comforter. Amazing victories and transformation happen in the presence of the Holy Spirit. "He said unto them, have ye received the Holy Ghost since ye believed? And they said unto him, we have not so much as heard whether there be any Holy Ghost. And

God wrought special miracles by the hands of Paul: So that from his body were brought unto the sick handkerchiefs or aprons, and the diseases departed from them, and the evil spirits went out of them" (Acts 19: 2, 11-12).

As reigning daughters of the King who have chosen to allow God to make us into *wonders*, this will, without fail, attract arrows from hell. It necessitates that we must adopt a warrior-stance. The blessings of the Lord are attractive to friends and foes. As such, you will need to fight. As God's prepared, authorised battle axe and skilled soldier we must be aware that we are never alone. Only engage in battles that are approved of the Lord (after enquiring of Him) and use only divine battle strategies, even if they don't make total sense to you and others. If it's God, victory is assured. Remember that the battle is already been won by Jesus Christ.

Thankfully, this isn't a fleshly fight because we would be no match for the enemy of our souls. Rather, the battle is of the Lord and it is He that sustains us and teaches us to fight. Yes, we are in a war, but it's "Not might, not by power, but by my Spirit, saith the Lord of hosts" (Zechariah 4:6). As such, we must allow the enabling power of the Holy Spirit not only to make us competent in using the different transformation tactics, but more importantly to make us into bona fide soldiers of the cross who have pledged allegiance to the King and His kingdom. As the interview with Private Rohan reflects, it requires discipline and a one-man band can't triumph in battle. It requires a team. Let's take the hand of a sister, a brother, a boy, a girl to fight for the King and together we can go forward.

The 4D warrior-stance makes you courageous as a lion. You show up in and to the battle with God-given strength and resilience knowing that you are not fighting for victory, you are fighting from victory! God made a covenant with Abram and said, "And I will bless them that bless thee, and curse him that curse thee." As a daughter of Abraham, you too have taken up your warrior-stance and are ready to become God's battle axe. You've also been skillfully trained to use the transformation strategies for battle. These are sure and promised victory armouries from the hand of God.

WARRIOR-STANCE TRAANSFORMATION TASK

1. In terms of the Reigning Dimensions regarding *Warrior-stance,* where are you? (Tick one)

Wonder ☐   Winning ☐   Waning ☐   Wandering ☐

2. Develop a Warrior-stance Declaration: Eg. I am an equipped, prepared, and ready soldier in the end-time army of the Lord!

_____

_____

3. Which of the Warrior-stance Transformation Strategies would give you the maximum impact now?

_____

_____

4. Set a SMART (Specific, Measurable, Attainable, Realistic and Time-bound) warrior-stance goal.

_____

_____

5. Motivation: Why is this goal important to you?

_____

_____

_____

6. Accountability: Which person or system will hold you accountable?

_____

7. Review Date:

_____

8. Reward: How will you celebrate achieving this goal?

_____
_____

Chapter Ten
Transformation Agent #10
WARDROBE

"Don't make fashion own you, but you decide

[who] you are, what you want to express

by the way you dress and the way to live."

Gianni Versace

The power of a woman's dress sense can't be overestimated. Having a functional wardrobe with items that flatter and represent you to the fullest is well worth the investment of time, money and energy. Be assured that it will yield an unlimited return on investment. Let's embark on the exciting journey to transform our wardrobes and jazz up our personal styling, which will change our lives! Are you one of the many women who are forever shopping for clothes and yet consistently complain of having nothing to wear?

It is not unusual for women to have bulging wardrobes stuffed beyond capacity, who then go into an absolute panic mode when we receive an invitation for a special event, scrambling to find something suitable to wear! Gok Wan, a

British fashion consultant, states that, "By making your wardrobe work for you, you'll be a collection of chic new looks richer and ready to feel fashion fabulous anytime, anyplace, anywhere. Because the one thing you never, ever have to cut back on is feeling gorgeous." To be the full expression of the reigning woman, we must be fashion-appropriate and the best that is possible for us!

Long gone are the days when in false humility and grossly inaccurate interpretation of Scriptures a Christian woman can afford to say, "Render your heart and not your garment". In the first place, the Scripture says, "Rend your heart, and not your garments" (Joel 2: 13). In other words, tear your heart, give God your heart and not vainly tear your garments as an inadequate substitute. So then, why is it vital that the reigning woman knows how to be appropriately attired? Clothes speak loudly. Hence, clothes matter. They matter very much. Rachel Zoe states, "Style is a way to say who you are without having to speak." We can't be women of wisdom, worth and wonder who honour and celebrate Jehovah, without dressing to complement this truth. What is the truth? The truth is you're wonderfully and fearfully made (Psalm 139:14) and you're God's wonder and ambassador with a brilliant assignment and destiny!

First Things First

The 'Foundation Garment' for *The Reigning Woman* is the Royal Robe of Jesus Christ. "Favour is deceitful, and beauty is vain: but a woman that fears the LORD, she shall be praised" (Proverbs 31:30). The fear of the Lord is the first 'brand' that must be the ultimate wardrobe must-have! As such, her dress sense is distinctively different yet arrestingly stunning! "Whose adorning let it not be that outward adorning of plaiting the hair, and of wearing gold, or of putting on of apparel; But let it be the hidden man of the heart, in that which is not corruptible, even the ornament of a meek and quiet spirit, which is in the sight of God of great price" (1 Peter 3:3-5).

No matter how attractively dressed a woman may be, if her attitude and spirit aren't sweet, they dim the splendour of her wardrobe. Every 4D reigning woman requires that the glory of God be upon her to turn heads. And not to turn just any old head, but to turn the right heads for the right reasons! Let onlookers see Christ in us.

In addition, the context for an effective wardrobe is thriving wellbeing; where our skin, hair, nails, teeth are in good condition. Importantly too, we must practise good hygiene and ensure that we smell amazing. Self-worth and wellbeing impact how we feel and our general health. Clothes can never substitute nor camouflage brokenness, low self-esteem and ill-health. They can only accentuate that which is already doing well.

Outer Garments

The wardrobe has always mattered to God. We shouldn't over-spiritualise things; how we present ourselves before God and mankind is very important. Huldah the prophetess, in 2 Kings 22: 14, was specifically identified as a "keeper of the wardrobe". Ask any royalty and they will tell you that fashion sense matters very much. Notice when a princess blunders in the wardrobe department that it becomes a negative press and when she gets it right there is approval and celebration. We are daughters of the King and like the kingdom royalty that we are, we must make our wardrobe speak and be a witness that the King of heaven is the Lord and Master of our lives and that we have fine taste and style.

Whenever we dress, our clothes must first pay us a compliment. This way, if no one else does, we still know we look amazing. No more sleep-walking through life. It's high time to stop using clothes to misrepresent ourselves. Sexually provocative and revealing dressing isn't befitting of an elegant woman of wonder. It says, "Look at my body, my mind and heart aren't asimportant!" Have you ever seen a reigning queen dressing provocatively? Is our clothing misrepresenting or even lying about us? We are deciding what clothes we wear. At least I'm hoping that we are the ones ultimately deciding how we are showing up in the world. Whilst it's alright to be inspired and within reason influenced by others in this area, we must refuse to be anybody's fashion slave, and by no means brand advertisement.

On the other hand, some women hide in their clothes. We do what I will now call a wardrobe settling. Settling for less than that which is possible. It is being acknowledged that for many reasons, we may not be able to dress well at present. However, once we are conscious of the truth that dressing appropriately matters, it will only be a matter of time that this mindset will be reflected in an improved fashion. Many women, including myself, have been there. This is why having healthy wealth and practising generosity are so important. Our 'Contribution DNA' will inspire us to help others to dress well.

However, be this as it may, it's time to be awakened women of God and let our wardrobe renaissance begin. Now call your name and say, "No more hiding." Let's be comfortable in our own clothes and our own skin.

Body Image

Being comfortable in our own skin is important. We know there are those who do cosmetic plastic surgery, but in general, the body God gave us is for a lifetime! Therefore, we ought to accept and love our own bodies in order to reign without distractions in this area. How do you view your physical body? Do you look at yourself with appreciation, wonder and respect? Do you look at your reflection in the mirror with grace-filled eyes? Or do you look at yourself with the eyes of a critic?

Some people, for various reasons, need help to love themselves completely. Seek help if you're struggling in this area. Since if this isn't in place, the most sophisticated wardrobe can't hide body-loathing. According to the *National Health Service*, body dysmorphic disorder (BDD), or body dysmorphia, "Is a mental health condition where a person spends a lot of time worrying about flaws in their appearance." This requires expert medical care. There may be a spiritual dimension to body loathing that will require deliverance.

Women's bodies come in different shapes and sizes, which are all beautiful and attractive. When we know the pros and cons of your own body shape, it will help us to better dress to complement our body shape with insight and confidence. As women, our bodies fall into the following generalised body shapes. It is important to know that there are multiple variations within each category. Hence, they mustn't be followed slavishly; rather as a general guide to support us making more informed wardrobe choices; not to imprison and label us: *Healthline* identifies the following body shapes:

1. **Hourglass:** With this body type, the waist is well-defined and the bust and the hip of approximately equal width; thus, creating the hourglass effect. This body type has more flexibility and the tailored look is usually very flattering.

2. **Rectangle:** This is when the waist measurement is approximately the same as the hip or bust and the shoulders and hips are approximately the same width. Using belts can create an indented waist effect.

3. **Triangle or 'pear':** In this shape, the hips are wider than your shoulder and bust. This creates the shape of a pear; narrow at the top and broader at the bottom. The waist is usually the area to accentuate.

4. **Inverted triangle or 'apple':** When your hips are obviously narrower than the shoulders and bust, it is considered to be an apple shape or the inverted triangle.

5. **Athletic**: This is very similar to the rectangle body shape having similar shoulder and hip measurements. However, this body type is usually muscular.

At this moment, take a pause and lovingly and honestly look at your body in a full-length mirror and determine the body shape that you have. You may have to do further research on these matters and or solicit the help of a fashion consultant or stylist.

Complement Your Skin Tone

Being unique includes your skin tone. Generally speaking, women's skin tone will be more suited to either warm or cool colours. To a much lesser degree, some women's skin tone is suited for both warm and cool colours! Accurate knowledge of your skin tone will transform your confidence in choosing colours in your wardrobe with greater intentionality and accuracy. When we no longer 'hit and miss' in our wardrobe colour scheme, we save ourselves time, energy and money. It will to some extent address the niggling thought that something doesn't quite suit us, but not knowing why. So, what are warm and cool colours? *Women's Fashion* state:

1. **Warm colours:** induce warmth because they usually remind us of things like the fire or the sun, such as yellow, red and orange. These are usually more suitable for a skin tone which is dark, olive or golden.

2. **Cool colours:** induce a cool feeling because they usually cause us to remember things like grass and water, such as green, blue, purple and violet. These are usually more suitable for a skin tone which is fair or pale.

If your skin tone is suitable for both warm and cool colours, consider yourself specially blessed in the wardrobe department, since you can wear clothes from a wider range of colours on the colour wheel!

We are all very unique and knowing what colours are most suitable is a big fashion win for women. Colour also has a huge impact on our moods, confidence and is a rather powerful instrument of communication. It even impacts our behaviour!

Wardrobe Dimensions of Reigning

• 1D Reigning: Wandering

In the *Wandering* 1D reigning dimension, there is an obvious lack of effort with our personal styling; being unkempt. In addition, we may not be unkempt in the classical sense of the word, but it also includes becoming a billboard for the world and its worldly values. For example, wearing clothes with bad language and images which are clearly not in keeping with holiness and temperance taught in the Scriptures. It's getting fashion attention for all the wrong reasons.

• 2D Reigning: Waning

In the *Waning* 2D reigning wardrobe, there is minimal effort. Whatever little efforts are made, it's not enough to represent Jesus, the King, and yourself with excellence. In this woman's dressing, she displays an I-don't-care-very-much attitude. On the other hand, there is also the error of over prioritising fashion at the expense of lasting values. This version of the 2D wardrobe exemplifies the mindset of the look-at-me syndrome. This is when pride and all its destructive 'cousins' begin a steady deterioration process. Everything about us should say, "Look-at-Jesus"; He's the only One worth intently looking at.

• 3D Reigning: Winning

In the *Winning* 3D reigning dimension of wardrobe, this woman has developed an effective signature style. In this category, she makes the effort to present herself well and be appropriately dressed. Her wardrobe is influenced by the protocols of her environments such as the workplace, business, place of worship, faith, educational establishments and the general cultural context. However, her personal style is still evident and appealing.

• 4D Reigning: Wonder

The woman of *Wonder* not only dresses with the 3D level of polish and suitability, but more importantly she dresses with the consciousness that she is royalty and she belongs to the King of heaven! Modesty and elegance are the gold standards for kingdom-minded dressing. She is not a slave to the fleeting trends of fashion. She doesn't misprioritise her spending and become neglectful of her wealth goals to keep up with the Jones in fashion. Instead, she adorns herself elegantly, befitting her sense of spiritual stance of righteousness. Her first 'branding' is with holiness and thereafter will only select brands in alignment with her core value of honour to Yahweh.

The 4D reigning woman of wonder is usually conscientious of where she sources her fashion items. Let's not indirectly support child labour and substandard pay; especially in some parts of the world where people are paid pennies for their labour. This usually ends up feeding the insatiable appetite for disposable fashion especially in the West. This has huge negative environmental consequences.

Let's be reminded that the essence of the battle in life is for our minds. Unfortunately, some people in the fashion industry have plugged into the mind game for the wrong reasons. Therefore, let's do our due diligence to remain an ambassador of Christ, even in our wardrobe. In fact, let's not only be defensive as we say no to unwholesome fashion and be courageous to debunk that which is against our Christian values. But importantly, let's go on the offensive and ask God to raise up amazing fashion labels which are in alignment with the Christian belief system; that will take a stand in providing wholesome fashion in a sin-darkened world. Their message will be intentional in honouring the King who reigns now and for eternity!

In a fashion sense, as much as the woman of wonder loves and appreciates herself, she is aware that her body isn't an objectof worship; God is! She knows and lives with the consciousness that her body is the temple of the Lord, and not her trophy. It's not the focus for the reception of glory and not the object of adoration. Rather, it is an instrument of exalting Jesus and to boldly take her stand in the world.

Do You Have the Wow Factor?

Dressing beautifully with a strong sense of God-consciousness is becoming of women who are kingdom ambassadors. In 1 Timothy 2:9-10, Paul instructs Timothy that, "Women should adorn themselves in respectable apparel, with modesty and self-control, not with braided hair and gold or pearls or costly attire, but with what is proper for women who profess godliness with good works."

When you identify your body shape, choose your most flattering colours and dress to complement your personality, you're likely to achieve what I call the Wow Factor! When we understand these key factors, choosing suitable fashion pieces usually gets easier as we become more experienced. However, let's not be afraid to ask for the help of a fashion stylist or a friend that is more experienced to assist us in this area. As we become savvy fashion shoppers, let's remember to keep within our budgets. We don't have to blow our budgets to look beautiful! Invest time and energy in researching where to buy quality wardrobe items at reasonable prices.

Invest in the Next Level You

Invest a portion of your time, energy and money to be a suitably attired reigning kingdom woman in her royal robe! Do whatever it takes. For example, in 2018 I did a wardrobe revamp with a reputable fashion consultant in London. It lasted for a little over four hours. However, this time, money and effort have yielded tremendous return on investment. When I got rid of all my fashion faux, that is, the fashion mistakes- be it because of the fit, the colour, the condition or the misguided combinations; it meant that every item which remained in my wardrobe has its place and has several suitable combinations.

In addition, my wardrobes were intentionally organised. As such, half of the larger wardrobe was designated for formal clothes and the other half for casual. The pieces that could fit well in both categories were placed at the end of the causal and the beginning of the formal categories. So, in effect, there was an infused third category. The second smaller wardrobe was used for work clothes. I now 'know' what is in my wardrobe. I will continue to replicate this wardrobe arrangement.

Prior to my wardrobe revamp, I had forgotten some of my clothes, some were not used for an extended period of time and sadly some were abandoned for years. People say, "Confession is good for the soul." Some of the clothes that were forgotten was the best fate for them; because they could not go with me to the next season. Others were abandoned gems. So now that I have set the stage, here are the multiple ways that a revamped wardrobe saves a boatload of time, energy and money.

1. This creates a well-ordered wardrobe which saves a lot of time and, as the saying puts it, "Time is money". As women, we spend a fair amount of time pondering what we will wear to the engagement party, baby blessing, presenting at the women's conference, and not to mention our first and follow-up dates with X or Y. An ordered functional wardrobe reduces the numerous try-ons and the needless perplexity.

2. It prevents unintentional double, triple, quadruple... spending on items you already have but don't remember that you have because they are out of sight, hence out of mind.

3. When you 'shop' in your wardrobe, it opens up your thinking with new fashion ideas. So, you don't have to do unnecessary spending and waste time shopping (whether online or in stores) because you have enough clothes, that with a bit of creativity, will give you the gift of dressing like the kingdom queen that you are. It is really true that there is always 'oil' in the house! Find your clothes 'oil'.

4. When you know your shape and most flattering colours, it prevents you from wasting money buying the wrong fashion items which don't accentuate your strengths and not to mention how brutal and unforgiving misguided fashion purchases are towards your 'none-strengths'. I deliberately refused to use the word flaws or

weaknesses; the good Lord knows we women can do without another baggage of labelling parts of our bodies as a 'weakness'. We have viewed our bodies as flawed for so long that it has become our default body image mindset. This disempowering thinking needs to go.

5. When I shop, I am more intentional because I have a fashion gap agenda to fill. This curbs impulsive buying. For example, when I did my wardrobe revamp, I identified a few gaps that I needed to fill- a black fitted blazer, two occasion dresses (initially I said three but as we went on and continued finding occasion fashion gems- I thought that two would be enough), black fitted leather blazer, short denim jacket, ankle boots and t-shirts. These will be informed decisions, not a spur of the moment budget-blowing spending that as women we sometimes engage in. This eliminated random shopping and bad fashion ideas.

These are but a few of the ways that being women which are clued up in the wardrobe department, no pun intended, can save money, time and energy. These crucial resources should be invested to have a lasting impact beyond our generation where they really matter; in the kingdom of God and our families!

Confidence: throne-room radiance

Our clothes, however lovely, cannot hide our body language! Our body language is never silent. Never. Never. Never. The greatest point of fashion leverage is our confidence. When God is the foundation of a woman's confidence, she is sheer dynamite! Not only is confidence in God important, but we must have confidence in ourselves too! There is no substitute for confidence and the lack thereof can't be hidden! When we know who we are and whose we are, we walk, stand and dress differently!

We must believe that we are the beloved of God and that indeed we can do *all things* through Jesus Christ, that gives us strength. We must also believe that God is able and so are we; because we are hooked up to the Source of all that is good. Everyone, without exemption, is inspired by extraordinary women who exude confidence. Even our biggest haters are enraptured by our greatness- the treasure in our earthen vessels. Our lives bear the invisible sign, 'God is at work'. Hence, it can be clearly seen that we are going from glory to glory by the hand of the Almighty.

The truth is, not everyone will be happy for you, so be prepared. When people hate you, they're simply paying you a backhanded compliment. You cannot be ignored, but they lack the graciousness to say, "You're amazing, continue shining". Without a doubt, you are on their radar, albeit they decided to be negative about your blinding throne-room radiance! This is why when God decides to roar and roll on your behalf, He will not go to the annex nor the back room to do it. No way. He will bless and elevate you in the very presence of your naysayers.

It is very important that we never let the throne room radiance swell our heads. Mismanaged confidence can quickly slip into pride and God resists the proud but gives grace to the humble (James 4:6). We must consciously put on the royal robe of humility. It is equally as important as confidence. Arrogance is never cute. Let's heed the instruction to, "Be clothed with humility...Humble yourselves therefore under the mighty hand of God, that He may exalt you in due time" (1 Peter 5:5-6). You're royalty by being connected to Christ. Therefore, be confident, yet walk humbly with the King!

Men and The Reigning Woman's Dress Sense

Men are usually very visual. So, for every reason, as women we need to take care of ourselves; not primarily for the benefit of men but by no means should they be excluded. Men and women sometimes view clothes and colours through different lens. I will not go so far as to say that men are colour blind, albeit to say there are sometimes significant differences. Even though we must dress to honour our uniqueness and personal style branding, every wise woman takes into consideration the dress taste of her spouse; if she has one. To ignore your spouse's dress sense is to do so to your own peril. God's people are destroyed for lack of knowledge (Hosea 4: 6)! "For after this manner in the old time the holy women also, who trusted in God, adorned themselves, being in subjection unto their own husbands" (1 Peter 3: 5). Yes, even in our dressing we must be considerate even as we celebrate ourselves. It doesn't have to be one or the other.

Our wardrobe can be a useful instrument to practice joyful and humble submission. Embrace the opportunity to deepen the intimacy with your spouse and others of significance to you. Let's diligently practise the highly rewarding and rewarded law of honour. In Romans 12:10 we are advised to, "Be kindly affectioned one to another with brotherly love; in honour preferring one another." How can we use our wardrobe to honour and prefer others?

This is not only related to spouses but also being

sensitive and compliant to the protocols in the corporate church, job, business and other such contexts. Let's be wise. If our clothes are going to cause others to stumble, cause the name of Christ to be blasphemed, shut certain doors of opportunities and possibly cause us not to be taken seriously in certain circles; is that moment of dressing *our way* really worth it?

The reigning 4D woman who has mastered the wardrobe transformation can skillfully use it to express her stylish unique self and honour the significant others in her life. Above all else, she also uses it as an opportunity of surrender and praise; even as she defers to and reverences God!

Women who adjusted their Wardrobe

Where God is taking us, beloved sisters, requires making a few adjustments in our wardrobe to facilitate representing Him well and to have maximum impact. Naomi knew the necessity of preparation before entering the presence of a man that matters! She advised her daughter-in-law, Ruth, to wash and perfume herself and put on appropriate raiment before going to the threshing floor of Boaz (Ruth 3: 3). Ruth could have said, "It's only a threshing floor for heaven's sake" or some such comment underscoring the fact that it was a plain and lowly threshing floor.

However, in obedience, Ruth did as she was instructed and the outcome is common knowledge. A widowed Moabite foreigner (who wasn't permitted to enter into the congregation of the Lord even unto the tenth generation-Deuteronomy 23:3), became Boaz's wife and later featured in the ancestry of the Saviour of the world, Jesus Christ (Matthew 1: 5)! Ruth knew that it wasn't the place that was the deciding factor. Rather, it was the man that was gracing the threshing floor that made all the difference, and that really mattered! Ruth's obedience changed everything and the rest really is history.

Not only can we adjust our wardrobe with good intentions, but it can also be done for negative reasons. Tamar in Genesis 38:13-15, 19 is a prime example of what we aren't to use our wardrobe to do.

> And it was told Tamar, saying, Behold thy father in law goeth up to Timnath to shear his sheep. And she put her widow's garments off from her, and covered her with a vail, and wrapped herself, and sat in an open place, which is by the way to Timnath; for she saw that Shelah was grown, and she was not given unto him to wife. When Judah saw her, he thought her to be a harlot; because she had covered her face. And she arose, and went away, and laid by her vail from her, and put on the garments of her widowhood.

Notice that Tamar used a veil to cover her face just as Rebekah did when she was about to meet her husband Isaac (Genesis 24: 64-65). However, their intentions were totally different! Tamar did it to deceive, entrap and execute revenge on Judah, her father-in-law; whilst Rebekah did it to show reverence to her husband. Tamar's positioning in the city and attire mistakenly classified her as a harlot! The expression of our sexuality and our clothing are closely linked and should be treated with the gravity that it deserves.

Let's learn how to upgrade our wardrobe...

WARDROBE TRANSFORMATION STRATEGIES

1. Detox: the gift of Goodbyes

We can never experience a wardrobe upgrade without learning the art of saying goodbye! It's time to say goodbye to our old season dressing. An upgraded wardrobe is an amazing gift you give to yourself and to the world. A new season demands new decisions. What will we do with our new knowledge (skin tones, body shapes, colour psychological impact, worthiness...to name a few) of the importance of dressing as kingdom royalty befitting our ambassadorial responsibility and privileges?

We have two options- carry on like before or changing to become the new confident well-dressed you. Only you get to make these decisions. First, enter the peak state of abundance and gratitude before embarking on this journey. If we are in the scarcity mindset, we will hold on to everything in our wardrobe- the good, the bad and the indifferent. Be committed to dress to complement your awakened identity and your forthcoming destiny. God is our Source and He isn't bankrupt nor in a recession. Hence, there is no need to be reluctant nor fearful to practise generosity. Cluttered hands have no capacity to receive God's best. When we release what is in our hands, the Father will release His top-notch quality to us.

Throw Out: If we are to dress our best, there are some items which are in our wardrobes that we must get rid of! The only place they should go is...out! Let's do our bit for the environment and recycle where possible in keeping with where we live.

Give away: There is a priceless feeling to be able to give away good quality clothes and accessories that will be of huge benefit to other people. Our fashion mistakes and or surplus will definitely be other people's fashion bonanzas!

2. Fashion Repurposing

This is reassigning wardrobe items for different use. For example, my smart black blazer was repurposed for work which was later replaced with a better fitting one.

3. Creating Your Own Fashion Box

Enough of thinking outside the box, why not create your own fashion box! Try taking informed fashion risks and pushing the boundaries using new combinations and accessories; embracing your new-found fashion confidence (in alignment with God's standards of course).

4. Discovering Forgotten Pieces

We all have some fashion gems that we have not seen for a very long time. These items can be drafted in to widen our fashion choices.

5. Upcycling

This is transforming something old or damaged and making it into something else. For example, you can cut the top off an old denim trousers or skirt and then use it to make a handbag. Insert a pretty scarf through its former waistband loops to make a very cute bow.

6. Repairing

Some wardrobe pieces can be rescued with adjustments being done by one or more of the following ways: changing buttons, to improve the fit inserting a few darts, pleats, and gathers, hemming, changing or strengthening colours by dyeing and adding details such as appliques and embroidery. Your decision to repair an item will be determined by the cost to do so (if you can't do it yourself) or if it is worth the time investment to do it. Sometimes a total gift of goodbye is better than the production involved in repairing it!

7. God Conscious Styling

Some people use fashion as an intentional insult and defiance to the reign of Jesus Christ. However, the more heart-breaking thing is that some people do so ignorantly. Begin to observe and think about some of the names, fashion statements (the use of expletives, vulgarity and obscene graphics) and styles of some brands. Our fashion is a reflection of our self-belief and our consciousness of God. We must be wise.

Fashion Hacks

- The fit of your clothes is everything. Clothes which are too tight, big, short, long, uncomfortable or revealing are not flattering, if we intend to be taken seriously as a 4D reigning woman representing the King of heaven. Certain adjustments may be as simple as moving a button or hemming. Fortunately, some of us can do our own alterations or know friends who can. If not, it is worth the investment to use the service of a tailor or dressmaker to adjust our clothing to attain a more bespoke fit.

- Let's not sacrifice our decency and comfort for style, this can be downright embarrassing, painful and senseless. A woman that is hobbling, grimacing and pulling up and down her clothes, certainly isn't making the right impression. Let alone being focused on the importance of the present moment because of her constant fidgeting.

- Invest in proper fitting foundation garments. This is a major investment, if not the single most effective fashion leverage and transformational decision. Foundation garments will significantly impact how the rest of your clothes fit and also how we feel. So, get the right size and style bra, knickers, body shapers (if used), petticoat; to name a few.

- Instead of always leaving your tops and shirts hanging out of bottoms (which sometimes create a less polished look; unless it's the oversized effect that is desired), why not try doing a full, half, centred or side tuck. This simple tweak can up-level your outfit.

- For those who would love to have a few designer pieces in your wardrobe without spending 'an arm and a leg', you can consider buying pre-loved items from charity shops and vintage outlets both online and in stores. Try shopping in charity shops in areas of higher socioeconomic neighbourhoods, you usually can tell the difference in the quality of the items in some of these shops.

- Just as garnish is used to complete a dish, clothes without accessories can look unfinished and possibly dull. The correct accessories can take your clothes to the next dimension of polished personal styling. So, work those shoes, handbags, belts, scarves, broaches, hats, jewellery, eyeglasses to name a few.

- Find out your skin tone and consciously choose the colour palette that is most flattering. For example, if your skin is classified as cool, choose the shade of colours that is most complementary. Vice versa. There are also those who are extra blessed that their skin tone is equally flattered by both warm and cool colours! The colour world is their oyster.

- Don't be afraid to experiment and have fun exploring your personal style. Don't get hemmed in (no pun intended) into anybody's fashion box. Have fun with lines, colour, retro, vintage and juxtapose combinations. For example, wearing a smart pleated skirt with trainers. Remember you're unique and your wardrobe should also reflect this truth! However, here is a word of warning. Gok Wan encourages us to exercise caution when buying prints; some are classics and timeless such as stripes, florals and geometrics, while others date quickly such as bright neon colours.

- We can implement a minimalist wardrobe by intentionally purchasing fewer clothes and ensuring that we are actually wearing the items in our wardrobes. However, every woman's wardrobe should contain basic pieces such as good quality t-shirts, smart black blazers, white shirts, pencil skirts and a little black dress.

- Use the correct dosage. I know, you're wondering what do I mean. There are certain fashion items which are more effective in small to medium well-considered dosages such as distressed rips, prints, retro/vintage, make-up, statement pieces and bright colours. For example, envision an outfit that has an animal-print scarf, belt, handbag and shoes all at the same time! One piece is usually enough; maximum of two pieces. Although, I respect the fact that it all boils down to personal taste and freedom of choice. However, it's best to err on the side of being understated rather than being over the top! Less is always more.

- Matching metals makes any mundane outfits look more polished. For example, if you are wearing shoes and using a handbag with eye-catching silver ornaments, then it's usually better to choose carefully selected complimentary silver accessories rather than choosing gold pieces. However, with careful consideration, this suggestion can be broken with tasteful results of mixing metals.

- Dress suitably for the occasion. Find out the dress code for the given event. If you ignore this cardinal rule, you may live to regret it in an eye-catching way. To err in this rule can be embarrassing and painful take another sister's word for it!

- Don't forget to smile. A warm smile is priceless. Not only for the fashion effect, but in all human interactions. In a fashion sense, your smile and your confidence can be considered to be your crown and sceptre, you can't reign without them! Critically examine your teeth and do whatever is necessary to take your smile to the next level.

The impact of an intentionally elegant woman is priceless. A beautiful, yet functional wardrobe is a powerful tool in a woman's life. Because we are so unique in our body shapes, skin tones, personalities and value systems, to create a wardrobe that works and is flattering, takes conscious efforts. There is no such thing as accidental elegance. Notably, it won't be attained in one attempt but must be cultivated over time. Whilst functionality and aesthetic appeal are important, so are other aspects of dressing as the 4D royalty we are meant to be.

A wardrobe overall or update doesn't simply expand a woman's ability to dress well. More importantly, it inspires a sense of confidence and even focus because she isn't distracted by the awareness that she isn't representing herself in her personal styling at the highest level that's possible.

As women who belong to Christ, the King, a call to modesty and holiness, even in our wardrobe, is not throwing cold water on our unique personal styling. In fact, it's quite the contrary, it's because we are amazing daughters of the Father, that we need to ensure that our wardrobe is representing us well. We must seize the opportunity to honour our responsibility to use everything about us, including our personal styling, to arise and shine for the glory of God.

Even in our wardrobe, we must fully surrender to the Lordship of Christ. In becoming a 4D woman of wonder with great impact we must use our wardrobe to indicate excellence, conscientious living and the holy brand of royalty; befitting our kingdom citizenship.

By the way, who is to say that a reigning woman can't be simultaneously modest yet attractively captivating? As women on assignment to represent the King of Kings and the Lord of Lords, yourself and the connections that matter; we can't afford to be inappropriately dressed. Appearance can either open or close doors. Our clothes can make us appear confident and ready for such a time as this or downright silly. Our clothes can be empowering or disempowering. Our clothes can be a bridge or a wall. Our clothes can make us look polished or rather unkempt. We must dress with the consciousness that as 4D royalty, the gold standards are integrity, purpose and excellence. What is your wardrobe saying about you? Let's apply selected fashion hacks and wardrobe transformation strategies to update or do a complete make-over of our wardrobe. We will testify that it's well worth the effort!

WARDROBE TRANSFORMATION TASK

1. In terms of the Reigning Dimensions regarding *Wardrobe,* where are you? (Tick one)

Wonder ☐   Winning ☐   Waning ☐   Wandering ☐

2. Develop a Wardrobe Declaration: Eg. My wardrobe represents me well as the royal wonder that I am!

_____

_____

3. Which of the Wardrobe Transformation Strategies would give you the maximum impact now?

_____

_____

4. Set a SMART (Specific, Measurable, Attainable, Realistic and Time-bound) wardrobe goal.

_____

_____

5. Motivation: Why is this goal important to you?

_____

_____

_____

6. Accountability: Which person or system will hold you accountable?

_____

7. Review Date:

_____

8. Reward: How will you celebrate achieving this goal?

_____

_____

FINAL THOUGHTS

The Reigning Woman!

We've been on a journey. Throughout this book, we've looked at what it means to reign and how the *Transformation Agents* are used in the needed process of changing to look like the ideal Template of Jesus Christ.

"Come reign with Me, for Me and through me", says Jesus Christ, the King of glory! We are called to reign in Christ; *now* and for *eternity*! What we do with this call, determines the pathway, altitude and outcome of our lives. Jesus has given Himself to us and that is fixed. Albeit, what we do with the priceless gift is up to the choices of our free will. Our experience of the Gift must be worked out (Philippians 2:12) and if the Gift isn't accepted, that will create a particular experience as well.

We can't go on an intentional journey with the King of all ages and remain the same. There must be startling, noticeable or even subtle changes in us and around us. We can't come in contact with the Change-maker and simply be unimpacted! Jesus is the Catalyst of all catalysts. Martin Luther King Jr. profoundly said, "We are confronted with the fierce urgency of now."

The Word of God and our words are the cornerstones of our reign. If we desire and intend to live a life of fulfilment, significance and great impact, it must be built on the unshakable foundation of God's Word. In turn, when we allow God's Word to change our words, we will become powerful women in God's hand; soaked by His Word. As Word-soaked women we can go forth to worship God according to the knowledge of His truth. Theodore Effiong's observation regarding the effect of God's Word deserve due consideration:

When Israel left off their dependence and fixation for the book [God's Word], God left them. Everything they tried failed. They were all children of God but nothing was working for them. I am always amazed and flabbergasted whenever I see believers, servants and followers of the Most High God wallowing in frustration, backwardness and abject poverty. I feel like screaming at them because they are the cause of their own misfortunes. When Israel embraced the book, God lifted them so high above all the nations of the earth. When they abandoned the book, God brought them down to the dust.

Wow! Let's take a moment and reread Effiong's scalding thought. Father have mercy upon us all! It is little wonder God told Joshua that the recipe for *good success* is His Word. Yes, people can always win and have success. However, they cannot have *good success* without the Word of God. I deeply believe that if we want to build lives like skyscrapers, we must build them on the Word of God. Indeed, it is the only foundation that can bear the weight of our destinies!

The Word creates the worship and the worshippers which are approved by God! The worship of the woman of wonder is different from those who have settled for success, those who are waning and certainly those who are wandering. She has been shaped to embody a living sacrifice; she has come to agree that it's her reasonable standard for worship. Over time, she has broken free from the limiting constraints and confines of self-promotions and conflicting denominational traditions.

She isn't an overnight wonder. Oh no. She is in God's Slow Cooker of becoming a vessel of honour fit for the Master's use. She is Word-based and she worships with her everything! This, in turn, creates a rock-solid sense of worthiness which makes her unmovable and abounding in the Lover of her prosperous soul. Her self-esteem and confidence are built on that which doesn't move; Christ the unshakable One! She is secure in the Lord.

As the woman of wonder grows deeper into the image of Christ, she exudes an almost tangible sense of dominion. She is awakened to the need to practise self-care to become and do that which Christ would have her to be for His honour. She also brings value to the lives of countless others.

Her service is marked by an ever-present warmth, that is delightful. She intentionally displays the nature of the Divine, whose image she bears with integrity. She has been bruised, battered and broken, but she has been healed by the Healer. Every day she awakens to go on a mission to love; anybody and everybody. She is a change agent and carries grace and glory. Her impact is felt near and far.

The Reigning Woman has found her place as an ardent worker in the vineyard of the Lord. She has joined with other kingdom servants to do the ministry of the King with passion and humility; which has a remarkable impact on her environment. This woman of wonder has strength but she also has feminine softness; but for sure she isn't a softie.

She has allowed God to do a special work in her life and now she is a wonderful trophy of His workmanship. She has also worked on herself and then does her work with commitment and zeal. Her life is marked with fruitfulness and divine favour; going from glory to glory.

The work that she has both become and does, ushers her into increasing levels of wealth. Her wealth, whatever its definition and quantification, is on a mission to make God's name great and to impact lives.

The Reigning Woman has been so transformed that she is the "battle axe and weapon of war" of the Lord (Jeremiah 51:20)! Consequently, Satan wants to stop her, but he can't. As a surrendered and equipped soldier of the cross, she is aware that El Gibbor, the Warrior Champion God, has never lost a battle. Hence, she has nothing to fear. The battle is not hers, it's the Lord's, who is mighty in battle and is the Triumphant King!

Finally, *The Reigning Woman* of wonder knows that her physical presentation and personal styling matter. She does all that is possible to be attired with elegance and aesthetic appeal. At the same time, she never forgets her royal kingdom identity that she belongs to and represents the holy God. She is a billboard of His glory.

She also knows that the work of transformation will never end. She still has work to do for every Transformation Agent. Nonetheless, a woman that knows God, can be strong and do exploits (Daniel 11:32).

The Reigning Woman is committed to become a *wonder*. She refuses to settle not even for *winning* and her days of *waning* and *wandering* have been served eviction notice. She has heeded the mandate to reign with a sense of urgency now and oh how her soul excitedly awaits eternity!

I hereby raise a toast to *The Reigning Woman* who has embarked on the journey of becoming totally transformed and having great impact!

Shalom.

Your Servant and Transformation Catalyst,

Dr. Donna M. Sherwood

NOTES

Introduction

1. Effiong, Theodore. *The Lost Art of Waiting Upon the Lord*: The School of the Seer VOL. II. Kindle Edition.

2. Martin Luther King, Jr., https://www.carnegiefoundation.org/blog/the-fierce-urgency-of-now/ Accessed 06/02/2021

Setting the Stage

1. A. W. Tozer quoted in Warren W. Wiersbe, The best of A.W. Tozer (Pennsylvania: Christian Publication Inc., 1980), 79.

2. Mark Twain, https://www.goodreads.com/quotes/505050-the-two-most-important-days-in-your-life-are-the Accessed 03/03/2021

3. James Strong, *Strong's Exhaustive Concordance of the Bible*. (Grand Rapids: World Publishing, 1980 #7965), 154.

Transformation Agent # 1: Words

1. Pearl Strachan, https://www.goodreads.com/quotes/235842-handle-them-carefully-for-words-have-more-power-than-atom Accessed 01/12/2020

2. Cindy Trimm, https://www.youtube.com/watch?v=GICAB3wWLDE Accessed 03/12/2020

3. A. W. Tozer quoted in Warren W. Wiersbe, *The best of A.W. Tozer* (Pennsylvania: Christian Publication Inc., 1980), 61.

Transformation Agent # 2: Worship

1. Darlene Zschech, *Worship Changes Everything* (Minnesota: Bethany House Publishers, 2015), 19.

2. Strong Exhaustive Concordance, strongs/greek/4352.

3. A. W. Tozer quoted in Warren W. Wiersbe, *The best of A.W. Tozer* (Pennsylvania: Christian Publication Inc., 1980), 131.

4. John Wesley. https://gracequotes.org/ Accessed 01/12/2020

5. Hanmer Parsons Grant, https://www.dictionary-quotes.com/we-must-free-ourselves-of- Accessed 03/03/2021

6. Charles Spurgeon, https://www.azquotes.com/quote/703823 Accessed 23/02/2021

7. Dr. Donna Sherwood. *Bible Advocate* (Bible Advocate Press: March/April, 2020), 22-28.

Transformation Agent #3: Wisdom

1. Mike Murdock, https://wisdomroombookstore.com/scripts/prodview. asp?idProduct=136 Accessed 03/01/2021

2. Socrates, https://www.goodreads.com/quotes/4097 Accessed 04/01/2021

3. John Whitmore, *Coaching for Performance* (Finland: Nicholas Brealey Publishing, 2002), 40.

4. Napoleon Hill, *Think and Grow Rich* (Rockville, Maryland: Manor Thrift, 2008).

5. Daniel Goleman, *Emotional Intelligence* (London: Bloomsbury Publishing. Kindle Edition, 2019). 9, 11, 20, 22.

6. Ibid.

7. The Maxwell DISC Certification Training: Introduction to Behavioural Analysis Online Training Course. 2018

8. John C. Maxwell, *The 15 Valuable Laws of Growth* (New York: Hachette Book Group, 2012), 16.

9. Institute of Health and Human Potential. https://www.ihhp.com/meaning-of-emotional-intelligence/ Accessed 23/02/2021

10. Daniel Goleman, *Emotional Intelligence* (London: Bloomsbury Publishing. Kindle Edition, 2019).

11. T. D. Jakes, https://www.youtube.com/watch?v=iUzlTV_5x4E Accessed 05/11/2020

Transformation Agent #4: Worthiness

1. Louise L. Hay, http://www.womenheal.org/ Accessed 21/01/2021

2. Eleanor Roosevelt, https://www.brainyquote.com/quotes/eleanor_roosevelt_161321 Accessed 28/02/2021

3. Robert A. Baron and Donn Byrne, *Social Psychology* (Massachusetts: Allyn & Bacon, 2000) 160.

4. Rentsch and Heffner (1994) quoted in Robert A. Baron and Donn Byrne, *Social Psychology* (Massachusetts: Allyn & Bacon, 2000) 161.

5. A. W. Tozer, https://www.goodreads.com/quotes/700558 Accessed 21/12/2020

6. Eleanor Roosevelt, https://www.brainyquote.com/quotes/eleanor_roosevelt_161321 Accessed 28/02/2021

Transformation Agent #5: Wellbeing

1. Maxime Lagace, https://www.wisdomquotes.com/health-quotes/ Accessed 25/12/2020

2. Office for National Statistics (UK) https://www.ons.gov.uk/peoplepopulationandcommunity/wellbeing/bulletins/personalwellbeingintheukquarterly/april2011toseptember2020 Accessed 28/02/2021

3. Biotanical Health (USA, 2008).

4. Catherine Geissler and Hilary Powers, *Fundamentals of Human Nutrition* (Churchill Livingstone Elsievier, 2009), 135

5. Hippocrates, https://guidelineshealth.com/health-care/let-food-be-thy-medicine-and-medicine-be-thy-food/ Accessed 28/01/2021

6. Catherine Geissler and Hilary Powers, *Fundamentals of Human Nutrition* (Churchill Livingstone Elsievier, 2009).

7. Michael F. Roizen and Mehmet C. Oz, *You: Staying Young: Make Your Real Age Younger and Live Up to 35% Longer* (HarperCollins Publishers. Kindle Edition, 2013).

8. Ibid.

9. Gideon Skinner, Research Director at Ipsos MORI https://www.kcl.ac.uk/news/how-the-uk-is-sleeping-under-lockdown Accessed 28/02/2021

10. Brené Brown, *Daring Greatly* (Penguin Books. Kindle Edition, 2012), 10.

11. Serenity Prayer, https://www.lords-prayer words.com/pdfs/ the_serenity_prayer.pdf Accessed 18/01/2021

12. John and Stasi Elderedge, *Captivating* (Nashville, Tennessee: Tomas Nelson, 2005), 181.

Transformation Agent #6: Warm-heartedness

1. Ann Landers, https://www.inspiringquotes.us/quotes/2d7I_6Y7QyP cb Accessed 03/03/2021

2. Brené Brown, *Daring Greatly* (Penguin Books Ltd. Kindle Edition, 2012), 2.

3. Corie Ten Boom, https://www.goalcast.com/2021/02/10/corrie-ten-boom/ Accessed 10/03/2021

4. Emmet Fox, https://www.inspiringquotes.us/author/7983-emmet-fox/ Accessed 20/12/2020

5. Dr. Gary Chapman, *The 5 Love Languages*. https://www.5lovelanguages.com/ Accessed 14/02/2021

6. Ibid.

7. Ibid.

Transformation Agent # 7: Work

1. Alexander Bell Graham, https://www.brainyquote.com/quotes/alexander_graham_bell_390795 Accessed 02/03/2021

2. Rabindranath Tagore, https://www.brainyquote.com/quotes/rabindranath_tagore_134933 Accessed 20/02/2021

3. Bill Johnson, *A Promise Driven Life* https://www.youtube.com/watch?v=bJKa6EE5ekY Accessed 20/11/2020

4. Jim Rohn, https://www.goodreads.com/quotes/7898460-learn-to-work-harder-on-yourself-than-you-do-on Accessed 11/03/2021

5. Whaid Rose, African Regional Convention Notes (Offinso, Ghana, 2018).

6. Max Lucado. *Cure for the Common Life* (Nashville: W Publishing Group, 2005), 1.

7. George Sheehan, https://www.quotes.net/ Accessed 02/02/2021

8. Socrates, https://www.bing.com/search?q=quote+the+unexami ned+life+is+not+worth+living Accessed 03/04/2021

9. Brian Tracey, *The 21 Success Secrets of Self-Made Millionaires* (San Francisco: Berrett- Koehler Publishers, Inc, 2001)

10. Ibid.

11. John Wesley, https://www.azquotes.com/ Accessed 21/03/2021

12. John C. Maxwell, LEADUK Transformation Leadership Conference Notes (Birmingham, UK. 2020).

13. John C. Maxwell, *How Successful People Think* (New York: Center Street, 2009) XX1.

14. Brian Tracey, *The 21 Success Secrets of Self-Made Millionaires* (San Francisco: Berrett- Koehler Publishers, Inc, 2001).

15. Sir Thomas Buxton, Taken from a Plaque at The Mico University College, Jamaica. 1992

16. Doug Fields, *Purpose Driven Youth Ministry* (Grand Rapids: Zondervan Publishing House, 1998), 104.

17. Edward Russel-Walling, *50 Management Ideas* (London: Quercus).

18. Brian Tracey,
https://www.azquotes.com/quote/837138 Accessed
12/12/2020

Transformation Agent # 8: Wealth

1. Andrew Carnegie,
https://www.goodreads.com/author/quotes/23387.An
drew_Carnegie Accessed 21/01/2021

2. Effiong, Theodore. *The Lost Art of Waiting Upon the Lord*: The School of the Seer VOL. II. Kindle Edition.

3. UK Economy Latest - *Office for National Statistics* (ons.gov.uk) Accessed 27/01/2021

4. Mike Murdock, *Why Men Stay Poor* (Texas: The Wisdom Center, 2014), 3.

5. Jaachynma N E Agu,
https://www.goodreads.com/author/quotes/5040334.J
aachynma_N_E_Agu Accessed 21/01/2021

6. Farrah Gray, azquotes.com Accessed 29/12/2021

7. Earl Nightingale, Change Your Life in 19 Minutes with Earl Nightingale
https://www.youtube.com/watch?v=6tbHYvH347A&
t=229s   Accessed 27/01/2021

8. Brian Tracey, *The 21 Success Secrets of Self-Made Millionaires* (San Francisco: Berrett- Koehler Publishers, Inc, 2001).

9. John Shedd,
https://www.goodreads.com/quotes/1388-a-ship-is-
safe-in-harbor-but-that-s-not-what Accessed
21/09/2020

10. UK Economy Latest - Office for National Statistics (ons.gov.uk) Accessed 27/01/2021

11. Trading Economics, https://tradingeconomics.com/united-kingdom/interest-rate Accessed 11/02/2021

12. UK Economy Latest - Office for National Statistics (ons.gov.uk) Accessed 27/01/2021

13. Dave Ramsey, https://www.ramseysolutions.com/debt/how-the-debt-snowball-method-works Accessed 29/03/2021

Transformation Agent # 9: Warrior-stance

1. Linda Evans Shepherd, https://www.goodreads.com Accessed 14/02/2021

2. Alysia Helming, https://www.alysiahelming.com Accessed 14/02/2021

3. Charles Spurgeon, https://www.brainyquote.com/quotes/charles_spurgeon_155622 Accessed 12/12/2020

Transformation Agent # 10: Wardrobe

1. Gianni Versace https://www.harpersbazaar.com/fashion/designers/a1576/50-famous-fashion-quotes/ Accessed 13/03/2021

2. Gok Wan, *Work Your Wardrobe* (London: Harper Collins publisher, 2009), 13.

3. Rachel Zoe, https://huffpost.com Accessed 02/02/2020

4. National Health Service https://www.nhs.uk/conditions/body-dysmorphia/ Accessed 18/2/2021

5. https://www.healthline.com/health/women-body-shapes#10-common-shapes Accessed 18/2/2021

6. Women's Fashion, https://womensfashion.lovetoknow.com/What_Colors_Look_Good_on_Me Accessed 01/02/2021

7. Gok Wan, Work Your Wardrobe (London: Harper Collins publisher, 2009).

Final Thoughts

1. Effiong Theodore, *Why Certain Men are Poor, Remain Poor and Die Poor:* (Kindle Edition. University of Wealth), 15.

2. Martin Luther King, Jr., https://www.carnegiefoundation.org/blog/the-fierce-urgency-of-now/ Accessed 06/02/2021